The CHURCHILLS

A Family Portrait

CELIA LEE AND JOHN LEE

 ST. MARTIN'S GRIFFIN  NEW YORK

ALSO BY CELIA LEE
Jean, Lady Hamilton 1861–1941: A Soldier's Wife

ALSO BY JOHN LEE
A Soldier's Life: General Sir Ian Hamilton 1853–1947
The Warlords: Hindenburg and Ludendorff
The Gas Attacks: Ypres 1915

THE CHURCHILLS
Copyright © Celia Lee and John Lee, 2010.
All rights reserved.

Quotations from Winston S. Churchill reproduced with permission of Curtis Brown Ltd, London on behalf of the Estate of Winston S. Churchill. Copyright © Winston S. Churchill.

Quotations from Clementine Churchill reproduced with permission of Curtis Brown Ltd, London on behalf of Clementine Churchill. Copyright © Lady Mary Soames.

Quotations from Lord Randolph, Lady Randolph, Jack, and Peregrine Spencer Churchill copyright by kind permission of Mrs. Peregrine Spencer Churchill.

Materials belonging to the late Lord Randolph Spencer Churchill and his late wife the late Lady Randolph Spencer Churchills (Jennie); the late Major John Strange Spencer Churchill (Jack); the late Gwendeline Spencer Churchill (Goonie); and the late Mr. Henry Winston Spencer Churchill used by kind permission of Mrs. Peregrine Spencer Churchill.

Unless otherwise noted, images appearing between pp. 136 and 137 are used by kind permission of Mrs. Peregrine Spencer Churchill.

First published in hardcover in 2010 by St. Martin's Griffin in the US—a division of St. Martin's Press LLC, 175 Fifth Avenue, New York, NY 10010.

St. Martin's Griffin are registered trademarks in the United States, the United Kingdom, Europe and other countries.

ISBN: 978-0-230-11220-9

Library of Congress Cataloging-in-Publication Data
Lee, Celia.
    The Churchills : a family portrait / Celia and John Lee.
        p.   cm.
    Includes bibliographical references and index.
    ISBN 0-230-61810-3 (alk. paper)
    (paperback ISBN: 978-0-230-11220-9)
    1. Churchill, Winston, 1874–1965—Family.   2. Churchill, John Strange Spencer, 1880–1947—Family   3. Churchill, Randolph Henry Spencer, Lord, 1849–1895—Family.   4. Churchill, Randolph Spencer, Lady, 1854–1921—Family.   5. Great Britain—History—19th century—Biography.   6. Great Britain—History—20th century—Biography.   I. Lee, John, 1946-
II. Title.
DA566.9.C5L358   2010
941.084092'2—dc22
[B]

2009039972

A catalogue record of the book is available from the British Library.

Design by Letra Libre, Inc.

First St. Martin's Griffin paperback edition: June 2011

P1

In memory of

Peregrine Churchill

1913–2002

"Peregrine had a burning loyalty to the truth, which he often saw as overwhelmed by innuendo and bad research. He was a great man who was devoted to history and saw Sir Winston in a balanced way, virtues and faults both."

—Richard M. Langworth, editor of *Finest Hour,*
from a letter of condolence to Peregrine's wife,
March 22, 2002.

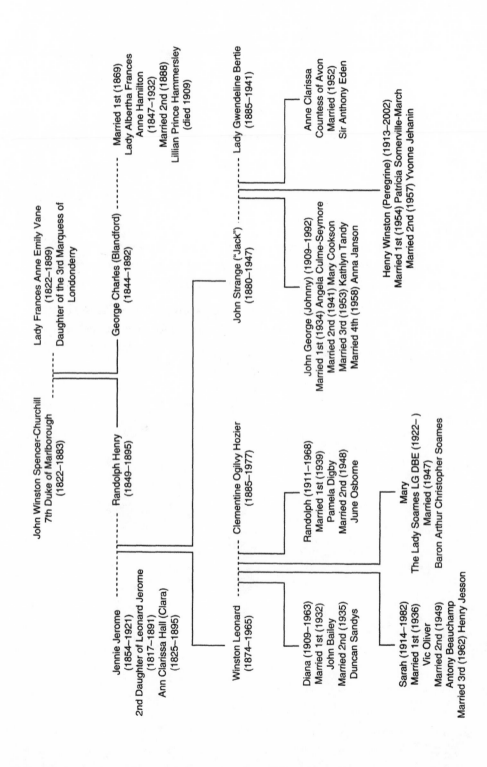

John Winston Spencer-Churchill
7th Duke of Marlborough
(1822–1883)

Lady Frances Anne Emily Vane
(1822–1899)
Daughter of the 3rd Marquess of
Londonderry

Jennie Jerome
(1854–1921)
2nd Daughter of Leonard Jerome
(1817–1891)
Ann Clarissa Hall (Clara)
(1825–1895)

Randolph Henry
(1849–1895)

George Charles (Blandford)
(1844–1892)

Married 1st (1869)
Lady Albertha Frances
Anne Hamilton
(1847–1932)
Married 2nd (1888)
Lillian Prince Hammersley
(died 1909)

John Strange ("Jack")
(1880–1947)

Lady Gwendeline Bertie
(1885–1941)

John George (Johnny) (1909–1992)
Married 1st (1934) Angela Culme-Seymore
Married 2nd (1941) Mary Cookson
Married 3rd (1953) Kathlyn Tandy
Married 4th (1958) Anna Janson

Anne Clarissa
Countess of Avon
Married (1952)
Sir Anthony Eden

Henry Winston (Peregrine) (1913–2002)
Married 1st (1954) Patricia Somerville-March
Married 2nd (1957) Yvonne Jehanin

Winston Leonard
(1874–1965)

Clementine Ogilvy Hozier
(1885–1977)

Randolph (1911–1968)
Married 1st (1939)
Pamela Digby
Married 2nd (1948)
June Osborne

Mary
The Lady Soames LG DBE (1922–)
Married (1947)
Baron Arthur Christopher Soames

Diana (1909–1963)
Married 1st (1932)
John Bailey
Married 2nd (1935)
Duncan Sandys

Sarah (1914–1982)
Married 1st (1936)
Vic Oliver
Married 2nd (1949)
Antony Beauchamp
Married 3rd (1962) Henry Jesson

Contents

Illustrations appear between pages 136 and 137

Introduction

Our story focuses on four members of the immediate Churchill family: Lord Randolph, his American wife Jennie, and their sons Winston and John (Jack). By considering them as a family, and, in particular, by bringing young Jack fully into the picture, we are better able to understand the lives of this remarkable group of people. Lord Randolph Spencer Churchill was the second son of the 7th Duke and Duchess of Marlborough, John and Frances Churchill, who lived at the stately Blenheim Palace, Woodstock, Oxfordshire in England. In 1874, Lord Randolph married the stunningly beautiful Miss Jennie Jerome, second daughter of Leonard and Clara (née Hall) Jerome of New York.

Earlier in that same year, Lord Randolph had been a newly elected Conservative MP (member of Parliament) for his home constituency of Woodstock, sitting in the House of Commons of the British Parliament at Westminster in London. Jennie, who was well-educated, and fluent in French and German, and an accomplished pianist, took an immediate interest in politics that would last for the rest of her life. While Randolph would rise politically to become a cabinet minister in the government, Jennie diligently promoted his career, even to the extent of campaigning for him in an election to retain his seat in Parliament, which was unheard of for a woman in Victorian Britain. Jennie would become established as a society hostess, mingling with the top tier of aristocratic society, including the Royal Family, and in particular befriending Edward, Prince of Wales, and his wife Princess Alexandra. The Prince was the elder son and heir of Queen Victoria, the reigning monarch.

The Churchills' elder son, Winston, would grow up to be a soldier, and while he was still quite young he became a successful politician and cabinet minister, following in his father's footsteps. When he was in his mid-sixties the Second World War (1939–45) broke out between Britain and Germany, and he became prime minister in May 1940, at an hour of great danger to his country. It is as Britain's wartime prime minister that he achieved a leading role on the world stage, credited with leading Britain to victory in the war. It was this phase of his life that made him famous and for which he is mostly known in the world today.

The Churchills' younger son, John, far exceeded his brother at school and was frequently top of his class. He served as an army officer in both the Boer War in South

Africa in 1900 and the First World War during 1914–18. He would, however, vanish into obscurity, and few people today know of his existence. This is the first complete portrait of the family, and Jack's story is central to understanding the family dynamic.

PROFESSOR OF PSYCHOLOGY Keith Simonton, in his 1994 book *Greatness: Who Makes History and Why,* discussed great men. Writing of Winston Churchill's "never surrender" attitude in the Second World War, Professor Simonton discovered the striking pattern that firstborns and only children tend to make good leaders in times of crisis, as they are used to taking charge. Then comes the astonishing assertion, "Churchill, as an only child, was typical." A sidebar to an illustration of Winston repeats the question "Was being an only child a factor in his greatness, as well as his defeats?"[1]

We are happy to reveal that Winston was not an only child. His brother, John (always known as Jack), was born in Dublin, some five years and two months after Winston. The brothers loved each other dearly, and Jack was frequently of service to Winston in unsung ways.

Winston is, by popular ballot, "the greatest Briton" who ever lived. Many millions of words have been and continue to be written about him in books, articles, the press, and a journal, *Finest Hour,* devoted entirely to preserving his memory and the lessons for the world today.[2] With a few honorable exceptions, most of this writing mentions Jack either in passing or not at all. To fully integrate Jack into the family history is the only way to begin to explain the many contentious issues that bedevil writings about the Churchills.

Jack's younger son, Peregrine, intended to write a new study of his Uncle Winston, which would endeavor to reinstate Peregrine's father in the family history. Having completed biographies of General Sir Ian Hamilton, and his wife Jean, Lady Hamilton, we were introduced by Mrs. Barbara Hamilton to Peregrine and his wife, Yvonne, in July 2001. After several meetings and discussions it was suggested that we might assist Peregrine, then eighty-eight years old, in organizing the papers and research for this work. This cooperation was only just getting under way when, in March 2002, Peregrine died unexpectedly. At the request of his widow, we have undertaken to write a new look at the Churchill family in the spirit in which Peregrine intended, and have been given unrestricted access to Mrs. Churchill's copyrighted material.

NOTE ON CURRENCY

Throughout the text we generally reference monetary figures for that particular time period; however, readers may be interested in their international and modern equivalents. Between 1874 and 1876, £1 was equal to $5.50. From 1877 to 1939 £1 was equal to $4.80, except in 1920, 1921, and 1932.[3] Between 1861 and 1901, £1 was worth nearly £70 in 2001 values.[4]

One

LOVE AT FIRST SIGHT

1873–1876

*In 1873, Queen Victoria was on the throne in England, and the British Empire was
at the height of its power. The Queen's elder son, Prince Albert Edward the Prince of
Wales (known as Edward or Bertie), was viewed by British subjects as a king in
waiting. Parliamentary affairs were dominated in the House of Commons by two
main parties. The Liberal Party, which was in power at this time, was led by William
Ewart Gladstone, prime minister from 1868 to 1874, 1880 to 1885, and 1892 to 1894.
The Conservative Party (Tories) was led by Benjamin Disraeli (Dizzy), prime minister from February 20, 1874, to April 21, 1880.*

It was August 1873, the week of the annual yacht races at Cowes on the Isle of Wight, known as Cowes Week. High society from the United Kingdom and Europe were in attendance. Mrs. Leonard Jerome and her daughters had been invited to a prestigious reception and ball aboard HMS *Ariadne.* Held in the presence of the Prince and Princess of Wales, the event was intended to introduce members of the visiting Russian Imperial family to English society. Where the printed invitation said "To meet," Mrs. Jerome's second daughter, Jeanette (Jennie), had written in the name "Randolph." This delightfully romantic touch by the nineteen-year-old American was the beginning of a whirlwind romance.

Having known the splendors of the court of Napoleon III before the defeat of France in 1870, Mrs. Jerome had raised her three daughters to have a high regard for European society. She had taken a pretty little cottage, the Villa Rosetta, with a garden and facing the sea, at West Cowes. The Russian Imperial family was staying close by, with Queen Victoria at Osborne House,[1] and the ball on August 12 was for the younger Russian Royals' entertainment. In this age, before electricity, dancing was from 3:30 P.M. to 7:30 P.M. on an English warship bedecked with lanterns and draped with the national colors of Great Britain and Imperial Russia. The guests, in their finest clothes and jewels, were serenaded by a band of the Royal Marines.

Jennie, resplendent in white gown and diamonds, attracted enormous attention. She was, quite simply, stunningly beautiful. Lord Randolph Churchill had seen her whirling about the deck and stood staring, spellbound by her dark good looks and sparkling blue-gray eyes.[2] The Honorable Frank Bertie, a junior Foreign Office clerk, was a neighbor of Randolph's in Oxfordshire, and also knew the Jeromes in Paris. It therefore fell to him to introduce the couple. Jennie later recalled the exact words: "Miss Jerome, may I present an old friend of mine who has just arrived in Cowes, Lord Randolph Churchill."[3]

Jennie was intrigued by this English aristocrat. He was of medium height and slim build, pale of complexion, fair-haired, and had a full mustache. His blue eyes were a little protuberant. He was immaculately dressed and charming to speak to. Though he was no great dancer, he seized the moment and asked Jennie for the next quadrille. At the earliest opportunity he made excuses to leave the floor, and they sat together on deck, sipping champagne and talking of the many things they had in common. Both had traveled widely in Europe, and both were fluent in French and German. But what drew them most closely together was their intense love of all things equine. Both rode well, hunted to hounds, and were enthusiastic race-goers.

They were quite lost in each other's company until Mrs. Jerome, anxious that her daughter was too long away from the dance floor, appeared and whisked her away.

After this brief encounter Jennie prevailed on her mother to invite Lord Randolph and his friend Colonel Edgecumbe to dinner the next day. She enlisted the support of her elder sister, Clara, and they practiced piano duets to entertain and impress their guests. Barely twenty-four hours after she met him, Jennie confided to Clara that she had "the strangest feeling that he is going to ask me to marry him." Her mind was made up. "I am going to say yes." After dinner, Randolph confided to Edgecumbe that "he admired the two sisters, and meant, if he could, to make 'the dark one' his wife." At dinner, Jennie had cleverly mentioned that she strolled along a certain quiet path at the same time each day. Sure enough, the following day Randolph was waiting on the path for her. Alone at last, they resumed their animated conversations. After their tryst, Jennie asked her mother to invite him to dinner again that evening. Mrs. Jerome was alarmed at the speed with which this relationship was moving. She had her sights set a little higher than the second son of a duke for her daughter, but she issued a formal invitation nonetheless. Mrs. Jerome excused herself after dinner with a headache, but left Clara as chaperone. Randolph and Jennie strolled in the garden on that beautiful summer evening. The moment was perfect for a proposal of marriage. Jennie accepted. They agreed not to say anything to her mother, "as she would not understand the suddenness of it." Randolph, hopelessly in love, changed his plans and stayed at Cowes four more days, and they saw as much of each other as they could.[4]

At the end of Cowes Week, Jennie told her mother that she was betrothed to Lord Randolph, and the reaction was everything she might have feared. "She thought we were both quite mad and naturally would not hear of anything so precipitous." She forbade Jennie to see or write to Randolph, and early in September, returned the family to Paris.[5]

LORD RANDOLPH Spencer Churchill was the second surviving son of the 7th Duke of Marlborough (John Winston Spencer Churchill) and his wife, Frances Vane, daughter of the 3rd Marquis of Londonderry, with large estates in Ireland. This was a union of two of the great Conservative families in the land. The Churchills' family seat was the huge and imposing Blenheim Palace, at Woodstock in Oxfordshire, built to celebrate the victories of one of England's greatest soldiers, John Churchill, the 1st Duke of Marlborough. But the family was strapped for cash due to the enormous financial drain of the upkeep of the house and estate.

Born on February 13, 1849, at 3 Wilton Terrace, Belgravia, London, Randolph was raised as was usual for an aristocratic child in Victorian England. He was given into the care of nannies and governesses and seeing his parents perhaps once a day, before going away to a boarding school, Eton, at about age eight. He did moderately well at school, but the Duke had occasion to write to Eton, almost apologizing for his son's behavior. "He is a boy who is readily moved, has a quick sense of right and wrong. . . . His great faults are want of self control in his language, temper and demeanor and an imperiousness of disposition to those under him."[6]

Randolph's health was always precarious, and he had a weak heart. Still, his father was grooming him to be the Conservative member of Parliament for Woodstock. In 1864, aged fifteen, Randolph delivered a political speech on behalf of his father, which was successful. He toured Europe, improving his grasp of French and German, and on his return he sat his matriculation exams. Having passed into Merton College, Oxford, he studied history and law. He developed an interest in chess and became a founding member of the university chess club. He once took the world champion, William (Wilhelm) Steinitz, to thirty-three moves before losing, though the grandmaster was playing blindfolded. In 1870, he graduated with a second-class honors degree, having narrowly missed a first.

Jennie's father, Leonard Jerome, was a successful businessman in New York. He was not above making a large fortune by blatant manipulation of stock prices through the good offices of friends who were leading financial journalists. When he wasn't busy in the corrupt world of New York politics, he worked briefly as U.S. consul in Trieste. A great patron of the opera, he often engaged opera singers, who became his mistresses. His wife, Clarissa, bore him three living daughters — Clarita (who called herself Clara), born in April 1851, Jeanette (Jennie), born on January 9, 1854, and Leonie, born in August 1859. Peregrine Churchill said that Jennie's mother went to stay with Leonard Jerome's brother Addison and his wife Julia at 426 Henry Street, Brooklyn. A terrific snowstorm blew up, and Clarissa went into premature labor and could not be moved. She gave birth to Jennie in their house while the snow outside was several feet deep.[7] The Jerome girls had nannies and governesses, and as good a private education as money could buy, with the proper emphasis on the genteel arts — music, drawing, and languages.

In 1858 Leonard provided the family a palatial home in New York. It had a ballroom fit for 300 guests, a theater that could seat 600, and a dining room for 70. In 1867, the couple separated, but they remained on friendly terms and never divorced. With a good financial settlement, and money of her own, Mrs. Jerome was able to move to Paris.

Mrs. Jerome and Clara soon became intimately acquainted with the court of Napoleon III, forming a particular friendship with the beautiful Empress Eugénie. Mrs. Jerome was ambitious for her daughters, with the goal of marriage into the European aristocracy. The Franco-Prussian War in 1870 brought an end to her plans, and in September the Jerome women fled to England. Leonard came as quickly as he could and installed them in London's prestigious Brown's Hotel. The girls continued their piano lessons, Jennie having been taught in Paris by Stephen Heller, a noted Hungarian teacher and composer. An Austrian tutor walked the girls every day in Hyde Park as they perfected their German. France settled down, and in the autumn of 1871 the Jeromes were able to return to their house in the Boulevard Haussman.

AFTER COWES WEEK, Randolph returned to Blenheim Palace in a state of high excitement. His father was in Scotland, and on August 20, he wrote him a slightly clumsy letter, telling him that he had met the love of his life and wanted to get married:

> I love her better than life itself, and my one hope and dream now is that matters may be arranged that soon I may be united to her by ties that nothing but death itself could have the power to sever.[8]

Randolph received a frosty reply from his father, which ended with: "I only hope you will be guided by your mother and me." Marlborough immediately set in motion an investigation of Leonard Jerome's circumstances in America.[9] Jerome was held to be a well-known man with a fast reputation, whose large fortune was matched by his extravagant expenditures—and he had been bankrupt. There followed a letter to Randolph from his father: "Persons from the outside cannot but be struck with the unwisdom and the uncontrolled state of your feeling, which completely paralyses your judgment."[10]

His mother, too, delivered a wounding blow: "Under any circumstances, an American connection is not one that we would like."[11]

During their separation Randolph and Jennie wrote to each other of their undying love. A general election of members to Parliament was expected soon. He said that he would refuse to stand for Parliament unless he was allowed to marry Jennie and that "all tricks are fair in love and war."[12] He also confided to her that public life held no great charms for him, but he would do it if it pleased her. She responded that she was already excited about becoming the wife of a member of Parliament and was reading up on British politics.[13]

On the other hand, Mrs. Jerome had written to her husband, describing Jennie as hasty, rash, headstrong, and impulsive. She implored him to come to Paris and try to influence his favorite daughter, who idolized her father so. Jerome wrote to Jennie and begged her to think again.[14]

From the end of August, Jennie bombarded her mother with tearful entreaties to be allowed to marry. Randolph wrote to Mrs. Jerome often and would finally win her over. She acknowledged on September 9 that "you have quite won my heart by your frank and honorable manner."[15] She was later the first to give way, and told her husband she consented to the marriage. Jerome, guided by his wife, telegraphed that he would provide Jennie with a dowry of £50,000/$275,000, an allowance of £2,000/$11,000 a year, and leave her one-third of his estate.[16] This was a powerful incentive to a cash-strapped English aristocratic family, and it was implied by the Duke that he would agree to the marriage if Randolph stood as MP for Woodstock and won, but he wanted them to wait awhile.[17]

Then, at the beginning of November, Jerome found out about Marlborough's investigations into his affairs in New York and sent an angry telegram to his wife: CONSENT WITHDRAWN.[18]

Nevertheless, Jerome, having arrived in Paris at the end of December, set out to meet Lord Randolph in London, and they dined together.[19] With their shared passion for horse racing, they became the best of friends, but still Leonard withheld his consent to the marriage.

The general election was called. Randolph ran for MP for Woodstock against a formidable Liberal candidate, George Brodrick, who made heavy and sustained attacks on the way the Churchills had run the constituency in the past. Randolph put in some rather nervous performances but campaigned hard, visiting all parts of the constituency.

In February 1874, Randolph won a resounding victory by 569 votes to 404. He cabled Jennie immediately to expect him in a day or so.[20] The Duke then gave his consent to the marriage. Jerome wrote to Randolph: "I congratulate you most heartily."[21] In mid-February, the Duke traveled to Paris to meet the Jeromes. Mrs. Jerome found him "a perfect dear." Jennie, who had just turned twenty, conducted a charm offensive, playing Beethoven sonatas for him on the piano and discussing British politics with marked intelligence. The Duke took an immediate liking to her. He agreed to settle all of Randolph's existing accounts, grant him an allowance of £2,000 a year, and pay all his annual expenses as an MP. Leonard gave his consent and considered that a dowry of £50,000/$275,000 and a joint income of £4,000/$22,000 a year was sufficient for the young couple to start their life together.

The wedding date was set for April 15, 1874, at the chapel of the British Embassy in Paris. The Duchess said she was ill and the Duke could not go without her. However, Randolph's brother, Blandford, and three of his six sisters attended. The Jeromes spent lavishly—Jennie wore white Parisian satin, under Alençon lace, with a simple string of fine pearls and a corsage of American orange blossom, all designed to enhance her dark beauty. After a sumptuous wedding breakfast, the couple left in a smart coach for their four-week honeymoon tour of Europe.

The newlyweds returned to England in late May to live temporarily at Blenheim Palace. By then, Jennie was already pregnant with their first child. She was deeply impressed with the grandeur of the place. It was the first time she had met Randolph's mother and his other three sisters, but despite the warm greeting by the Duke the Churchill womenfolk remained stern and unforgiving, for their mother had not considered her good enough for Randolph. Jennie made a real effort to get to know them. She may have tried too hard and may have come off as simply showing off. She knew she was beautiful and she was always dressed in the height of fashion. Neither of these attributes applied to the Duchess and her daughters. Jennie was a vastly better pianist, and a truly accomplished horsewoman. Everything she did seemed to them calculated to offend.[22]

Nevertheless, Randolph and Jennie were the golden couple of the season. Clara and Leonie came to visit from Paris, and the two elder sisters attended balls together, but Leonie, aged sixteen, was too young. Girls did not "come out" in society until they were eighteen years old. Jennie was very popular with the young men, but as the pregnancy developed, she had to take proper care of herself. Soon she was denied the chance to ride, while Randolph went off hunting with the Heythrop Hounds, the Duke of Beaufort's famous fox and hounds hunt, which took place during certain seasons of the year. Jennie played the piano, viewed the oil paintings in the vast palace, and read in the magnificent library, but this was not what she had married for. She agitated for a home of their own, and in the summer Randolph rented a small house for them in London's fashionable West End: No. 1 Curzon Street, Piccadilly.[23]

It was during a visit to Blenheim in November 1874, when Jennie was out walking on a game shoot with Randolph, that she went into premature labor. She was rushed back to the house and, unfit to climb the stairs, was put to bed in a downstairs room. After a difficult eight-hour labor, the local doctor, Frederic Taylor, delivered Winston Leonard Spencer Churchill at 1:30 A.M. There had been no time to assemble the baby's clothes, and so he was dressed in some clothing given by the local solicitor's wife. In the days ahead it would become apparent that the new baby had red hair and blue eyes.

Winston was baptized on December 27 by the Duke's chaplain in the private chapel at Blenheim Palace, and was named after Randolph's father (whose middle name was Winston) and Leonard for his other grandfather. Randolph's great-aunt Clementina, Lady Camden,[24] was his godmother, and at Randolph's request Leonard Jerome was his godfather, though he is not thought to have made it from the United States on time.

In January 1875, the young Churchills returned to Curzon Street. Jennie had appointed Mrs. Elizabeth Everest, aged about forty years, as an experienced nurse and nanny. This single lady—"Mrs." was an honorific title—became an enormous influence on the Churchill boys. When Winston learned to talk he called her Woom, meaning woman. She is the "Woom" or "Woomany" to whom the boys constantly refer in their letters, an adored and adoring companion for twenty years.

Furnishing their new home proved costly, and money troubles were already beginning soon after Winston's birth. Leonard Jerome did not pay all of the expected dowry, and the Duke also seems to have failed to pay the full allowance he had promised Randolph.[25] The young couple seemed in denial as they vigorously embarked on establishing themselves in society. The Duke did, however, buy a leasehold for £10,000/$55,000 on a new house for them: No. 48 Charles Street in fashionable Mayfair. This was a four-story house where the couple could set up home properly for the first time. But it, too, had to be refurbished and redecorated. They hired an excellent French cook and a number of servants. They were able to entertain successfully, but at some expense. Jennie was thrilled whenever the Prince of Wales came to dinner. Being seated beside the future king of England was exactly what she had always aspired to. The Prince always complimented them on the meals served, and clearly enjoyed their company a good deal.

Randolph had his parliamentary duties to attend to; Jennie sometimes visited her family in Paris, taking baby Winston with her. Throughout, they kept up a delightful correspondence. Jennie wrote to Randolph after he had left her in Paris, circa the summer of 1875:

> It seemed so lonely not to find you dearest. I took particular pains to shut the door of your room. I could not bear the desolate look it had. . . . I hope your cold is no worse and remember only *6* cigarettes. . . . Please take care of yourself darling boy and come back soon to your lonely Jennie. . . . The baby is such a darling, he is growing so fat and nearly walks alone.[26]

Charles Street turned out to be a drafty house, and Winston was unwell. In October 1875, after a successful visit to the Newmarket races where he cleared £400/$2,200 in winnings, Randolph wrote "I still feel rather anxious about the baby. I hope you will be very careful of him in that draughty house."[27] Early in 1876, he was trying to rent a house in the country, which he felt would be healthier for them all. Letters from this period always send his love to "Skinny," their comical nickname for this plump baby.

Jennie was already concerned about Randolph's excessive smoking, and about the continuous minor ailments that seemed to dog him. Another undated letter, circa autumn 1876, shows what a close and loving family they made: "Tell me really how you are . . . please dearest get well and come back. . . . The baby is most flourishing, but he never will kiss me unless I say 'For Papa.'"[28]

THE CHURCHILLS had settled down to a happy family life, but soon they were to face an upheaval. Randolph's elder brother, George Charles, Marquis of Blandford (known as Blandford), was married, with family, and had been having an affair with Edith, Lady Aylesford, a former mistress of the Prince of Wales. On February 20, 1876, the Prince suddenly struck a high moral tone and wrote to Blandford demanding that he divorce his wife and marry Lady Aylesford.[29] An abusive row developed in which Randolph and Jennie took Blandford's side against the Prince. The Prince let it be known that he would never again enter a house where the Churchills were guests, and the family was suddenly dropped from invitation lists.

Two

AN IRISH "EXILE"

1876–1880

Ireland was in those days an integral part of the United Kingdom, and therefore sub-ject to the rule of the British government. Irish members of Parliament sat in the House of Commons. Queen Victoria was also Queen of Ireland, and she was repre-sented there by a viceroy, a titled English aristocrat. For some years, discontent had been growing in Ireland over problems with absentee landlords from England charg-ing exorbitant rents for lands and houses they owned there. When the poorer farm-ers could not afford to pay, the bailiffs evicted them. An Irish Home Rule League Party (later the Irish Parliamentary Party) had sprung up. They demanded an Irish Parliament in Dublin. In the 1874 general election they won fifty-nine seats. The "Irish Question," as it was referred to, would begin to dominate parliamentary busi-ness. In 1877, a famine in Ireland increased the demand for Home Rule. The Duke and Duchess of Marlborough became Viceroy and Vicereine, and Randolph and Jennie ac-companied them.

The Conservative prime minister, Benjamin Disraeli, was a great friend of the Duke of Marlborough and advised him to accept the position of viceroy of Ireland, in order to distance himself and his family from the upset with the Prince of Wales. His term of duties would last for three years and three months.

The installation of the 7th Duke of Marlborough as the new viceroy, in December 1876, was a major state occasion. The Duke wore a full-dress uniform, and his family and staff entered the city of Dublin in a cavalcade of coaches to a salute of cannon fire. The cheering crowds could see that Lord and Lady Randolph had brought their two-year-old son, Winston, in the carriage with them. After the fashion of the day, he wore a white satin frock, with petticoats, and a royal blue coat, with his red hair done up in ringlets, hanging to his shoulders, and tied with a white ribbon. Jennie thought he should be given the chance to participate in this, his first great state event.

The duke and duchess lived in the Viceregal Lodge in Phoenix Park, Dublin. Randolph, who was appointed as his father's (unpaid) private secretary, lived in the "Little" White Lodge close by, with Jennie, Winston, Mrs. Everest, and a small staff.

Randolph and Jennie quickly took to the life of the Anglo-Irish gentry, with its heavy emphasis on riding, hunting, fishing, shooting, and sailing.[1]

During one vigorous ride, Jennie was galloping through a farmyard gateway when a gust of wind blew the gate shut and her horse crashed into it, spilling her from the saddle. She later recalled:

> Luckily I fell clear, but it looked as if I might be crushed underneath him, and Randolph, coming up at that moment, thought I was killed. A few seconds later, however, seeing me all right, in the excitement of the moment he seized my [hip] flask and emptied it. For many days it was a standing joke against him that *I* had the fall, and *he* had the whisky![2]

A contemporary record of Jennie's beauty at that time was made by Lord D'Abernon (Edgar Vincent), the former ambassador to Berlin and an international banker in Turkey. He saw Jennie on a formal occasion at the Viceregal Lodge where all eyes were turned on her. She wore a diamond star on the front of her black hair, "its lustre dimmed" only by "the flashing glory" of her blue/gray eyes. "Universally popular," she stood out from amongst the crowd, "radiant, translucent, intense." To these attributes he added that she possessed a "cultivated intelligence," "kindliness," "high spirits," and a "wish to please."[3]

The member of Parliament for Woodstock had duties to attend to in England, and Randolph was obliged to spend time in London away from his family. His letters to Jennie always said he was "dying" to get back to her, and that he was bored.

In his maiden speech to Parliament (March 1874), he had added his voice to the opposition to turn Oxford into a new territorial military center, suggesting it would become a garrisoned city like London, Dublin, or Edinburgh, with troops on hand to control an unruly populace. The Lord Mayor of Dublin took exception to Randolph's characterization of his city as lawless and in need of patrolling.[4]

Disraeli (Dizzy, as he was known) had a quiet word with Randolph at that time about his performance in Parliament. Randolph had taken almost no part in future debates that session, speaking only occasionally on matters relating to his Woodstock constituency.

In Ireland, however, his interest in politics developed when he was thrown into the company of some very impressive intellects. Chief among them was Lord Justice Gerald FitzGibbon, the law adviser at Dublin Castle, seat of British rule in Ireland. He dealt with questions of law from every part of the country and from every department of government. He was also the center of a circle of fine minds, meeting often to discuss politics and high culture. Through his great friendship with FitzGibbon, Randolph was drawn into this circle. It included the Roman Catholic priest Father James Healy, who became a regular visitor to the "Little" White Lodge, and who interested Jennie greatly in the issues surrounding Irish Home Rule (that is, a Dublin-based parliament separate from the London Parliament), to which Randolph was fiercely opposed. As he got to know this group better, Randolph came to rue his earlier description of Dublin as a "seditious capital."[5] In late 1877, he expressed his regret in the Commons, admitting, "I have since come to know Ireland better."[6] Through their interest in Irish politics, Lord Randolph and Jennie visited all thirty-two counties of Ireland.[7]

The spring and summer of 1876 in Ireland had been unusually wet, and that year the potato harvest was very poor, leaving a serious shortage of seed for the following year. When the bad weather continued throughout the summer of 1879, a most serious failure of all harvests, potatoes and wheat, and the lack of usable peat for fuel, led to very great hardship for the people of Ireland. Some poor relief was provided but was inadequate. There was famine, evoking memories of the more infamous "Great Hunger" of 1845–52, when 1 million people died of starvation.[8]

In late 1879, the Duchess of Marlborough set up her own Famine Relief Fund, with Randolph as its secretary.[9] Jennie became much involved in its work. Its purpose was to provide food, fuel, and clothing, especially for the elderly and the weak, and small sums of money to keep able-bodied men, temporarily in distress, out of the workhouse, which was a place of poor relief where they received one meal a day and a bed for the night.[10] Grants were also available to schools, that they might provide meals for the children. With the prestige of the Marlborough and Churchill names behind it, the fund attracted substantial gifts from Queen Victoria, the Prince of Wales, and all the great families of mainland Britain.[11] By March 1880, the fund had reached £88,000/$484,000. It raised in total over £135,000/$742,500 (today's equivalent of £8 million/$44 million).[12]

When Randolph was attending the Commons in London, Jennie wrote to keep him abreast of family matters in Ireland. In one letter she mentioned the fuss Winston created when she had to leave with the Duchess to carry out famine relief work:

> Winston has just been with me—such a darling he is—"I can't have my Mama go—& if she does I will run after the train & jump in" he said to me. I have told Everest to take him out for a drive tomorrow if it is fine—as it is better the stables should have a little work.[13]

In the course of administering these funds, often dispensed through local committees, Randolph and Jennie continued to visit different parts of Ireland, meeting large numbers of its citizenry, and experiencing poverty firsthand.[14] Together they had become more than familiar with Ireland's problems, and these times would have a lasting influence on them both. Their travels went a long way toward radicalizing Randolph's politics, and set him on a collision course with his own party in government. The Tory Party and government had no interest in providing money to the Irish, and many English absentee landlords, despite the famine, were still claiming unfair rents from impoverished Irish peasants and farmers.[15] On September 28, 1877, during a speech at Woodstock in which he discussed the rise of an Irish Nationalist movement and the disruptive role of its members of Parliament in the House of Commons, Randolph said:

> I have no hesitation in saying that it is inattention to Irish legislation that has produced obstruction. There are great and crying Irish questions, which the Government have not attended to. Who is it, but the Irish, whose eloquence so often commands our admiration, whose irresistible humour compels our laughter, whose fiery outbursts provoke our passions?[16]

Randolph became a formidable expert on Irish matters and now threw himself fully into politics. He took upon himself a survey of the need for educational reform. He criticized the diversion of funds to the Church of Ireland at the expense of other institutions. He persuaded the government to set up a small commission, on which he and Lord FitzGibbon sat, to enquire into the condition, management, and revenues of Ireland's schools. Fact-finding for this work also took him all around Ireland. Lord Randolph had become a man with a mission to solve the "Irish Question," a phrase used from the 1800s by members of the British government and the press to describe the Irish struggle for nationalism and independence.

Later that autumn in the Commons, he roundly condemned England's record, proclaiming that it had "years of wrong, years of crime, years of tyranny, years of oppression, years of general misgovernment to make amends for in Ireland."[17] This radical stance did not make him in any way sympathetic to the flourishing Irish nationalist movement, represented by the Home Rule League Party, under the chairmanship of Isaac Butt, a Dublin barrister. Butt was a member of Parliament and a moderate. But hovering in the wings was another party member and member of Parliament, the charismatic Charles Stewart Parnell. Parnell made inflammatory speeches in favor of Home Rule,[18] what we know today as a devolved parliament with its own elected members in Dublin. There was also a small band of revolutionaries, loosely referred to as the Fenians, who sought complete independence from Britain. This notion was anathema to Randolph, who would have liked to implement a huge range of reforms to improve the quality of life for all the Irish people, to give them equal status with the other citizens of the United Kingdom.

With a new confidence, Randolph was vigorously opposing the more militant policies of his own party and government. During the crisis occasioned by the Russo-Turkish war of 1877–78, it was to the great Liberal politician, Sir Charles Dilke, that he wrote, on February 7, 1878, suggesting ways that several Balkan provinces might gain their freedom from Turkey (which had the backing of Disraeli's government), and he even promised to enlist the Irish Nationalist vote for the project. He later told Dilke that he did not want these new republics to fall under some Russian or German prince who would be a mere puppet under the guise of a constitutional monarchy. This son of a duke had no great regard for aristocratic rule. As a war fever swept through England, Randolph denounced it in the Commons, saying: "I think the Conservative Party are gone mad."[19]

JENNIE'S LIFE had certainly not turned out as she might have planned. She and Randolph adored the two-year-old Winston, and there were pleasures enough to be had in the company of the Irish and Anglo-Irish gentry—but it was not the same as the glories of "the Season" that she had so recently been a part of, that great round of balls, banquets, and festivities that defined the lives of the British aristocracy.

Jennie was supportive of Randolph's newfound interest in politics. There was the possibility of advancement in this field, and Jennie would become fiercely ambitious for her husband. The famine in Ireland gave her some meaningful work to do, something cruelly denied to women of her class and station. It even brought her a little closer to her austere mother-in-law. She greatly enjoyed the opportunity to share in Randolph's work as they traveled about Ireland together.

But he was increasingly absent, needing to attend sessions of the House of Commons. Letters between them in 1877 began to indicate that Jennie was feeling "lonely and wretched"; his replies begged her not to be angry with him. He sent her a fine new saddle, and was "relieved" when she said how much she liked it. Jennie's sisters, Clara and Leonie, visited her on occasion in Ireland.

Their dear son, Winston, was a constant topic of interest. In Jennie's letters to Randolph a precarious "W" began to appear at the bottom, as Winston added his first attempts at a signature. He was a greatly indulged and boisterous child. "Winston is here making such a noise I can hardly think of what I'm writing. . . . Clara & Winston send their love."[20]

The letters at this time are full of the usual stories of child development and baby talk: "I bought Winston an elephant this afternoon which he has been asking me for some time, & I was on the point of saying to the shop-woman 'An ephelant.' I just stopped myself in time," and "Winston is flourishing and has learnt a new song, 'We will all go hunting today, etc.'"[21]

News of winter colds brought concern from the absent father, who wrote on September 18, 1877: "I shall leave for Ireland Monday night and be with you Xmas day morning. . . . I am rather uneasy at your account of little Winston and hope you will get the Dr. to see him." Winston had been a robust baby, but the atrocious wet weather in Ireland was giving him regular chest trouble. This, and the weakness in the male line of his family, seems to have left him prone to ill health. In December 1877, Randolph considered bringing Winston back to England to rest in a sanatorium, but it was not necessary.[22]

In 1878, Winston's portrait was painted by the Dublin artist P. Cyron Ward. The most remarkable features were still his mass of red ringlets, tied in ribbons, and his beautiful blue eyes. Mrs. Everest took him walking in Phoenix Park most days when the weather permitted. With his head filled with stories told by her and the servants, he expected to encounter "Fenian ruffians" at any moment. "I gathered these were wicked people and there was no end to what they would do if they had their way."[23] There were anti-British demonstrations by the Fenians in and around Phoenix Park, and the nurse was always wary. Mrs. Everest and Winston set out one day to a pantomime at the theater only to find it had been burnt down.[24] While out riding his donkey one day in 1879, Winston had a serious fall and was badly concussed.[25] Both parents were greatly alarmed, and he was to suffer painful headaches for years to come—an added trial for a by now somewhat delicate child.

On April 14, 1879, Randolph sent birthday greetings to his mother and took the opportunity to let her know just how happy he was at that stage in his life: "I write to wish you many happy returns for your birthday to-morrow, which is also, as perhaps you may remember, our wedding-day; and having been married five years I begin to feel highly respectable."[26]

Winston had the constant attention of Mrs. Everest, and Jennie read to him on a regular basis. At around age four, Mrs. Everest introduced him to a book called *Reading Without Tears* and began his proper education. This was in preparation for the appointment of a governess, who would be brought in one day a week to teach lessons. Winston took an immediate dislike to her and to the whole idea of compulsory learning. He later recalled her as the "steadily gathering shadow"[27] over his daily life, and how he would run away and hide in the extensive garden shrubberies. The descent into "a dismal bog called sums,"[28] and the knowledge that his mother "sided with the Governess almost always"[29] was a blow to the little chap. This display of rebellion, and inability to adjust to any degree of discipline, bore all the hallmarks of an overindulged, not to say spoiled, child. Jennie did get stricter with him, but it was the start of a series of misadventures relating to Winston's education.[30]

Winston created the impression, perhaps unintentionally, that his mother did not give him enough attention, when he wrote that he remembered her in Ireland wearing a riding habit, "fitting like a skin and often beautifully spotted with mud," and that she and his father "hunted continually" on their large horses.[31] There is a very fine photograph of Jennie looking beautiful in just such a costume.

Sometime late in June 1879, Jennie and Randolph conceived their second child, and his arrival Jennie declared to be her most joyful experience in Ireland.[32] Once again, Jennie took good care of herself, giving up her riding interest, but finding time to accompany Randolph on his school inspection tours. For a second time, however, she was not able to carry the baby to full term. On February 4, 1880, she delivered John Churchill prematurely into the world. His younger son, Peregrine, told us that his father was described as a "blue baby," after a difficult birthing, and baptism had to be arranged very quickly. The full name given the infant was John Strange Spencer Churchill. John was for his paternal grandfather; Randolph and the duchess always called him Jack in honor of the famed 1st Duke of Marlborough, who won the battle of Blenheim in Bavaria. The name Strange was for the 5th Earl of Roden, John Strange Jocelyn, who stood in at very short notice as godfather.

Jack had blue eyes and fair hair, though his hair would darken to jet black like his mother's. The arrival of a new baby was, of course, a source of upheaval in the household. To the five-year-old Winston it was something of a mixed blessing, as he rarely saw other children. Jennie had brought the Jerome rocking chair from her family home in America and used it to rock Winston, but now rocked Jack.[33] It would be a while before Jack would be a playmate. Meanwhile, Winston lost the undivided attentions of his mother and Woomany and had to share them with a brother. This is usually resented by a first child and, as an entirely natural development, need not be exaggerated. If his mother or Mrs. Everest was attending to Jack, then the other was free to devote her time to Winston. Most famously, Winston described how he "loved" his mother "dearly—but at a distance," and implying that Mrs. Everest was his one constant companion and "confidante."[34]

By 1880, the Duke of Marlborough's thirty-nine months as viceroy were coming to an end. A general election had been called in England for April 2, 1880, so Randolph, Jennie, and family returned home early in March. They lived in a hotel near Blenheim Palace until their latest new house, 29 St. James's Place, Mayfair, London, could be got ready.[35]

Randolph worked very hard to retain his seat at Woodstock. He wrote to his mother on March 21 that he was campaigning from nine o'clock in the morning until eleven at night. Bad weather in England had also seen the rural workers suffer hardship, and the Blenheim Estate land agent had not handled the tenants who worked on the estate with a great deal of tact. In a small community like Woodstock, where those in charge at Blenheim Palace were expected to set an example and treat people fairly, it would have detracted from the family's reputation that numbers of estate workers were allowed to sink into poverty during the Duke's absence. Luckily, the splendid work the whole family had put into the Duchess's Famine Relief Fund in Ireland earned them a good deal of political sympathy in Oxfordshire. Thus, while the Conservative Party crashed to a heavy defeat in the election,[36] Randolph retained his seat by 512 votes to 452. To examine the causes of their defeat, the Conservatives would set up a Central Committee tasked with "reforming, popularising and improving the party organisation."[37] Randolph would become a major force in party and national politics.

Three

A POLITICAL
STAR IS BORN

1880–1882

The Liberal Party won the April 1880 British general election. Their leader, William Ewart Gladstone, became prime minister and would remain so until 1885. In the months and years ahead, Lord Randolph Churchill would be at the forefront of the battle to discredit the Liberals in any way he could and prevent their policies being passed in bills through Parliament. He started by preventing a Liberal, Charles Bradlaugh, from taking his seat because he refused to swear the oath of office on the Bible. In the meantime, the Land League arm of the Irish Home Rule League Party was gathering momentum under the leadership of Charles Stewart Parnell. Home Rule was anathema to the Conservative Party, and Lord Randolph was now viewed as an expert on Irish affairs.

The newly elected House of Commons assembled for its first session on May 5, 1880. The Liberal member of Parliament for Northampton, the atheist Charles Bradlaugh, caused an uproar by refusing to take the religious oath of allegiance on the Bible, which was also the oath of office required of all elected members before they could take their seats. When the Liberal government, anxious to get on with other matters, suggested setting up a committee to investigate the issue, Randolph swung into action and delivered one of his most brilliant speeches; it was for the whole Parliament to decide the matter, he insisted. Bradlaugh's atheism was of no particular interest to Randolph, but he seized the opportunity to cause deep embarrassment to the new Liberal administration. He immediately became the darling of the Conservative opposition, both in the House and in the country, and his speeches dominated the press.

The affair was dragged out for months. Randolph drove such deep wedges into the ranks of the Liberals that the government was defeated by 275 votes to 230 on the issue. When Bradlaugh eventually agreed to take the oath, Randolph gleefully led a revolt that denied him the chance to swear an oath he so obviously did not believe in. The largely Tory press loved every moment of it, and Randolph's fame was established as the scourge of "the enemy." It was not until 1886 that compromise was reached with a different wording than usual and Bradlaugh took his seat in the Commons.[1]

The defeat in the 1880 general election had been a shock to the Tory establishment, and their critics seized an opportunity to begin a campaign for change within the party. Randolph joined a group calling themselves the Fourth Party (allowing the Liberals, Conservatives, and Irish Nationalists as the first three). This group included Sir Henry Drummond Wolff, member for Portsmouth, a senior figure in the Conservative Party; John Gorst, member for Chatham, whose organizational skills led Disraeli to credit him with the electoral victory of 1874; Lord Randolph Churchill; and the new member Arthur Balfour, nephew of Lord Salisbury, who was somewhat more loosely associated with them. These four sat together on the opposition front bench and met regularly and in secret. They devised strategies to fight the Liberals and also to galvanize what they saw as a thoroughly inadequate Conservative opposition. Randolph's acerbic wit was given free rein. He could be rude to the point of vulgarity and made as many personal enemies as he made friends in his own party. For example, the leader of the opposition in the Commons, the heavily bewhiskered Sir Stafford Northcote, was promptly nicknamed "The Goat"; Lord Randolph poked fun at him at parties. He called two Conservative members, W. H. Smith and Sir Richard Cross, "Marshall and Snelgrove," which was the name of a garment makers company, implying they were only tradesmen, and jeered at "the old gang" in the Commons.[2]

The first political battle in Parliament in February 1880 was over the Employers' Liability Bill, in which the Liberal government tried to offer some protective legislation to their working-class supporters while not simultaneously overburdening their powerful manufacturing backers. The bill was meant basically to redress inequalities in the position between employers and workers in the cases of accidents at the workplace.[3] Hastily put together, it was riddled with anomalies. The Liberals expected the official opposition to argue in the interests of the capitalist class against new liabilities being laid upon them, and were astonished when Lord Randolph and the other members of the Fourth Party denounced the bill as not strong enough in protecting the interests of injured workers, and proceeded to expose its inadequacies. Randolph poured ridicule on the Liberals and easily emerged as the real champion of the working class on this issue. By the time the bill was passed through Parliament later that year, it had been altered beyond recognition. Employers were to be held fully accountable for the conditions of their employees and the machinery in their workplaces.[4]

Every piece of legislation brought before the House in this session found the Fourth Party well informed and in a combative mood. Their arguments were often more progressive than the "left" of the Liberal Party, and as for the old Tory leadership, they simply ignored it entirely.

One important figure deeply impressed by the Fourth Party was Benjamin Disraeli, now Lord Beaconsfield.[5] He personally encouraged Wolff and Gorst in their work, and shortly before his death in April 1881, he predicted to Sir William Harcourt, Liberal member for Oxford, that Lord Randolph would become a powerful figure in the Conservative Party: "When they come in they will have to give him anything he chooses to ask for and in a very short time they will have to take anything he chooses to give them."[6]

STILL VEXED at the social ostracism caused by the rift with the Prince of Wales, Jennie took great pride in Randolph's success. She clearly hoped it would bring them some social advancement. A note of July 12, 1880, to her mother in Paris was only a little short of a begging letter, with its heavy emphasis on their shortage of money, but it evinces a deep understanding of her husband's character. Winston was still a handful:

Dearest Mama

Old Everest got a cold and I had to give her a holiday—and she is still away. Luckily I found a very good monthly nurse who looks after the Baby [Jack].

Winston is a very nice boy, and is getting on with his lessons, but he is a most difficult child to manage—so much for the infants.

You will be glad to hear that R.[andolph] has been covering himself with glory, and I am told he has made himself a wonderfully good position in the House. Last Monday he spoke on an Irish Question which interests all the landlords at the moment, and he has made a _really_ splendid speech—everyone says so—and Gladstone got up and answered him for an hour. . . . When this Government goes out (which they say will be soon) I fancy R. and his boon companion Sir Henry Drummond Wolff must be given something. I am only so afraid of R. getting spoilt—he would lose half his talent if he did. I keep reminding him of it. London is very gay just now. I haven't been to many balls as I simply can't afford to get dresses and one can't always wear the same thing. Besides I am not bidden to the ones I want to go to and I do not care about the others. This week I am going out every night, tomorrow to the opera; I was sent a box. . . . [7]

I shall send Winston and John to Ventnor [with Mrs. Everest to the Isle of Wight] for a month. Money is such a hateful subject for me just now don't let us talk about it.[8]

Jennie attended many of the debates at the House of Commons, and her dinner table saw many schemes hatched by the Fourth Party. By a delicious irony they lived right next door to "The Goat." The group became fast friends, and as Gorst and Balfour were both music lovers, Jennie frequently joined them at concerts. She and Balfour played the piano together very well.

FROM OCTOBER 1880, Parnell and an organization known as the Land League started a campaign in Ireland called "Captain Boycott." They encouraged tenants to refuse to pay their rents, and to resist evictions, and attack land agents and bailiffs acting for absentee landlords. Gladstone proposed to remedy the situation by introducing land reforms alongside a coercion bill to maintain law and order. The Land Act was to provide fair rents fixed by land courts for a period of fifteen years; tenants could be evicted only if they did not pay rent; a tenant who wanted to give up farming could do so and sell his lease. From April 1, 1881, the House of Commons sittings were entirely dominated by Irish affairs. Randolph spoke passionately against the coercion bill, defending the "high qualities" and "many virtues"[9] of the Irish people, and deploring this act that would criminalize many men seeking to protect their homes and families. He caused great disquiet in the ranks of the Liberals as he ruthlessly exposed just what an illiberal bill this was. Although 250,000 tenants had their rents reduced, guarantees of tenancy seemed pointless to those who could not afford to pay their rent, and no help was provided to those already in arrears. In October, despite a calming of the situation in Ireland, Parnell and the leaders of the Land League were seized and imprisoned in Kilmainham Gaol.[10]

Randolph was working so hard in the political sphere that he was nearing exhaustion. Partly to get out of London and into the fresh air, partly to save money, and partly to continue political discussions with his father, the family moved into Blenheim Palace for some months. It was good to be able to ride and hunt in Oxfordshire, and the naturally friendly and exuberant Jennie did all she could to make the stay pleasant. But the hostility of her mother-in-law was an insuperable barrier. On November 21, 1881, Jennie wrote to her mother expressing her abiding unhappiness at Blenheim:

It is such ages since I've seen you. It is really too long.

I quite forget what it is like to be with people who love me. I do so long sometimes to have someone to whom I could go and talk. Of course, Randolph is awfully good to me and always takes my part in everything, but how can I always be abusing his mother to him—The fact is I *loathe* living here. It's not on account of its dullness, *that* I don't mind, but . . . it is gall and wormwood to me to accept anything or to be living on anyone I hate. It is no use disguising it, the Duchess hates me simply for what I am—perhaps a little prettier and more attractive than her daughters. Everything I do or say or wear is found fault with. We are always studiously polite to each other, but . . . it is rather like a volcano, ready to burst out at any moment. . . . Meanwhile our money affairs are pretty much like everyone else's it seems to me, hard up notwithstanding Papa's generous "tips." . . . Randolph is obliged to spend so much in a political way. . . . You don't know how economical we try to be.[11]

The beautiful and vivacious Jennie would never win the favor of her mother-in-law. Clearly, Randolph defended his wife from much of the criticism. Jennie's idea of being economical would almost certainly be at variance with the normal use of the word. However, much of the young Churchills' money was being eaten up in paying for political dinners, entertaining, and hiring halls for large public meetings.

For Winston's seventh birthday, in November 1881, he was given the first of what grew into a huge collection of toy soldiers, which interest would eventually lead him into an army career. The collection was added to that Christmas and at all subsequent festivities. At this age, like most boys, Winston was noisy, boisterous, and disruptive. Jennie spent a good deal of her time engaging his interest and attention, while Mrs. Everest saw to the two-year-old Jack, who was already a quiet, placid, well-behaved child, with a slightly serious aspect. Winston saw this inherent goodness as something of a challenge, something to define himself against. Sir Henry Drummond Wolff, when he visited, asked Jack if he was a good boy, to which the little chap replied, "Yes, but brother is teaching me to be naughty."[12]

Peregrine Churchill preserved his grandmother's only diary for the year 1882.[13] It gives us a faithful picture of the sort of life Jennie led. In January, they were still resident at Blenheim Palace, and the diary describes a contented family scene. Jennie was attentive to her husband and her sons. She regularly recorded having given Winston his lessons, taking him for walks, and reading to the children.

The other principal activity that she recorded was her painting, which she indulged in almost every day. It had been part of her genteel upbringing, and she had developed the interest further in Ireland. Her sister Clara was an early model to practice her skills in portraiture. Back in London, she took lessons from Mrs. Henrietta Ward, a notable English Victorian painter, who later wrote, "Lady Randolph Churchill showed a decided talent for painting . . . and on more than one occasion was accompanied by her son Winston, a delightful little boy in short trousers."[14]

We have the testimony of Peregrine, with whom his father lived in his later years, and from whom he learnt a good deal of the family history, that first Winston, and later Jack, were taught to draw and paint by their mother. Both boys regularly illustrated their letters within the family, and Jack would keep up the tradition in writing to his own children when they went to school.

The diary, besides dutifully recording the weather every day, holds many references to domestic contentment, including playing billiards with the duke and other Churchills, to charitable duties with the duchess, giving out blankets to the poor, and to attending political meetings with Randolph. Among the many friends she recorded visiting or being visited by was Lady Blanche Hozier (née Ogilvy), the mother of Winston's future wife, Clementine.

On a foggy February 4, 1882, Randolph, Jennie, and their family moved back to their London home in St. James's Place. She resumed her painting on a daily basis, which included portraits of some of their close friends,[15] and was getting back into life in the capital city when things took a dramatic turn for the worse.

Jennie recorded in the diary that in mid-February, Randolph's health collapsed completely. Officially diagnosed as an acute inflammation of the mucous membrane, it was a result of his working too hard, coupled with his serious chain smoking of very strong Turkish cigarettes and Cuban cigars. It led to a deterioration of his immune system, leaving him vulnerable to other infections. His principal physician was Dr. Robson Roose, a specialist in nervous disorders who had written a number of medical studies on the strain on some men of hard mental work. Randolph's enemies began to circulate the slur that he was ill with syphilis, but nothing in his medical reports, which record his treatment, indicates any such disorder.

Mrs. Everest took the boys away to Blenheim Palace for the duration of their father's illness. It would be five months before Lord Randolph could return to the House of Commons. Despite his doctors ordering a complete rest, there were streams of visitors coming to see him and to argue questions of policy and strategy. While there was a day nurse in attendance, Jennie personally looked after Randolph every evening and coped with the crowds who came to see him.

Randolph's condition worsened toward the end of February, and he suffered a physical collapse. Still he would not reduce the number of visitors he received or refrain from the excitement of politics.

One entry in Jennie's diary on March 2 was significant, recording for the first time a visit by Count Charles Kinsky, a personal friend of Randolph's through their shared passion for horse racing. Jennie had first met him in 1881 and would become very greatly attached to him in the future. For eleven days there are no entries in the diary as Jennie coped with the crisis in her husband's illness. Randolph began to improve. Jennie, able to take one break from her bedside duties, recorded something of a turning point in her place in society. After a party at the home of Lord and Lady Salisbury on March 15, she was taken on to a ball given by Randolph's eldest sister, Cornelia, Lady Wimborne. This kindly woman was working to heal the breach with the Prince of Wales, and the Prince and Princess Alexandra were present at the ball without any major upset in protocol. They did not actually meet Jennie, and she recorded that the ball was "not wildly exciting," but it was the first small step toward reconciliation.

Jennie took Randolph away to a hotel in the Crystal Palace area of London, then still quite rural in aspect and a much better environment for a convalescent. The children were able to visit there, in the company of their aunt Cornelia. Jennie attended closely to her husband, taking him for improving walks and keeping near him as she got on with her painting and reading.

Randolph improved a good deal by the end of March, which is more than can be said for their finances. Considerable extra expense was being incurred. The doctors who attended Randolph, one of whom was a Harley Street specialist, Oscar Clayton, FRCS,[16] had to be paid. Leonard Jerome was in arrears with Jennie's allowance. On March 20 they had been obliged to send four of their best horses to Tattersalls, the livestock auctioneers, for sale,[17] but even then only two were sold, with the other two failing to make the reserve price. The £142/$681 gained would not have made much of a dent in their spiraling debts.

Mrs. Everest and the Marlborough family took good care of Winston and Jack. The gap in ages between the brothers meant it would be some years before Jack could really become a playmate. Winston had his cousins to play with in the wonderful grounds of Blenheim Palace. Jack, though still a toddler, was getting his first access to his brother's toy soldiers. In one of the first letters from the seven-year-old Winston, to his "dear Papa," dated March 20, he hopes he is getting better, and makes reference to the many primroses he sees at Blenheim. He had evidently picked up on the idea that these were the late-lamented Disraeli's favorite flower. After this charmingly precocious observation, he sends "Best love to you and dear Mamma."[18]

Jennie was very tired during this ordeal. She sometimes recorded in her diary that she read all through the night as she kept a close eye on Randolph's health. Her painting sustained her all the while, though oils and canvases did not come cheap. Through a harsh winter, she finally curtailed the number of visitors, and Randolph improved a good deal. They were able to return home, with the children, to St. James's Place on April 1. On the doctor's advice they immediately arranged for Jennie and Randolph to go for a long trip to America, where the cleaner air was expected to assist his recovery. It would also keep him away from the hurly-burly of politics, for the stream of visitors had resumed the moment he returned to London. They would be able to see Jennie's father and have a serious talk with him about her allowance, as well as see Clara and Leonie, who were both visiting their father at that time.

Leaving the children at Blenheim, they traveled to Liverpool, accompanied only by Jennie's maid Gentry and Randolph's faithful valet Thomas Walden. They sailed for America on April 21 and had the most awful crossing. The weather was very bad, and they were both seasick. Jennie's diary recorded the consolations of painting, playing the piano, and reading. At last, on May 2, they docked in New York, and the Jerome family were all there to greet them. Leonard and Randolph always got on well, through their shared love of the races. Despite continuing bad weather, they enjoyed a lively time of visits to friends, to the theatre, the racetrack, and eating out.

HISTORIC EVENTS in Ireland brought the holiday to an abrupt end. In April, Parnell had been released from prison. On May 6, in Phoenix Park, Dublin, Irish revolutionaries (Fenians) stabbed to death Lord Frederick Cavendish, the chief secretary, and Mr. Thomas Henry Burke, the permanent under secretary to Earl Spencer, the recently appointed viceroy of Ireland. Randolph saw that this would create a new crisis in that troubled country and insisted on returning to England. The Irish Coercion Act, which had been passed in April 1881, was due to expire in September. On May 17, Jennie described "an enormous crowd" of family and friends seeing them off from New York. Headwinds made it a rough passage, but otherwise the weather was warm.

The Churchills were back in St. James's Place on May 27, and the dizzying round of visitors and dinner parties resumed at once. Randolph may have been eager to return to the political fray, but his doctors certainly did not agree. They advised that his improvement was fragile, that he should avoid crowds and take further rest and fresh air. London in general was smoggy and unhealthy, and their house had a peculiar, ill-smelling miasma about it. Rather than suffer a further spell at Blenheim with her detested mother-in-law, Jennie began to look for a home in the country.

Jerome had provided some much-needed funds, enabling Jennie to gleefully record one of her favorite pursuits on June 7: "Shopped all the morning." She rented a "cottage," Beech Lodge, in Wimbledon, and the Churchills moved in on June 8. A photograph of it shows it to have been an airy, elegant mansion of a place, which was fully staffed with servants. Its spacious lawns and rose garden provided a fine setting for some rest and relaxation. They spent a very happy summer there with the boys. Being able to rent out their London house helped their finances somewhat. Beech Lodge was sufficiently removed from London to reduce the usual stream of visitors to Randolph's immediate family, the pals from the Fourth Party, and some of Jennie's American friends. The fine weather allowed for lots of painting, and there were visits to Blenheim, where Winston was delighted to find the yeomanry cavalry encamped.

On July 3, Randolph finally returned to the House of Commons and immediately took up the reins as the scourge of the Liberal government. He led a fight against an attempt by the Liberals to legislate for a two-thirds majority being required to pass new laws. If a simple majority got one elected to Parliament, he argued, why should that not be enough to win a vote in the House? He so discomfited the Liberals that they had the unusual experience of seeing all the Irish Nationalists line up behind this firebrand Tory radical against them.

Randolph got even more radical when Britain waged war on Egypt. In 1875, Egypt had become debt-ridden, and Benjamin Disraeli, then prime minister, bought Egyptian shares that came up for sale in the Suez Canal. Britain's interest in Egypt was thereby greatly strengthened. There had been nationalist disturbances over the years, and Egyptian military officers rose up against the government in February and September 1881. In May 1882, France and Britain each sent small naval squadrons to protect their respective interests. On June 11, Egyptians rioted in Alexandria and killed about fifty Europeans, including three British military personnel. The British responded by bombarding Alexandria on July 11. Arguing that Egypt was descending into anarchy, threatening the Suez Canal (located about 180 miles to the east), the British government sought international support for an invasion of Egypt, but without success. Acting alone in August 1882, they carried out large military operations, and 25,000 British soldiers descended upon Egypt. Within two months they captured the Suez Canal and defeated the Egyptian army at Tel-el-Kebir. The Egyptian officers had led a revolt against Ottoman Turkish rule as part of a process of modern reforms. Britain selfishly looked only to defend its own financial interests in the country. Randolph had actually backed the revolt of Egyptian officers and saw the British interference there as a "wicked war, an unjust war, a bondholders' war."[19] Again it took a leading Tory to expose this illiberal government move.

The Fourth Party was developing a philosophy known as "Tory Democracy." They could see that the "old gang" of Tory leaders was hopelessly out of touch with the mass of the population. Randolph and his friends wanted to devise a political program that would directly represent the interests of the working people. They would address the issues that mattered to them—housing, education, health, national insurance, access to common land and open spaces, museums, libraries, galleries. Many of these advanced ideas, well ahead of the Liberals in social awareness, would challenge the interests of powerful backers of the Conservative Party. The Fourth Party relished these fights. Seeing the dead hand of the "old gang" on the Central Committee, they backed a new organization called the National Union of Conservative Associations (NUCA). When Randolph was put up for election to the committee, it split fifty-fifty, and he was only successful with the casting vote of the chairman. Randolph wrote to Wolff on September 28 that he intended to "declare war against the Central Committee and advocate the placing of all power and finance in the hands of the Council of the National Union."[20] Success at the national conference of the NUCA gave Randolph a platform from which to launch his bid for the high office that everyone felt was his due.

While her husband resumed his spectacular political career, Jennie set about finding a school for Winston. Like all boys of his age and class, it was time for him to go to a preparatory school. It has to be said that both parents agreed that this rather difficult, overindulged boy would probably benefit from the disciplined routine of a boarding school. Together they finally decided to send him to St. George's, Ascot. Founded in 1877 by Mr. Herbert William Sneyd-Kynnersley, this was an impressive modern school, with small classes (ten boys to a tutor), electric light, a fine swimming pool, gymnasium, and playing fields, with an intelligent program of out-of-school visits. At £55/$264 a term, it was expensive and fashionable.

Jennie accompanied Winston there on his first day, November 3, 1882. They set off together in a carriage to the railway station. Winston always remembered that his mother gave him as pocket money three half crowns, which he awkwardly dropped on the carriage floor. After a private interview with the headmaster, she left him in the care of the school. His parents could have had no idea what a hellish place they had delivered him to.

Four

A SHOOTING STAR
BURNS OUT

1882–1886

In March 1883, reconciliation finally took place between Lord Randolph and the Prince of Wales. Almost at once, Lord Randolph was forced to take a break from politics following a nervous reaction to the sudden death of his father (July 1883). That November, the Fourth Party set up a new political organization, the Primrose League, that admitted women into its ranks. On June 18, 1885, Lord Randolph became secretary of state for India in a minority Conservative government led by Lord Salisbury.[1] Following a general election in 1886, when the Conservatives once again commanded a majority, Salisbury appointed Lord Randolph leader of the House of Commons and Chancellor of the Exchequer.

At just a few weeks before his eighth birthday, in November 1882, Winston was nearly a year older than most of the other boys starting at St. George's School, and hence a year behind in the expectations of his masters. His first letters home to both his parents were, however, a convincing declaration of his happiness at school. On December 3 he wrote:

> My dear Papa
> I am very happy at school. You will be very pleased to hear I spent a very happy birthday. Mrs Kynersley [sic; the headmaster's wife] gave me a little basket. I am going to send a [school] Gazette wich [sic] I wish you to read. With love and kisses, I remain your loving son
> Winston.[2]

He wrote a similar letter to his mother.

There was a regular exchange of letters between Jennie and Winston, and there are references in them to her visits to the school, but mostly it was Mrs. Everest who visited. Winston was begging for a visit almost as soon as he arrived, and Jennie probably thought it best not to give in or it would unsettle him.

Later that year, Randolph was ordered by his doctors to take another holiday in the fresh air. He was touring in Algeria when, on December 17, Jennie penciled a note to him from their latest new home, 2 Connaught Place, saying she was ill and in the care of Dr. Laking.[3] She wrote that her mother and Leonie were nursing her. Jennie was much sicker than her doctors told her: It was the onset of typhoid fever. Mrs. Jerome feared for her daughter and brought in the eminent doctor Sir William Gull.[4]

Randolph sent a telegram on December 28, expressing his great alarm at the news of Jennie's illness, and there followed an exchange of letters and cables between the two, each expressing love and concern for the other. Randolph had started for home, and had reached the south of France on New Year's Day 1883, when he heard the worst was over. He wrote:

> My darling, I have been in such a state of mind about you ever since last Thursday. . . . I could not bear the idea of your being ill without my being with you to look after you; particularly when I remembered how you use to look after me when I was ill. . . . Why dearest if anything happened to you my life would be broken.[5]

Winston was also home from school ill, and Randolph's letter continued that he expressed his sorrow that "little Winston has not been well."[6]

And so it went on, with Jennie saying she was wretched at causing him any worry, "Your letter made me cry," and Randolph replying, "I should have been sent for. It would have done me good to look after you." He sent her a little oyster knife for her twenty-ninth birthday and wanted her to join him on his way home in the south of France.

Jennie, having had a slight relapse, wrote to Randolph on January 3, saying Dr. Laking insisted she was not strong enough to travel to France. She wrote to him again, on January 16, telling him that Sir Henry Drummond Wolff had told her Thomas Chenery, the editor of *The Times,* had said Randolph was the only man who could lead the Conservative Party, and that other senior Conservatives were "praising him up."[7]

Winston had been only over a month at school, and Jennie was displeased to receive an invoice for a full three-month term. She wrote to Randolph, making some observations on Winston's behavior:

> As to Winston's improvement I am sorry to say I see none—He can read very well, but that is all. . . . The first two days he came home he was terribly slangy and loud. . . . He teases the baby [Jack] more than ever. It appears he is afraid of me.

It is unclear whether Winston was afraid of his mother because he associated her with the school regime in which she had placed him or whether he had been warned by the doctor, Mrs. Everest, and his grandmother that he must keep his distance from his mother because she was ill.

Winston's school report showed him at the bottom in his class of eleven boys, but they had had a year's start on him as seven was the age to begin preparatory school and Winston was nearly eight when he arrived. Randolph was more concerned about the flare-up of Winston's chest trouble. On January 5, he wrote to Jennie, "I am so glad to hear that Winnie is right again. Give him a kiss from me. Goodbye my darling, I think always of you." Jennie had sent Winston with Mrs. Everest to Brighton for his health for two weeks. On January 16, Randolph wrote, "Love to the children. I suppose Winston will go back to school in a few days. Give him a little money from me before he goes."

Jennie would not have been allowed to see Winston or Jack while she was ill with such a contagious disease. Nor would she have been welcome at St. George's School for fear she might infect the children. If she had been fully fit and well, she might have pondered why Winston had become "afraid" of his mother.

In *My Early Life* Winston tells of the bestial regime of floggings indulged in by the headmaster, Sneyd-Kynnersley.[8] Further evidence is provided by the artist Roger Fry, who, when he was head boy at St. George's after Winston's time there, had to assist in the punishment:

> the culprit was told to take down his trousers and kneel before the block over which I and the other boy held him down. The switching was given by the master's full strength and it took only two or three strokes for drops of blood to form everywhere.[9]

Winston wrote in his memoirs that he hated the school and the "life of anxiety" he led there for nearly two years. "Two or three times a month . . . delinquents were . . . flogged until they bled freely, whilst the rest sat quaking, listening to their screams."[10] Yet, his letters home remained deceptively cheerful. Why he uttered not one word of his troubles to either his parents or Mrs. Everest remains a mystery. Was it pride or embarrassment? Was it fear induced by the power figure that was Sneyd-Kinnersley? Did he think he deserved punishment for being naughty, and that this was the normal regime at school?

AT THE END of January 1883, Randolph returned to London, invigorated from France, and he was much in demand at meetings all around the country. He spent a great deal of time mastering his speeches for these occasions and memorized them so that his delivery was all the more remarkable.[11]

Then, in March, reconciliation took place with Edward, Prince of Wales. Jennie arranged a dinner at 2 Connaught Place at which her famous French cook provided a memorable banquet. The Prince and Princess of Wales arrived, perfectly on time, itself a mark of respect. At once, Princess Alexandra drew Jennie up from her deep curtsey to embrace her and say, "We haven't played Bach for a long time!"[12] Winston and Jack were brought downstairs to meet the Royals, and Prince Edward gave them each a small gift. The dinner was a huge success. On being offered a choice of two soups, the Prince promptly helped himself to both. He expressed his delight, not least because "You are not an American food faddist, Lady Randolph."[13] With this dinner, the Randolph Churchills were immediately restored to the highest rank in society. Restaurants and London clubs would compete for their patronage. The Prince also began to bestow expensive gifts of jewelry on Jennie, and she was soon a guest at his famous country house parties, not always in the company of her husband. Jennie was now at the height of her power and beauty in society. She had the grace and manners to light up any room she entered. She was charming and witty and clever, and when she entered a ballroom every head turned to gaze at her.

The Prince invited beautiful women to parties at his country estate, Sandringham House, Norfolk, with the express purpose of seducing them into his bed and those of his friends. From this time the Prince wrote notes to Jennie that would eventually run into hundreds, all of which are preserved.[14] Anita Leslie, Leonie's granddaughter, wrote extensively in her books *Edwardians In Love* and *The Marlborough House Set* about the Prince and the free lovemaking that took place at Sandringham House.[15] The married women and men who participated were nicknamed the "Marlborough House set" after the Prince's London residence, the name having nothing to do with the Marlborough family. The Prince had a string of mistresses and illegitimate children over the years, which is well documented elsewhere. He would only have shown such interest in Jennie for sex, and his attentions to her then, and after her husband's death, followed the pattern of his behavior with his other mistresses, such as Daisy, Countess of Warwick, and Alice Keppel. We can therefore safely assume that Jennie somewhat discreetly joined the long list of the Prince's conquests at about this time. The dire state of her husband's health and his constant absences from home, exhausting himself making speeches, would mean that exuberant, vital Jennie would increasingly be driven to seek comfort elsewhere.[16] It was Peregrine's opinion that Randolph was more or less impotent from the time of his serious illness in 1882.

In April 1883, Count Charles Kinsky, a military attaché at the Austrian Embassy in London, won one of the leading horse races of the year, the Grand National at Aintree in Liverpool, riding his own horse Zoedone. Kinsky was a popular hero of the time in the racing newspapers and the London gentlemen's clubs. He was the son of Prince Ferdinand Kinsky, an ancient and powerful Austrian family. Their dazzling palace still stands in Vienna today. Kinsky was an intimate of the Prince of Wales, and like Jennie he was part of the Prince's notorious "Marlborough House set."[17] The Prince was an opportunistically keen believer in free love for his aristocratic friends, which involved the changing of sexual partners. At his London and country homes and the country houses of his friend the maids ensured that the bedrooms of adulterous couples were next to each other.[18] These activities were not meant to lead to marital splits or divorce; quite the reverse. Neither were they meant to lead to long-term relationships. Unmarried men were included, but single women were not involved. Jennie, who was now part of the Prince's elite inner circle, flouted the rules when soon after the Grand National she fell head over heels in love with Kinsky and began a strong physical relationship with him. Kinsky had an apartment at Clarges Street in the fashionable Mayfair area. It would become their love nest, and Kinsky retained it for the rest of his life with a butler to look after it. Jennie loved Kinsky for many years, without ever doubting her love for her husband.[19] Both men offered her something she needed; Kinsky was a great lover, and Randolph, so she thought, would become prime minister. There is no reason to suppose that Randolph ever knew of her adultery.[20]

THERE SOON CAME a blow that led to another collapse in Randolph's fragile health. On July 4, 1883, he and Jennie dined with his father and mother at Blenheim Palace. The duke was in fine fettle. Next morning came the terrible news. As Jennie recalled it: "At eight o'clock . . . we heard a knock at our bedroom door, and a footman stammer out: His Grace is dead!"[21] The duke had died in his sleep of a heart attack at the age of sixty-one. Randolph had loved his father deeply and never failed to greet him with an arm around his shoulder and a kiss on the cheek. The shock to Randolph led his doctors to recommend that he go to Germany and take the healing waters and bracing mountain air at Gastein. Randolph, Jennie, and Winston went there for a holiday, leaving Jack in the care of Mrs. Everest. They went on daily mountain treks in the fresh air, and even made the acquaintance of Otto von Bismarck, the German chancellor, whom they met along the way.[22]

That summer of 1883, Jennie and the boys spent at Blenheim Palace, a more congenial destination now that the Dowager Duchess was no longer the chatelaine there. At the death of the 7th Duke their elder son, George Charles (Blandford), automatically acceded to the dukedom as the 8th Duke of Marlborough. Frances now became the Dowager Duchess, and was obliged to move out of the palace to live in her London residence, a mansion, No. 46 Grosvenor Square. At Blenheim, Winston could run riot with his favorite cousin, Blandford's son and heir, Charles Richard, Duke of Sunderland, always known as Sunny. Jack, now nearly four, was able to join in some of their wild games.

THAT DECEMBER, Sir Henry Drummond Wolff was begging Randolph to return to the fray in Parliament, but he replied from Blenheim, "I am not up to it physically or mentally . . . it is very melancholy here—sad recollections at every moment."[23] The family spent the rest of 1883 at Blenheim Palace.

The Fourth Party had been toying with the idea of a mass membership organization to extend the principles of Tory Democracy. There was a tremendous amount to be done, as poverty, hunger, ill health, bad housing, and illiteracy still prevailed throughout large parts of the United Kingdom. The Fourth Party wanted to tackle the boards of health, local government departments, the dwellings of and for the poor, compulsory national insurance, temperance, education, the preservation and reclamation of common grounds and open spaces as recreation for the masses, along with people's parks, museums, libraries, and art galleries.[24] These were to be added to the reforms in Ireland, and to support for the nationalist reforms in Egypt. There was also the problem that women were not allowed to play any effective part in politics, and it would be many years before they could vote in an election.

The Primrose League, an organization for spreading the principles of the Conservatives in Great Britain, began to be formed immediately after the unveiling of Disraeli's statue[25] in the Commons, April 19, 1883, but it was not officially launched until November 17. One of its crucial aims was to encourage and help members to improve their professional competence as leaders. But it was also a charitable organization giving money to the poor to help educate them and buy them clothes and shoes. The founders, mainly the Fourth Party, included Randolph, Gorst, Wolff, and Sir Alfred Slade, a veteran of the Crimean War. They had opened its ranks to women, and Jennie and the Dowager Duchess were among those ladies who organized the first committee. Men and women were made Knights and Dames and wore primrose badges. Subsequently a separate Ladies Branch was formed. The founder of the Ladies Grand Council was Lady Borthwick (afterward Lady Glenesk), and the first meeting of the committee took place at her house in Piccadilly in March 1885. The League's popularity soared, and its membership rose from 957 at the end of 1884, to 11,366 in 1885.[26] Jennie played a leading role in the League, and it would become the power base for Randolph's great struggle with the old leadership of the Conservative Party.

Despite her newfound political activities, Jennie still had to attend to her children. She received a school report (undated, but presumably midterm 1883) for Winston, showing little improvement. He was again last, in a class of nine, and the number of times late for class nineteen. While the report said that he was very good at history, his spelling was "about as bad as it could be," in math he "could do better than he does," but he "does not quite understand the meaning of hard work."[27] He had now been at St. George's School six months, and the expensive education was not bearing much fruit, but his parents persevered, presumably in the hope that he would improve. Winston's final school report for the year, sent in December, showed some improvement; he was eighth out of eleven in his class.[28] His letters home remained cheerful, stressing how well he sometimes did in gymnastics. His letter to his father on December 9 ended affectionately with one big kiss (X), followed by lots of little kisses. At about the same time he wrote to his mother, who had obviously spoken to him sternly about his behavior: "I will try to be a good boy." In this letter he reported that he had received a nice letter from Jack, not yet four years old, "but I think Everest held his hand."[29] That Christmas, Winston's army of toy soldiers swelled to over fifteen hundred.

By February 1884, Winston reported to his parents that he was "very happy indeed" and had the chance of a school prize if he worked hard. As a reward for this effort, his father sent him a fine copy of *Treasure Island,* which he read many times with great pleasure. Even this seems to have annoyed some of his tutors, who resented his obvious talent for reading not being displayed on the texts they set for him. It was a letter of February 24 that should have alarmed his parents. In the space of a few lines, written in unusually bad, cramped handwriting, he asks three times if someone could come and see him soon. Against his signature he drew a face with sad, downcast eyes. This plea was ignored by his busy parents,[30] who were completely distracted by the prospect of a general election, though a date had not yet been announced and it was still some way off.

The Churchills appear to have been under the impression that Winston was happy at school. A further diversion was that Randolph's safe seat at Woodstock was to disappear in a proposed redrawing of electoral boundaries. He was preparing to have to declare himself as a candidate for the large Central Division of Birmingham, which was held by the popular Liberal, John Bright. It is likely therefore that so long as their son was happy they were not greatly perturbed by his reports. A further school report for March/April 1884 showed he had improved in his lessons, but his behavior had worsened drastically. "Conduct has been exceedingly bad. He is not to be trusted to do any one thing"; "is a constant trouble to every body and is always in some scrape or other"; "number of times late, 20 —very disgraceful."[31] In his May/June report, Winston improved considerably, though by June/July the report was again mixed.[32]

That July, Winston suffered a bout of illness, and Jennie came to the school and took him home. He would never return to that awful place. Maurice Baring, of the famous Baring's Bank family and who in adulthood became a writer and dramatist, had attended St. George's School just after Winston left. Baring later recorded:

> Dreadful legends were told about Winston Churchill. . . . He had been flogged for taking sugar from the pantry, and so far from being penitent, he had taken the Headmaster's sacred straw hat from where it hung over the door and kicked it to pieces.[33]

Winston, who still suffered from a weak chest and was prone to severe bouts of asthma from the time of the prolonged bad weather in Ireland, was treated by the Churchills' family doctor, Robson Roose, who was called in to attend to him. Roose was the physician at St. Andrew's home for boys in Brighton and had considerable experience in treating children. From later correspondence between Roose and Lord Randolph, when Winston was taken ill again at a later date, the doctor stated that in dealing with his high temperature he used "stimulants, by the mouth and rectum."[34] It would seem likely, therefore, that it was in the course of this treatment that Roose first saw Winston's bottom and discovered the terrible signs of the repeated beatings he had endured in silence. Peregrine said the wounds had festered. Sneyd-

Kynnersley's abuse of Winston was much talked of in the family for years afterward. Peregrine related a story of how, one day, when Winston was already an experienced swordsman at Harrow Public School, he decided to settle the score. He set out to St. George's School, Ascot, to tackle the headmaster, unaware that he had died of a heart attack the year after Winston left the school.

By happy coincidence, Dr. Roose's son, Bertie, went to a very well-run school in Brighton, and he strongly recommended it to Jennie and Randolph. The healthy climate and moderate regime would be a double benefit to Winston. In September 1884, shortly before his tenth birthday, Winston began at The Brighton School, which was actually in Hove, Sussex. The school was run by two spinster sisters, Charlotte and Kate Thomson, Charlotte being the headmistress.[35] Flogging was not permitted there, and Winston recalled that he was allowed to learn things that interested him— French, history, poetry, riding, and swimming. His enthusiasm for stamp collecting was ignited. By this enlightened method, employing kindness and sympathy, the Misses Thomson aroused his interest in the classics, so vital for entry into the great public schools like Eton and Harrow. By another coincidence, the school was near to Robson Roose's practice, so if Winston was taken ill the doctor could be called in immediately. With Bertie Roose as a friend to help him settle in, Winston's marks improved immediately, and his letters home were more frank and open. Jennie had obviously asked him not to hide things from her, and he solemnly wrote that he was telling her everything that was happening in his life. He would ask if Mrs. Everest could come and visit him, with Jack. He sent his love to his brother and said he could have some of his artillery from the model armies at home to play with.

RANDOLPH HAD RECEIVED hints from Lord Salisbury that he would be the next secretary of state for India. In anticipation, he sailed for India on December 3, 1884. Jennie and the two boys saw him off. Jennie's younger sister, Leonie, had married an artist, John Leslie, from County Monaghan, Ireland. Partly to save money and partly to keep Jennie company, the Leslies moved in to live with her while Randolph was away. The £20/$96 a month they contributed to the household expenses was useful to cash-strapped Jennie.

Despite his fine start at Brighton School, Winston was already in trouble. Miss Charlotte Thomson wrote to Jennie on December 17 that, during a drawing examination, some dispute arose between Winston and the boy next to him over a knife needed for their work. It ended with Winston receiving a stab wound to the chest.[36] Dr. Roose attended to the injury, which was about a quarter inch deep, and brought him safely home to his mother.

Randolph's response to this incident in a letter to Jennie from Beejapore, January 19, 1885, was of the boys-will-be-boys kind. "What adventures Winston does have;

it is a great mercy he was no worse injured," and "tell little Winny how glad I was to get his letter which I thought was very well written."[37]

Randolph returned from India in March and was greeted with acclaim by the Conservative Party and kept busy with meetings all around the country. Both Winston and Jack were now fully aware of how famous their father was. Winston told his father in a letter on April 8 that he would be very proud if he would write to him, and also began importuning him for copies of his autograph, whole pages of them. He said it was to give to his school friends and some admiring teachers. Peregrine said Winston was also selling the signatures to augment his pocket money.

WINSTON FLOURISHED under the benign influence of the Misses Thomson. His position in class improved steadily—he actually came first in classics—and though his health remained a little delicate, he became an accomplished rider and finally learned to swim. Nevertheless, he still managed to come last in conduct. His many letters invariably contained some requests for more cash, for food, or proper riding apparel, and he asked about Mrs. Everest. His parents seem to have complied with all his requests.

THE CHURCHILLS MAY have seen Randolph as steadily climbing the political ladder to become prime minister, but there were obstacles. Sir Stafford Northcote (The Goat) had been leader of the Conservative Party in the Commons from 1876, and Lord Salisbury had an eye to becoming the prime minister following an expected Conservative victory in the next general election. In June, over a seemingly innocuous amendment to a budget speech, the Liberal government slumped to a defeat by twelve votes. Gladstone had to offer his resignation to Queen Victoria. As there was a lot of parliamentary business outstanding, it was not an appropriate moment to call an election. Instead, Queen Victoria sent for Lord Salisbury and asked him to form a minority Conservative administration. Salisbury asked Randolph to become secretary of state for India, and he accepted.[38]

Randolph now entered the government on a salary of £5,000/$24,000 per annum, a very considerable sum in those days. Jennie was thrilled at this advancement, and his sons were bursting with pride. Politics had become Lord Randolph's *raison d'être*. He was driven by a need to achieve important things in his life. At the expense of his health and personal relationships, he drove himself hard, sustained by insomnia, strong coffee, and tobacco.

The new post meant that Lord Randolph was a government minister, and under the parliamentary rules he was obliged to resign his seat and stand for re-election. His Woodstock constituency still existed. He was so completely immersed in his work at the India Office in London and so confident of winning that he wrote to his constituents explaining that he would not be able to campaign among them. Instead, Jennie would campaign on his behalf. She became the leading light of his reelection effort, together with his sister, Georgiana, Lady Howe, and leading Conservatives such as Wolff, George Curzon, Alfred Milner, and St. John Brodrick.

Jennie reveled in the bustle of electioneering, and she was very good at it. She and Georgiana covered the whole constituency in a horse-drawn carriage decked out in Randolph's racing colors—pink and brown. A local rhymester made a popular jingle referring to the prowess of "that Yankee lady."

Randolph wrote to Jennie: "If I win, you will have all the glory." And glory there was when, on July 3, 1885, the declaration gave Randolph 532 votes to the radical Liberal Mr. Corrie Grant's 405, double his majority of the 1880 election. Jennie gave a victory speech at the Bear Hotel, Woodstock, and the Prince of Wales sent her his congratulations. Winston was enormously proud of his father, and even the five-year-old Jack was excited by all the activity.

As secretary of state for India Randolph appointed his friend General Sir Frederick "Fred" Roberts as commander in chief of the army in India. Randolph was an enthusiastic supporter of railway construction in the Indian subcontinent, and also had to wrestle with the defense issues raised by Russian expansion in Central Asia up to the borders of Afghanistan.

The months following his election to the cabinet were the busiest days of Lord Randolph's political life, and the amount of work he got through astonished all who knew him. Still an expert on Irish affairs, he strove to keep the Irish Nationalists "on side" with his government in the Commons. He went through some difficult times with the Protestant Orange Loyalists, who saw every concession to the Irish Nationalists as some sort of betrayal. He was always in demand for giving speeches to Conservative organizations around the United Kingdom. On September 13, 1885, Lord Salisbury had written to advise him on the enormous strain he was under. Later that month, Randolph took a holiday, salmon fishing in Scotland, where he was able to entertain his newly appointed commander in chief of the army in India, General Sir Fred Roberts, and learn more of India's military problems before the general left to take up his command there.

In November, Lord Randolph authorized a British invasion of Burma, where King Theebaw[39] operated a most hostile regime against British commercial interests and subjects, and was something of a tyrant. His father, King Mindon, had made Theebaw prince of the northern state of Thibaw. King Mindon had died in October 1878, leaving thirty sons who could make claims to the throne. Theebaw then massacred twenty-seven of his brothers and their families, and installed himself on the throne. At that time, half of Burma had been under British occupation for thirty years. In 1885, Theebaw was dethroned, his people rejected a protectorate, and Burma was annexed to the British Empire on January 1, 1886 .

THAT SEPTEMBER, Jennie had been very active in charitable work, focusing on Lady Dufferin's Medical Fund for Women, which in turn supported the work of the National Association for Supplying Medical Aid to the Women of India. Randolph wrote to her from Scotland, praising her work, and putting her in touch with the editor of *The Times,* on September 27: "I should advise you to get hold of Mr. Buckle and fascinate him, and get him to write you up."[40] That December, at Buckingham Palace, Queen Victoria honored Jennie's work by personally bestowing on her the Insignia of the Order of the Crown of India. After kissing the Queen's hand, Jennie stood in a fine black velvet dress, so heavily embroidered with jet beads that the Queen struggled with the medal and drove the pin into her chest. Jennie cherished the pearl and turquoise cipher, and it features in many photographs of her in evening dress.[41]

Randolph had little time during these politically turbulent months to visit Winston at school. However, Winston and Jack looked upon their father as a great man, and Jennie saw him as the future prime minister and expected to be the first American lady to enter No. 10 Downing Street. In the summer of 1885, Jennie had determined that Winston had to do better at school, and she told him that she had engaged for the holidays a governess who would give him some lessons every day as he was being groomed for one of the public schools like Eton or Harrow. Winston declared that he had never had to work through the holidays before, that it was "against his principles,"[42] and that even one hour a day of study would hang like a dark cloud over him and quite spoil everything. The governess was appointed, and even when they went to the Isle of Wight on holiday, she continued his tuition. Watching the Cowes Week Regatta and driving himself about in a little donkey cart were, apparently, no compensation for the relentless strictures of the unkind governess, "so strict and stiff."[43] He was now lionized at school as the son of such a famous politician, something he had never enjoyed at St. George's, and he supplied his friends with autographs of both parents.[44]

The general election was finally called for November 23, 1885, by which time Randolph's Woodstock seat had been abolished and he had to stand for Central Birmingham. His mother, as a Dame of the Primrose League, and Jennie canvassed the whole of the Central Division of Birmingham, street by street. Frances Marlborough was not too proud to go into the factories and address the workingmen and was loudly cheered. Randolph narrowly failed to win. Nevertheless, he won reelection, for a vacancy had occurred in the London elections, which took place the following day. The official candidate stood down in his favor, and Lord Randolph stood again and won the seat of Paddington South, which he would retain for the rest of his life. The Liberals, though now in the majority, could no longer automatically rely on the Irish Nationalists (who had secured eighty-five seats), and they declined to form a new government. Salisbury therefore continued to head a minority government, but it was soon defeated in the Commons. On the last day of January 1886, Gladstone formed a new Liberal administration, and Lord Randolph lost his job.

DURING THE ELECTORAL campaign, Winston had read in the newspaper that his father had paid a fleeting visit to the Orleans Club in Brighton, where he was in the habit of meeting up with his political friends. He had failed to call at the school to visit Winston, who wrote him a wounded letter on October 20, saying he was "very disappointed" and supposed his father was too busy to see him. His stamp collection, he said, stood at 708, and he badly needed a new album. His "mild request" for seventeen shillings and sixpence was in the nature of a fine on an errant parent, and one that was willingly accepted by an affectionate father. Winston wrote to his father again, on November 28, that he hoped he would get in at Birmingham, but he was so late sending the letter that the election was already over.

Winston had grown protective of his younger brother. Jack was now six years old, and we can deduce from a letter to him from Winston on February 10, 1886, that he was doing well at his lessons at home. The letter had several lines, in French, congratulating Jack on the improvement in his writing, and giving news of the recent riot by unemployed workers in Trafalgar Square, London, illustrated with a suitable drawing. Winston admired Jack's drawings of cannon firing, and advised him to work hard at home to avoid having to go to school for as long as possible. Winston was obviously maturing at Brighton, and showing a commendable interest in Jack's development. He clearly wanted to spare him the "ordeal" of going to school. He even promised to teach his younger brother the rudiments of Latin on his next stay at home. Mrs. Everest regularly brought Jack down to Brighton for short breaks, and the boys loved each other's company.

AS PRIME MINISTER again, Gladstone would support Home Rule for Ireland. Randolph's love of the Irish people and his passionate fight for reform in Ireland's affairs were meant to make it a fully functioning and prosperous part of the British Empire. He never at any stage thought a Home Rule parliament in Dublin would solve its problems, and he was completely opposed to the United Kingdom being broken up in this way. Gladstone brought forward a Home Rule Bill for debate in the Commons. Lord Randolph rushed over to Belfast to address the Protestants of Ulster as they organized against the proposals. At a huge public meeting in Belfast's Ulster Hall on the night of February 22, 1886, he appealed to the loyal Catholics of Ireland to stand with the Protestants for the union with Britain. The Catholic Bishops were all Conservative,[45] and Randolph hoped they would oppose Home Rule and influence their congregations. The speech—a call to prepare to resist the imposition of Home Rule—was inflammatory. Despite Lord Salisbury congratulating him on a speech "to which no Roman Catholic could object,"[46] communal violence had broken out in the north of Ireland, and innocent men and women were killed and injured.

Another (family) crisis arose around the beginning of March,[47] when Winston was taken ill at school during very cold weather. His chest trouble turned to pneumonia, and he was in peril of his life. The remarkable Dr. Roose, whose practice was in the road next to the school, with a dedication that sprang from his admiration for Randolph's politics, canceled all his London appointments, and moved into a room next to the sick child to monitor his condition and nurse him through the crisis. Jennie was informed on March 13, and rushed immediately to Brighton, followed by Randolph, but initially Roose would not allow them near their son. They stayed in the nearby Bedford Hotel, communicating by frantic notes with the doctor. Roose wrote to Lord Randolph twice on March 14, apprising him of the seriousness of his illness but that he was optimistic for his recovery. He wrote again, March 15, at 1:00 P.M.: "We are still fighting the battle for your boy. His temperature is 103 but now he is taking his nourishment *better.*"[48] Between March 12 and 17, Winston's temperature had edged up and up, peaking at 104.3 degrees, before he pulled back from the near-fatal crisis. As Winston gradually recovered, a flood of relieved congratulations issued from all the great names in British society. The Prince of Wales halted a line of audience in order to ascertain how Winny was progressing.

In the midst of this family crisis, Lord Randolph still had to keep an eye on political matters and especially to the threat of the Home Rule Bill. Gladstone had made a statement to a packed Commons on March 10, at which the Prince of Wales was present. On March 29 and 30, Gladstone published letters in the press saying the proposed parliament would have powers equal to the Constitution of Canada, meaning the Irish would elect their own members to a Dublin parliament.[49] Joseph Chamberlain left the Liberal Party and as a member of the Liberal Unionist Party newly formed that year, led a public campaign against the bill. Despite a stirring speech by Gladstone in the Commons the government lost the vote on Home Rule by 341 to 311, and Parliament was dissolved on June 27. In that extraordinary year, 1886, another government had fallen, and another election was called.

From April to June 1886, the ever-popular Randolph had made as many speeches on Home Rule and other issues in Birmingham and Manchester as he did in his South Paddington constituency. Confident of retaining his own seat, and before the ballot took place, he went on a fishing holiday to Norway. Once again, Jennie and his mother would fight the campaign for him through the Primrose League, and Jennie would keep him abreast of all the news. He wrote to her from Torresdal on July 19: "This is doing me a lot of good. I felt very seedy leaving London, and it took me some days to get right. . . . I expect the Tories will now come in, and remain in some time. It seems to me we want the £5,000 [minister's salary] a year badly."[50] Randolph won comfortably with 2,576 votes to his opponent's 769.

Meanwhile, Winston had recovered well from his illness, and was able to congratulate his father on his election. To his mother he declared in a letter of July 13 that he was "bankrupt and a little cash would be welcome."[51] Letters to Jack discussed their model armies and how they would build barricades together in the summer holidays.

When the results of the election were declared, the Conservative Party had a majority, 316 seats; the Liberals 191; the Irish Nationalists, led by Charles Stewart Parnell, 86; and the Liberal-Unionists, composed of disaffected Liberals, led by Lord Hartington, 78.[52] Hartington and Chamberlain then formed a political alliance with the Conservatives in opposition to the Home Rule Bill.

After the huge electoral loss for the Liberals, Gladstone resigned on July 20, and Lord Salisbury became prime minister. Salisbury asked Randolph to be the leader of the House of Commons as well as Chancellor of the Exchequer, and he accepted.

Being leader of the House meant that Randolph was a member of the cabinet. He was responsible for arranging government business in the House. A great deal of time was devoted to bills, acts of parliament, and ministerial statements. Randolph had to organize the use of the time to accommodate these matters, and to making regular announcements to the House as to what business would be put before Parliament for discussion. He may also have been called upon to stand in for the prime minister in his absence at Prime Minister's Question Time.

Lord Randolph was now openly talked of as the next prime minister, though he was still only thirty-seven years old. It would not have pleased Lord Salisbury to have been upstaged in this way in the newspapers. Both Jennie and the Dowager Duchess could hardly contain their excitement as he edged nearer to the highest office in the land. His closest friends noted an alarming increase in his already excessive smoking.

Parliament sat from August 19, 1886, and Randolph took no summer vacation to be with his family, apart from weekends. He worked hard as chancellor, instituting financial reviews of all the spending departments of government. He dedicated himself to a program of reform in Ireland, but the Irish Nationalists would not forgive him for his role in defeating Home Rule, and opposed him bitterly at every turn.

RANDOLPH'S WORKLOAD and the strain he was under were taking their toll on the Churchills' domestic situation. In August, Jennie perceived that he was acting in a cold and distant manner toward her, and wrote letters confiding in her mother-in-law. Unfortunately these letters have not survived, and we know of the situation only from Frances Marlborough's lengthy letters of reply. It is possible to deduce that Jennie's friend Lady Mandeville was spreading gossip about town that Randolph had a mistress. The woman in question was the beautiful and promiscuous Gladys, Lady de Grey. Despite her long-standing sexual relationship with Kinsky, Jennie took this news very badly and, in an extraordinary exchange of letters, asked Frances if there was any truth in the story and what she, Jennie, should do about it. It may be that what Jennie really feared was that Randolph had found out through gossip that she was secretly seeing Kinsky. Frances could not resist suggesting that Jennie's own lifestyle contributed to the stories, and strongly advised her not to add fuel to the flames by talking of her troubles to her so-called friends. On September 8, Frances wrote to Jennie:

> Accept your present worry and anxiety patiently and strive to dispel it by the exercise of DOMESTIC VIRTUES!! looking after the Children and the new cook etc—avoiding excitement and the Society of those Friends who, while ready enough to pander to you, would gladly see you vexed or humbled, as they no doubt are jealous of your success in society. . . . I *know* in his Heart he is truly fond of you—and I think I ought to know.[53]

Jennie fired off three letters of reply in forty-eight hours, and clearly she was very agitated about the situation. Frances replied, asking her to be calm, chiding her impetuous disposition, and offering to speak to Randolph. Jennie's concerns went on for some months, and in October Frances tried further to calm her, writing: "Perhaps he is full of other things. I *cannot* believe there is any other woman."[54] Leonie suggested in a letter to Clara that Jennie was imagining it and that even Kinsky thought so.[55] Jennie's affair with Kinsky was periodic. Leonie said he was never true to her and took other women to his bed, including the Prince of Wales's mistress Daisy Warwick.[56] It was only in later years that Jennie would become dependent upon Kinsky to the point of considering marrying him. The trouble with Jennie, Leonie felt, was that she was so used to admiration from other men that, having temporarily waned, she now thought Randolph was not paying her sufficient attention.

Randolph's notes to Jennie at this time were fairly curt and businesslike. The strain of parliamentary duties had induced in him temperamental outbursts that even the closest of his friends had commented upon with some anxiety. Modern medical opinion now suggests that Randolph may have suffered from bipolar disorder, possibly genetic in origin, that would manifest itself in mood swings under too much pressure.[57] It can border on manic depression during stress, and must have made him difficult to live with sometimes.

We can only wonder if the domestic peace at Connaught Place had been disturbed by similar outbursts of rage over the state of the household expenses. Jennie's income was not covering the amount she was spending, shopping and buying expensive dresses from Paris. It is more likely that Randolph was concerned about her lack of consideration in this respect and became withdrawn instead of approaching her immediately on the subject. Frances wrote a firm letter to Jennie on September 26, explaining that she had had a long talk with Randolph, occasioned by his needing to ask for her signature on yet another huge loan to settle (purely temporarily) their chaotic financial state, and that it was the first she had heard of their money worries. She begged Jennie to "give up that fast lot you live with, racing, flirting and gossiping. . . . You will be happier I know *once* you break off with the past and live for a better and more useful existence." She again reassured Jennie that she had "no cause for jealousy," and urged her to stop discussing her private affairs at social gatherings, as the stories made their way all around society and back to Blenheim.[58] Gladys de Grey was a good friend of Randolph's—she was interested in politics and often discussed the politics of the day with him—but there was no basis for the lurid tales circulating about them. Frances wrote firmly to Jennie, on October 3: "I still believe you have no cause for jealousy of that Lady."[59]

That September, Randolph really shook up the Treasury over excessive spending, denouncing them as "a knot of damned Gladstonians." His first great budget was a profoundly reforming document. Slashing away at many wasteful aspects of finance, and increasing death duties, stamp duties, and taxes on luxuries, he planned to produce a surplus of government income over expenditure, helping local government with grants and cutting income tax from eight pence to five pence per pound. The government departments that would feel the biggest cuts were the army and the navy. Randolph was always incensed at the way governments seemed to embroil themselves in "foreign adventures," and these curbs on the armed forces were one way of limiting such policy. From late October to December 1886, he was bombarded with complaints from his colleagues over his stringent policy. Salisbury indicated that the army and navy budgets would have to be maintained; Randolph replied that he could not continue to serve unless they both made significant cuts.[60] Jack and Mrs. Everest had accompanied Winston back to Brighton School after the summer holidays. Perhaps aware of the difficulties between his parents at home, Winston wrote to his mother September 7 that Jack sent her "millions" of kisses, "and I send you double!"[61] Winston was thriving in the kind, healthy atmosphere at school, with lots of swimming and riding. He was even trying for a classical prize.

Randolph had so exhausted himself in his work that he had gone off with a friend, Thomas Trafford, for a tour of Europe, taking in Paris, Berlin, Dresden,

Prague, and Vienna, traveling incognito as Mr. Spencer in an attempt to avoid the press following him. From Vienna, where he was socializing with Charles Kinsky, he wrote to Jennie, on October 12, a letter that shows how famous he had become and how the close attention of the press to celebrities is not a new phenomenon:

> I am hopelessly discovered . . . At the station yesterday I found a whole army of reporters, at whom I scowled in my most effective manner. Really it is almost intolerable that one cannot travel about without this publicity. How absurd the English papers are! Anything equal to the lies of the *Daily News* and *Pall Mall* I never read: that *Pall Mall* is most mischievous . . . The reporters have been besieging the hotel this morning, but I have sent them all away without a word.[62]

His letters to Jennie were friendly without being effusive, and he was sending back presents of Bohemian glassware that he hoped she would like.

ON DECEMBER 20, 1886, Randolph embarked on the last great political gamble of his life. After a meeting with Queen Victoria at Windsor Castle, he returned home and wrote out a letter of resignation, and sent it to Lord Salisbury and gave a copy to the editor of *The Times*. He later explained that he had intended this to force Salisbury into a serious discussion of the issues raised by the budget. He did not, however, tell either his wife or his mother, both of whom were astonished when they read it next morning in the newspaper. Jennie was too crushed and miserable to ask for an explanation.

Clearly, Randolph expected Lord Salisbury to concede the point that Randolph had pledged in public to carry through this budget and that he could not, in all conscience, remain in office if his own government would not support him. He badly misjudged Salisbury's reaction. The prime minister circulated the letter to cabinet colleagues and, on December 22, replied that he could not support cuts in military expenditure in what he considered to be dangerous times.

Randolph replied that he thought the Conservative government's foreign policy was "at once dangerous and methodless." That Salisbury had accepted his resignation without so much as an interview, he took as a calculated blow at Tory Democracy. Having resigned at Christmas, he would have no opportunity to explain his reasons to the assembled House of Commons.[63]

In a letter to Lord Salisbury, after Randolph's death, the Dowager Duchess revealed how utterly devastated her son was at the way Salisbury accepted his resignation without further discussion. She had gone to Salisbury, personally, and begged him to relent, but "your heart was hardened against him."[64]

Five

A HAPPY FAMILY AGAIN?

1887–1889

Lord Salisbury, leader of the Conservative Party,[1] continued as prime minister throughout the period 1887–89. At the end of 1886, Lord Randolph Churchill had resigned as a cabinet minister but retained his parliamentary seat of South Paddington, which he held for ten years. The Prince of Wales stood by him. In 1887, Queen Victoria had been fifty years on the throne, and Lady Randolph Churchill and Winston attended the Queen's Golden Jubilee. Later that year, against the wishes of his mother and the government, the Prince supported the Churchills on an unofficial political visit to the Czar and Czarina of Russia.

The year 1887 could hardly have started any worse for Jennie. Fearing for the state of her marriage, she was reeling from the disappointment of Randolph resigning his ministerial posts of leader of the House of Commons and Chancellor of the Exchequer without having the decency to inform her. On January 14, she received a shocking letter from Arthur Brisbane, the London correspondent of the New York *Sun*. He asked if there was any truth in an article he had received for publication that she and Lord Randolph were to separate. Jennie handed the letter to Randolph. That same day, Randolph fired off a blistering reply to Brisbane, wondering how an American gentleman could circulate statements so utterly false, and libelous.[2]

Brisbane's letter came as a wake-up call to them both. Randolph realized that the frenetic energy he had expended on political work had come at a heavy price to his family. The rift with Jennie was patched up, but Randolph had been unwell all through Christmastime, suffering from his nerves, lying on a couch in his private room smoking cigarettes.[3] He could not rest and recover in London as the press pursued him everywhere, his resignation being a hot topic. In search of fresh air, and to calm his shattered nerves, Randolph went off on February 9 on a tour of the archaeological sites of Algeria, Tunisia, Malta, and southern Italy. Jennie wrote him all the news she gathered at the many parties and dinners she attended.

In her letters there was always news of the children. Jack's seventh birthday was noted ("How time flies"), and Winston had been to a pantomime in Brighton, where he had rounded on a man who hissed a reference to Lord Randolph, saying, "Stop that row, you snub nosed Radical!"[4] Randolph was so delighted by this display of filial loyalty that he asked for Winston to be sent a sovereign. Following a dinner with the Salisburys, Jennie wrote to Leonie in Ireland at the end of February of how exasperated she had been that just at the moment when Randolph could have achieved anything he desired, he had thrown it all away in a gamble that had backfired. She said she believed "in the bottom of my heart" that his "head was quite turned" and that "he thought he could do *anything*." However, she had forgiven him and was busy with her painting and music. Randolph has "been so much easier and nicer since that I ought not to regret the crisis. He writes most affectionately & very often & I hope all will be righted when he returns."[5] To Randolph she wrote on March 5:

> you are good to me & I trust you utterly, & don't care twopence what they say—Enjoy yourself as much as you can & come back well, ready to fight the

whole lot—And if you are only glad to see me, & understand how much I think of you & all that you are to me—I shall be quite happy.[6]

Lord Randolph returned to London at the end of March and resumed his seat in the House of Commons in April, in time to see a budget passed that accepted the cuts in military spending that he had sacrificed his career over.

WINSTON'S LETTERS from Brighton were full of good news, of his progress at sports (football and cricket), and his assertion that he was "blessed with that inestimable treasure, good health." He was playing Robin Hood in an opera, and his friend Bertie Roose was Maid Marian. Jennie allowed him to come home to attend Queen Victoria's Golden Jubilee, June 20, and he was invited with his mother onto the royal yacht *Britannia* to be introduced to the Prince of Wales and his son George, later King George V. He also went to Buffalo Bill's Wild West Show and got to meet the great man.

In July, Mrs. Everest took Winston and Jack to Ventnor, on the Isle of Wight, to commence their summer holidays. Their mother and father joined them there in August for Cowes Week. At one party the Prince of Wales gave each of the boys a beautiful gold tiepin, set with a diamond. Winston immediately lost his, and the Prince gave him another. Jack kept his tiepin carefully all the days of his life and handed it on to his younger son, Peregrine.[7]

Following his return to school, Winston wrote his mother an abject apology, August 24, for his bad behavior while at home. The following letters all stressed how well he was doing in his lessons, and he wanted the autographs of both his mother and father for friends at school.

Later that summer, Randolph was discussing a school for Winston with his brother-in-law, Edward Marjoribanks, who introduced him to the idea of Harrow Public School. Randolph wrote to the headmaster, the Reverend Dr. James Welldon, and also explained about Winston's delicate health. It elicited a warm response, and Welldon said he would be delighted to find a place for Lord Randolph's son.

Winston wrote and thanked his father for the choice. Jennie took Winston back to Brighton for his last term of 1887, and was pleased to see him settle in well. He came at the top in history, ancient history, Bible history, and algebra, and second in geography and arithmetic. He would win prizes for English and Scripture by the end of the year. He took up boxing, and was doing well at riding and swimming. He still managed to come last, or nearly last, in conduct.

In September 1887, aged seven years and seven months, Jack began boarding at Elstree Preparatory School, in Hertfordshire. His earlier fair hair had turned dark and curly like his mother's, and he was tall and slim, blue-eyed, and resembled his father as a child. If there has been less to say about him until now, it is because he was a very well-behaved child, of a placid and serious disposition.

Jack's early letters, as may be expected, were a little homesick. "Do you miss me much? I do you. I hope Papa is quite well give him my love and a million kisses, also to you." This showering of affection on their parents was the hallmark of both boys in their letters home. However happy he was at school, Jack still counted the days till he got home: "My dear mama, I got my hamper on Wednesday. I hope you are quite well. I am very happy. There are only 5 more weeks before the holidays. The exams are going to begin very soon." His dear "Woom" (Mrs. Everest) was never far from his thoughts as, after a trip with her to Brighton to see Winny riding, this kind little boy wrote to Jennie on October 20: "Please dear Mama will you send Womany some money very soon as she is very low down indeed."[8]

IN THE LATE autumn, Randolph decided to take Jennie away on holiday to Russia. With the backing of the Prince of Wales, they would make a highly publicized visit to the court of the czar and czarina. In December, before leaving, they visited the boys at school, giving them generous gifts of money. Randolph went to Brighton to see Winston. The Misses Thomson were in such admiration of Randolph that they gave all the boys a half holiday.

On arrival at St. Petersburg, the Churchills were received like visiting royalty. Czar Alexander III invited them to the Gatschina Palace, which Jennie described as Russia's Windsor Castle. Every day they were the guests at some aristocratic party. There were troika drives in the country or skating by day, balls and dinners, theatre and the opera by night. Each had a private audience, Randolph with the czar, Jennie with the czarina. She wanted to know everything about society, fashion, and political life in England, and showed Jennie the many beauties of the palace. The czar received Randolph with great affection and, over shared cigarettes, got onto serious matters. He wanted Randolph to know, and presumably to convey home, that Russia was absolutely no military threat to Britain and its Empire, contrary to many stories in the newspapers.[9] Randolph wrote letters to the Prince of Wales keeping him informed of progress with the czar.

After a fabulous New Year's Eve party in St. Petersburg as guests of the czar and czarina, Randolph and Jennie went on to Moscow. They then left Russia for a ten-day visit to Berlin, where they were invited to a royal command performance at the opera, and were formally introduced to Emperor Wilhelm and his court.[10]

MEANWHILE, BACK in London, Winston and Jack had spent Christmas with Aunt Leonie and Uncle Jack Leslie. Winston wrote to his mother December 27 saying that they drank the Queen's health and his parents' health, and went to Uncle Jack's house and played games. They had also been taken to pantomimes, and Winston had met his favorite adventure author, Rider Haggard.[11] On December 30, Mrs. Everest had been taken seriously ill. Dr. Robson Roose had been called in, and initially he feared she had diphtheria. He moved Winston and Jack into his London house. Winston wrote to his parents from there, on December 30, that Mrs. Everest was not so ill as at first feared. And again on January 12, 1888, it was "more Quinzy than Diptheria." He solemnly reported that he was glad she had not died.[12]

For the remainder of the holidays Winston and Jack were first taken to Blenheim and then to their grandmother's London house, 46 Grosvenor Square. There were more visits to pantomimes and the theatre.[13] But writing to Randolph on January 23, their grandmother admitted that she was glad when Winston went back to school:

> I do not feel sorry for he is certainly a handful. Not that he does anything seriously naughty except to use bad language, which is bad for Jack. I am sure Harrow will do wonders for him for I fancy he was too clever and too much the boss at that Brighton school.—Jack is a good little boy and not a bit of trouble.[14]

Jack was well settled into Elstree School. On his eighth birthday (February 4, 1888), he wrote to his mother asking her to come down and see him, with the very specific instruction to "bring a hamper and 2 tins of sardines." However many times Jennie visited her boys, it was never enough for them. Mrs. Everest was a very regular visitor, bringing hampers of food, sweets, clean or new clothes, and the ever-needed pocket money. Peregrine said it was remarked at Elstree with what care and attention Jack greeted Mrs. Everest and walked with her around the school.

In his last term at Brighton, Winston worked hard to prepare for the Harrow entrance examinations. His father had given him some good advice on how to handle the exams. Winston should do the most "paying questions first"—those carrying the highest marks—and tackle the others later.[15] Winston's account of the exams themselves, taken on March 15, 1888, is open to question. He had just had an attack of mumps, but for him to say that he couldn't answer a single question on the Latin paper, which he merely adorned with an inkblot and several smudges, sounds like an amusing story told for effect.[16] Dr. Welldon, assured by Miss Charlotte Thomson at Brighton School that he was capable of good work, would let very little stand in the way of the young Churchill passing into Harrow. Randolph visited Winston at Brighton to tell him just how pleased he was that he had passed.

Winston went up to Harrow on April 17, and with his cousin Dudley Marjoribanks and two boys from his year at Brighton School also there, he settled in quickly. There were 550 boys in the school, and they were taught in purpose-built teaching blocks and resided in separate living accommodations.[17] Harrow was an expensive school. At £80/$384 a term, plus £38–40/$184 board, it was among the most expensive of public schools, nearly double some of its competitors. All additional but often compulsory activities, including music, games, specialist science, and workshop, were paid for separately. Winston suggested that all the other boys seemed to have much more pocket money than he, and reminded his mother, on April 21, that she had promised he "should not be different to others."

Welldon personally saw to it that Winston was taken into a special house run by Mr. Henry Davidson, where he would be coached along gently until he was ready to enter Welldon's house. Academically, he was put into the bottom class of the school, the third division of the fourth form. He excelled at English and history, always struggled with the classics, but did notably well at mathematics.

Most significantly for his future career, that May, he took the first opportunity to join the Harrow School's Rifle Corps. He proudly told his father in a letter June 3 that he was competing for an English prize and had to learn a thousand lines of Macaulay. Sadly, however, there was a malaise at the heart of this good news. On July 12, Mr. Davidson wrote to Jennie a long and heartfelt letter, setting out their concerns:

> I have decided to allow Winston to have his exeat [weekend at home]: but I must own that he has not deserved it. I do not think that he is in any way *wilfully* troublesome: but his forgetfulness, carelessness, unpunctuality, and irregularity in every way, have really been so serious, that I write to ask you, when he is at home to speak very gravely to him on the subject. . . . Constantly late for school, losing his books, and papers, and various other things into which I need not enter—he is so regular in his irregularity, that I really don't know what to do: and sometimes think he cannot help it. As far as ability goes, he ought to be at the top of his form, whereas he is at the bottom.

Clearly Jennie must have given Winston a good talking to at home because his performance improved somewhat, and he won the prize for a word-perfect recitation of—as it turned out—1,200 lines of Macaulay from memory.

For the summer holidays, Mrs. Everest took the boys to stay with her married sister and husband, Mary and John Balaam, in Ventnor, on the Isle of Wight. They loved these jaunts out with Woomany, and their days were filled with good, healthy exercise. John Balaam, chief warden at the high security Parkhurst Prison, was able to regale Winston and Jack with stories about criminals and their adventures, rather like the ones in Charles Dickens novels. Everest, while still on duty, could also be on vacation with her relatives; it was a happy arrangement for all. Winston could report to his mother that "Jackey" went to bed saying, "Well I think that *has* been a successful day." He thought that he and Jack ate "about a ton a day." A stay at Blenheim Palace rounded off their holiday.

On returning to Harrow in September, Winston found himself denied the "remove" (promotion to a higher class) that he might otherwise have expected. This was clearly a punishment for general bad behavior. But in November, his class undertook a special study of three of William Shakespeare's plays. Winston wrote to his father proudly on November 7 that he had come fourth out of twenty-five boys, having been awarded a score of 100 marks (amounting to the total for each of the components of the literary work), and the boy who came top had 127.

After their return from Russia, Jennie and Randolph enjoyed a renewal of their close relationship. The break from politics had done Randolph good. Together, they took great interest in the races and had made some shrewd purchases of racehorses that would perform well and earn useful prize money. The most outstanding was a beautiful black mare, the L'Abbesse de Jouarre. In June 1888, "the Abbesse," as the Churchills referred to her, won the Prince of Wales Handicap, with a prize of £1,000/$4,800, and then went on to win a number of other prestigious races.[18] The prize money would help sustain the Churchills' finances through difficult times.

In June, also, Randolph received an honorary doctorate of law from Cambridge University. A short holiday in August in the beautiful south of France was especially invigorating. Life was good.

BY HIS FOURTEENTH birthday, November 30, 1888, Winston had a fine collection of soldiers, all perfectly organized into a British infantry division and a cavalry brigade, with the correct artillery. Jack was a regular playmate, with his own collection. By a "Treaty for the Limitation of Armaments," devised by Winston, Jack was restricted to only colored troops, with no artillery. Soon after his birthday, Winston was marshaling his army at Blenheim Palace when his father paid him a visit. After a detailed inspection of some twenty minutes, Lord Randolph asked his son if he would like to go into the army. Winston immediately replied that he would, and his career was decided upon. Perhaps his father had observed in Winston the flair of the famous 1st Duke of Marlborough.

Lord Randolph wrote to Dr. Welldon conveying this important news and visited Harrow soon after to see Winston and his masters. Christmas was spent at home at Connaught Place. The boys so overindulged themselves, eating too much and singing themselves hoarse, that they were both ill. Jack recovered quickly and was taken to see the circus. Winston had a prolonged sore throat and a slight fever and confessed in a letter to his mother, January 2, 1889, to being "horribly bored & slightly irritable," made worse by the "awful rot" of having to spend part of his holidays in bed. The doctor's son and Winston's friend from his Brighton School days, Bertie Roose, came and sat with him and kept him company. At the end of January a short break with Mrs. Everest in the bracing air at Ventnor prepared the boys for their return to school.

Jack's letters were always, if sometimes unintentionally, amusing. In the autumn of 1888 the whole country was aghast at the series of murders in London's Whitechapel district attributed to the notorious Jack the Ripper. Randolph may well have discussed them with his friend, Henry Mathews, the Home Secretary, at home over Christmas. Like any boy of his age, Jack would have been all agog at these sensational events. He signed off his letters in February 1889 "Jack, not the Ripper." He was always aware of his father's troubled health, and almost every letter contains some reference to it. He sent regular and detailed reports on the school sports teams. His letters contained as much news of Winny as they did of himself, and he was able to report that he was already fourth in his class. His reading ability improved apace, and Jennie sent him the _London News_ and the _Daily Graphic,_ and took out a subscription for him to the monthly _Strand_ magazine. He was well informed in current affairs, the racing world, society gossip, and, of course, his father's political work.

Randolph had written to ask Welldon if he could take Winston into a more senior house in the school, meaning in fact the Headmaster's House.[19] Welldon replied, on April 2, saying that it was already arranged that Winston would be so promoted after Easter. By way of reward, Randolph sent Winston the money for a new bicycle. In September he would enter the army class at Harrow and begin his serious preparation for entry into the Royal Military College Sandhurst, where he would eventually train to become an officer in the army.[20]

DESPITE HIS RESIGNATION as a cabinet minister, Randolph remained a popular speaker in the House of Commons. In July 1889, he gave one of his most charming and witty speeches in support of more money from the Civil List for the children of the Prince of Wales. He was much praised in the press and in the Conservative Party, with whom a reconciliation took place. The Prince of Wales looked upon him as a loyal friend.[21] Peregrine related a story that soon afterward, Lord Randolph returned home one day earlier than expected and found Jennie alone with the Prince. For any man to be found alone in the house with an aristocratic woman, whether she was married or single, was a serious breach of etiquette. Lord Randolph was furious and angrily ordered the forty-eight-year-old Prince out of the house.[22] Bertie, or "Tum-Tum," as Jennie laughingly referred to the Prince, had already found himself called into court, in 1869, as a witness in a divorce case between Lord and Lady Mordaunt. Harriet, Lady Mordaunt had entertained a number of lovers in her home and had given birth to a child that was not her husband's. The Prince of Wales had visited Harriet alone, when her husband was absent from home hunting. In court the Prince admitted to visiting the lady, but nothing more.[23]

Six

LOOKING FOR GOLD
AND FAMILY MATTERS

1890–1893

Lord Salisbury continued as prime minister in 1890. He had been steadily promot-
ing his nephew Arthur Balfour inside the Conservative government. Balfour (an
old acquaintance of Lord Randolph) and the Fourth Party had abandoned their prin-
ciples. Charles Stewart Parnell's successful leadership of the Irish Parliamentary
Party would end abruptly in 1891. Now out of office for good, Lord Randolph paid
more attention to his home and family and to Winston's examination prospects. In
April 1891, Randolph set off with a mining party to South Africa in search of gold.
That November, the somewhat ruthless Arthur Balfour became leader of the House
of Commons. July 1892 would, however, see the return of a Liberal government led
by Gladstone.

In the first school term of 1890, Winston graduated to the first division of the fourth form.[1] Lord Randolph was in regular touch with him, and on February 26, Winston thanked him for a postal order received safely, asked if he could come down and resuscitate the Conservative Club at school, discussed some of Randolph's recent political speeches, and ended with a cheery note, "Don't trouble to write because you are so busy."[2]

Letters back and forth between all parties—Randolph, Jennie, Winston, Jack, and Mrs. Everest—were all shared and read between them.[3] Jack kept his parents regularly informed of how well he was doing at school, usually with a reminder of how low his finances were that particular week. A little note just before a birthday was always useful as a reminder to his father so that he would send him money as a birthday present: February 1, 1890: "Dear Papa, I am quite well. I am ten on the fourth of this month . . . two more years till I can go to Harrow. I must work up. It is a very short term, but it is very cold. I am getting on in writing." The next letter, February 9, is by way of thanks for his birthday present and assured his father that "I have not spent a shilling yet," and that he was saving it for the holidays.

Randolph made a point of sharing his winnings at the horse races with the boys, particularly following some of the triumphs of the Abbesse, which won the Manchester Cup.[4] On May 3, Jack wrote, "Thank you so much for sending me £3/$14.40. It is a lot. I have been top of my form 5 times." The enclosed list showed that Jack had been awarded 300 marks, 65 marks ahead of the boys who tied for second.[5]

Randolph had also sent Winston £5/$24 as his share of the winnings. On June 12, however, Jennie had to write her son a very stiff letter, sent via Mrs. Everest:

You know darling how I hate to find fault with you, but I can't help myself this time. . . . Your Father is very angry with you for not acknowledging the gift of 5£ for a whole week, and then writing an offhand careless letter.

This brought to a head the dissatisfaction that his parents were feeling with fifteen-year-old Winston. He had been kept back from one examination because his work wasn't up to standard. Then, on June 1, he wrote a long and carping letter to his father about the drawbacks of the army class. It is a frank letter, not the sort of thing a boy who was afraid of his father would write. He complained that the army class meant a lot of extra work in the evenings and during weekends and half holidays. He didn't like the idea of having to go to a "crammer" (a school where a specialist teacher taught only the subjects required to pass the exam) so that Winston could get through the Sandhurst entrance examinations, and suggested instead going into the militia. This was an easier route to obtaining a commission in the army.

Jennie gave free rein, on June 12, 1890, to the disappointment both parents felt:

> Your report which I enclose is as you will see a *very* bad one. You work in such a fitful inharmonious way, that you are bound to come out last. . . . Your Father & I are both more disappointed than we can say, that you are not able to go up for your preliminary Exam. Dearest Winston you make me very unhappy—I had built up such hopes about you & felt so proud of you—& now all is gone. Your Father threatens to send you with a tutor off somewhere for the holiday. I must say I think you repay his kindness to you very badly.

Inevitably, Winston's conduct was now being compared, unfavorably, with the ten-year-old Jack: "There is Jack on the other hand—who comes out at the head of his class every week notwithstanding his bad eye. . . . Your loving but distressed Mother."[6]

In July, the boys returned for their summer holidays at Banstead Manor, a country estate conveniently close to the Newmarket Races, which the family had rented for several months, a sign of their improved finances. The Abbesse had made a tidy profit, and Randolph was elected to the Jockey Club because of her string of victories. This was a long and glorious holiday, with lots of visits from family and friends, including Jennie's lover, Count Charles Kinsky, a great favorite with the boys. Having transferred from the Paris embassy to London that June, Kinsky now lived in the neighboring estate. He set up a target range and began to teach Winston and Jack to shoot. The boys also formed, and operated successfully, a model farm at Banstead, in which they kept a menagerie of dogs, ponies, laying hens, and rabbits.

Randolph took the boys on a long visit to Cliveden House, the home of Hugh Lupus Grosvenor, 1st Duke of Westminster.[7] Jack wrote to his mother: "If the house had been built for us, they could not be better." Randolph wrote to Jennie, August 24, that he had taken Winston and Jack, together with Jack Leslie (his godson, later known as Shane) and John Millbank (Winston's friend from Harrow), on a trip up-river: "We made an expedition up the river to Oxford, sleeping the night at Wallingford. We nearly got as far as Abingdon [Oxford] the next day. The boys enjoyed it. Jack has at last got a pony to ride and had his first ride this morning. He is seemingly pleased."[8]

Winston and Jack returned to school in September. It was clear that Welldon, out of his high regard for Lord Randolph, was going to a good deal of trouble to see that they got the best out of young Winston. The boy really was working hard, especially at his drawing, an important subject for military cadets. Jennie was less pleased when Winston mentioned in one of his letters that he had taken up smoking cigars, given his father's health problems, and warned him against it.

IN THE WINTER of 1890–91 Randolph was once again advised by his doctors to holiday in warmer climes. He set out with two friends, via Monte Carlo and Rome, for Egypt. Jennie's letters kept him informed of the political situation at home. From Rome, on December 3, he wrote to her: "Your nice long letter was very pleasant to receive. I should like to get them very often." He could not help relishing the disarray caused to the Irish Parliamentary Party (still referred to as the Home Rule Party), led by Charles Stewart Parnell.[9] The sensational news was that Parnell's long-standing affair with an aristocratic, married English woman, Katharine "Kitty" O'Shea, with whom he was living in England, had got into the newspapers when her husband filed for divorce.[10] The scandal led to Parnell being deserted by the majority of his party.

WINSTON HAD TAKEN his examinations in December 1890. As soon as school broke up, Winston and Jack went with Mrs. Everest to Banstead Manor for a winter break. Everest wrote to Jennie on January 1, 1891: "They [Winston and Jack] danced all evening & were out before breakfast this morning & have been out with the keeper [and] killed 5 rabbit." The boys, she said, were "so happy" and "the pond is beautiful for skating. It is so much better for them than London. I am desired to enclose drawings of last night with their best love & kisses."[11]

When the exam results were announced, Winston had done well. Out of twenty-nine candidates, twelve had succeeded, and Winston came fourth. An overjoyed Jennie sent the good news to Randolph, now on his way home from Egypt, on January 26, 1891: "I think you might make him a present of a gun as a reward. He is pining for one, and ought to have a little encouragement." Upon his return home in February, Randolph bought Winston a gun.

THE CHURCHILLS' finances remained unresolved, so Lord Randolph decided to try something new. He raised a loan of £5,000/$24,000 from Lord Rothschild and set off at the end of April 1891 for southern Africa to look for gold. Rothschild protected his investment by supplying a fine mining engineer, Mr. Henry Perkins, to the expedition, which was led in the field by the experienced Major George Giles, and, in Mr. Hans Lee, had one of the best hunters in Africa to guide it and supply a plentiful diet of fresh meat. They trekked into Mashonaland, risking attack by Matabele tribes and wild animals. This was a very rugged journey, crossing difficult, largely unexplored country. The *Daily Graphic* commissioned a series of twenty letters from Randolph, at £100/$480 each. He sent back an entertaining account of his travels and adventures, which kept him in the public eye. The Churchill family, including the Dowager Duchess, followed Randolph's progress on a map.[12]

Jack was growing quite tall, and his appetite for food was seemingly insatiable; his letters to his mother in May that year bombarded her with requests for hampers and fresh fruit, all of which seem to have been supplied. If he thought his mother was falling behind in replying to this stream of letters, he would tell her so, as on May 10: "You have not written to me for a fortnight. Do write and tell me how Papa is and the family of animals. You are hidden away at Banstead. Do write and talk." This letter ends with the word "Do" repeated forty-five times!

Jennie visited Harrow regularly, and spoke with Welldon about Winston's progress in the army class. Then Winston wrote to his mother on May 17 to confess there had been "a deuce of a row" at school when he and four chums had smashed all the remaining windows in a derelict factory. He had been one of two boys caught and received a birching from Welldon. A record was written in the school's punishment book, which is today on view at the Churchill Museum in London's Cabinet War Rooms.

On May 27, Derby Day, Winston wrote to his father, in Cape Town, a letter full of detailed accounts of recent racing successes and the prospects for the Derby, which was won by the favorite horse, Common.

Like most small live-in communities, Elstree School could do little to prevent the spread of illness once contracted. During his time there, Jack wrote of "epidemics" and "outbreaks" of measles, mumps, whooping cough, chicken pox, influenza, ringworm, eye infection or "eye disease." He wrote of having influenza, colds, coughs, bilious attacks, and eye trouble. The glands in his throat were prone to flaring up, and he suffered from earaches that dogged him into adulthood. Just when he was looking forward to seeing an important cricket match at Lords, he came down with mumps. That the headmaster had offered to take him is an indication of how well liked he was at the school. Jennie bought him a new pony as compensation for missing the cricket.

THERE FOLLOWED A long summer vacation at Banstead. Jennie rode out often with her two sons and took them dining in restaurants. A note to Randolph would say, "The boys are very happy. Kinsky has gone out with them to put up a target. . . . Both boys ride very well—particularly Jack." Winston supervised a large force comprising his brother, cousins, and estate workers to build a two-room den, complete with moat and drawbridge, defended by catapults that fired apples at any attackers. Between these military adventures and the busy model farm of ponies, horses, chickens, rabbits, and dogs, the Churchills, Frewens, and Leslies spent an idyllic summer.

Given the lengthy delays in postal deliveries, Winston must have been delighted to receive a letter from his father, dated June 27:

Dearest Winston,

You cannot think how pleased I was to get your interesting & well written letter & to learn that you were getting on well. I understand that Mr Welldon thinks you will be able to pass your examinations into the army when the time comes. I hope it may be so, as it will be a tremendous pull for you ultimately. I expect that when you are my age you will see S. Africa to be the most populous & wealthy of all our colonies. I suppose Mama has read you my letters & that you have seen my letters in the *Daily Graphic*. . . . You would have enjoyed an expedition I made last week for shooting purposes. A regular gipsy life, sleeping on a mattress in a bell tent, dressing and washing in the open air & eating round a camp fire. The sport was very fair & wild & there was much variety of game to shoot. Here I have been examining gold mines & investing money in what I hope will be fortunate undertaking for I expect you & Jack will be a couple of expensive articles to keep as you grow older.

In a long and affectionate reply, Winston gave his father lots of news, including all about the abuse that his letters to the *Daily Graphic* were receiving from competing papers. He also explained that his request for "an antelope" was not, as his father had imagined, for a live one, but for a head to put up in his room at home.

Jennie meanwhile was in serious discussion with Welldon about Winston's future. She needed Randolph's help and advice and wrote at length from Connaught Place on September 25, hinting that Winston was at an age that he needed his father to take charge of him:

Winston will be 17 in 2 months and he really requires to be with a man. [He] will be all right the moment he gets into Sandhurst. He is just at the "ugly" stage—slouchy and tiresome. I managed to get a very nice little man from Cambridge—very clever spoke 12 languages.

Money was becoming a worry again. Horses could not be depended on to win races, and they were expensive to stable and feed. The family was back to relying on Jennie's income from the rented property in New York, the Jerome family home that was part of her dowry from her father, and the occasional gift of money from him. School fees were a serious drain on their finances.

HEARING FROM JENNIE that Arthur Balfour had accepted the office of leader of the House in his uncle's government, Randolph replied on November 23, "Tory Democracy, the genuine article, at an end!," and stressed his complete disillusionment with politics and his yearning to come home to his family. Salisbury had made Balfour chief secretary for Ireland in early 1887, and he had betrayed much of what Lord Randolph had fought for. He ruthlessly enforced the Crimes Act there, which imposed a kind of martial law to suppress disorder, earning him the name of "Bloody Balfour." Salisbury approved of Balfour's methods, and was reported to have said that the Irish must "take a good licking" before conciliation would do any good.[13] In breaking up demonstrations the police had shot and killed people and wounded civilians, and there were imprisonments.[14]

Financial constraints saw the Churchills giving up Banstead Manor in October, and, to Jennie's great chagrin, she had to let 2 Connaught Place for the winter and move in with her mother-in-law, who now lived at 50 Grosvenor Square. To Randolph she pined, "I know beggars can't be choosers but I feel very old for this sort of thing. . . . I shall be glad to get you back. . . . I feel rather low and lonely at times."

Welldon advised Jennie that Winston needed to improve his French, and despite his protests, he was sent to France for Christmas, to improve his language skills. His letters home seethed with resentment, about the "queer food," the cold, the lack of good company.

LORD RANDOLPH returned from South Africa a richer man than when he left. He landed at Southampton on January 8, 1892, bringing with him the antelope's head for Winston. Jack had accompanied his mother to meet him, and in an excited letter to Winston, he described how the press was there in great numbers. *The Globe* reported that Lady Randolph "nimbly ran across the dock" to greet her husband. Randolph was in vigorous good health, and had grown a beard. Jack described it as "horrid," and drew a picture of his papa in his letter to Winston. Jennie called it "a terror" and thought she might have to bribe him to shave it off.

Randolph and Jennie at once made plans for a holiday in Paris together. On learning this, Winston wanted to join them. Randolph made it quite clear from the outset that it was not the right moment for Winston to take time off from his studies and that he was expecting much better things from his elder son. He wrote on January 15, reminding Winston of his own disappointment at not doing better at Oxford:

> The loss of a week now may mean your not passing, which I am sure you will admit would be very discreditable & disadvantageous. . . . When I was going up at Oxford for "final schools" I took something of an extra week & consequently altogether neglected what was called "special subjects." I just missed the First Class degree and only took a Second, & I have often thought since what a fool I was to lose the chance of a First for a few hours or days amusement.

In the end the Paris trip was postponed due to the sudden death on January 14 of the elder son and heir of the Prince of Wales, Prince Albert Edward. In a letter to his mother, Randolph made some observations on the behavior of the Prince of Wales that reflects his own moral standards: "How very sad is this death of the poor Duke of Clarence. Perhaps this grief may bring them [the Prince and Princess] together more and put a stop to importunate affairs."[15]

The discovery of gold during Randolph's trip to South Africa resulted in his acquiring gold shares from the Rothschilds. The shares would show a steady growth over the next three years, and would eventually be valued at £70,000/$336,000. These funds greatly enhanced the terms of his will (made in 1883), whereby a trust fund was set up to maintain Jennie and his sons. The provisions were extended to make allowances, after the boys were married, for their children. As an executor to his will, Jennie would administer the proceeds of the fund.

Soon after his return home, Lord Randolph suffered a brief paralysis in his arm, which the doctor attributed to bad circulation. Gradually, though, in the weeks and months that followed, he began to suffer mood swings, and Jennie found him difficult to live with. Peregrine has said there were many arguments and their domestic situation had all but broken down. In March, Jennie went to Monte Carlo to the gambling casinos without him. Randolph and Winston read in the English press that her purse had been stolen, and Winston wrote to his mother and begged her to stop gambling.[16] Later that year, when talking to his friend Nathanial "Natty" Rothschild, Randolph revealed, "I suppose you know she [Jennie] is living with Freddy Wolverton."[17] It was probably the first time Randolph acknowledged that Jennie sought sexual gratification elsewhere. Frederick, Lord Wolverton, was a handsome young aristocrat and an intimate of the Prince of Wales and his circle, who seems to have seized his chance during a cooling off between Jennie and the wayward Kinsky, who was often away from England.

In February 1892 Randolph resumed his seat in the House of Commons, and his demeanor was remarked by fellow members as silent and reserved.[18] He recognized the growing power of organized labor, and saw that they were ill served by the Liberals. A delegation of coal miners had once aired their grievances to both Prime Minister Gladstone and Randolph, and they openly declared they got far more satisfaction from the Conservative lord than the Liberal premier. A general election was called for July 1892. Randolph was returned unopposed, whereas the Tories crashed to defeat. Gladstone formed yet another Liberal administration, and promptly recessed Parliament for the summer.

Randolph was, as always, "living on his nerves." In the autumn of 1892, Winston had been trying out his new shotgun in the garden and fired at a rabbit close to where his father was resting. Randolph flew into a rage, which demonstrably distressed Winston. Randolph relented and spoke reassuringly to his son. Winston later remembered the conversation as one of the longest and most pleasant he ever had with his revered father. They spoke of school life, of going into the army, and "the grown-up life which lay beyond."[19] The strain of the continual abuse Randolph took in his political life was evident. "Do remember things do not always go right with me. My every action is misjudged and every word distorted. . . . So make some allowances."[20]

In the results of the Sandhurst entrance examinations, sent out August 23, out of 693 candidates, Winston came 390th, a full three hundred places below those who passed. There was, however, an encouraging note from his army class tutor, Mr. Moriarty, saying that his marks and place were "very creditable for your first try."[21]

Jack, in another rite of passage, passed the entrance exams into Harrow at his first attempt. In September 1892, age twelve and a half, having entered the school a year early, he was the youngest boy there. To his great delight, Dr. Welldon agreed that Winston and Jack could share a room. By some administrative error, Jack arrived too late to take an arithmetic test. He was able to tell his father in his first letter that he passed the exam the next day. Jack took readily to the school life and was soon forging ahead with his studies. He was rewarded with the gift of a fine gold watch by his proud father, who wrote on September 25:

> I hope you will take great care of it as it is a valuable one. You must wind it carefully and slowly, never in a hurry and never hard. I was delighted to hear you got through the Arithmetic paper.[22]

Randolph sent Winston and Jack generous food hampers and responded to their constant demands for more money. Even the careful Jack was finding Harrow very much more expensive than Elstree, and his letters became every bit as money-oriented as Winston's. He had taken up photography as a hobby, and his parents bought him a camera. It was an added expense but would stay with him all his life. In those days photographs were made on glass plates, and some of his early attempts at practicing on his family have survived.[23] Jack immediately began an accounts book, and kept an accurate record of income and expenditure. It was a great boon to be able to share a room with his elder brother, and he was spared many of the rigors of the "fagging" system that made new boys perform menial services for the seniors. Before long, however, the studious Jack saw the drawbacks. Winston could be a noisy and disruptive companion. In November, Jack wrote to his mother that Winston was going off for a medical examination: "so I shall expect a quiet day. (I am longing for it); I do not get much peace when he is here."

At the beginning of October, Jennie was suddenly in a great deal of pain. She was attended by Dr. Robson Roose and the gynecological specialist Dr. Thomas Keith. Keith diagnosed (October 22), an "irregular tender swelling about the size of a hen's egg" behind the uterus—"an enlarged ovary and tube or boil or both."[24] Jennie was in such a bad way that Randolph wrote to the boys October 25 to warn them how ill she was. After two weeks of extreme discomfort, she did respond to complete rest and medication and gradually recovered.

ON NOVEMBER 9, Randolph's elder brother the 8th Duke of Marlborough (Blandford), aged forty-eight, was found dead on the floor at Blenheim Palace from a heart attack. It was a dreadful shock to Randolph. Blandford's son Charles (Sunny) became the 9th Duke. Randolph was now next in line to the title, with Winston next after him.

Once again, Randolph's doctors advised him to go south for his health, this time to the south of France. Before leaving, he had a nice letter from Winston, giving the news that Jack had set a new record at Harrow, for having received not one single line of punishment for the whole of his first term. (Neither was he ever punished for any misdemeanor during his whole time at either Elstree or Harrow.) Randolph also received a letter, on November 28, from Dr. Welldon, praising Winston's work but warning that he still might not pass the exams.

A holiday at Monte Carlo did Randolph some good, but it was over that winter of 1892–93 that he began to show the physical signs of a tumor developing in his brain. He suffered from vertigo, palpitations, and numbness of the hands, all of which would get steadily worse. Eventually his wonderful memory and his sense of hearing would both be affected.

Jennie, the boys, and the Dowager Duchess were staying at Canford Manor, near Bournemouth, the home of Randolph's sister, Lady Wimborne, for the month of January 1893. On January 10, while playing a boisterous war game, Winston found himself trapped on a bridge by his brother at one end and a cousin at the other. It was not in his nature to surrender, and he climbed over the bridge railing and leapt for the branches of the nearest pine tree. He missed and fell thirty feet. It was three days before Winston recovered consciousness.[25] Randolph rushed back from Dublin, where he had been in talks with FitzGibbon, and collected one of the finest surgeons in London as he sped toward Bournemouth. Besides concussion, Winston suffered a ruptured kidney and injury to his right shoulder. The doctors ordered a long rest from hard study or vigorous exercise.[26]

Later in January, Winston learned that, despite a general improvement in his marks across the board, he had again failed the entrance exam for Sandhurst. He was "awfully depressed," but Welldon was very encouraging. He sounded out the best of all the "crammers," Captain James, ex–Royal Engineers, whose famous school in West

London, known as Jimmy's, had a wonderful record for divining the questions before an exam and preparing his pupils to pass successfully. Captain James agreed to take on Winston, and Randolph visited him to discuss the requirements, and he wrote to the Military Secretary at the War Office to see if Winston was eligible for a commission in the Household Cavalry.

Jack returned to Harrow alone and roomed with two new boys. He was invited to join the Rifle Corps but very sensibly said he would wait and see if he could use Winston's uniform, as he knew it "cost such a lot." What he did have to cope with was demands relating to unpaid bills left by Winston at the school and a local shop. Jack wrote to Winston in January (undated) about some of these bills, which he was settling, and presumably Jennie or Winston paid the rest.

Jack was soon sent away from Harrow in early February when scarlet fever struck the school. Mrs. Everest took him to Margate, where the sea winds "blew away" his coughs and colds. One of the masters wrote to Winston, saying how popular Jack was at the school. "Everyone likes him, as indeed no one could fail to do."[27]

At the end of February, Winston started at Captain James's school to begin cramming.

By March 7, James found it necessary to write to Lord Randolph:

He has been rather too much inclined up to the present to teach his instructors instead of endeavoring to learn from them, and this is not the frame of mind conducive to success.[28]

Captain James wrote again on April 29: "I have no definite complaint to make about him but I do not think that his work is going on very satisfactorily."

There was another distraction in Winston's life: He had developed a lasting interest in politics. During the time he was at home recovering from the fall at Bournemouth, he met MPs who were friends of his father's when they were dining with his parents and at the dinner table had engaged in discussion with them about the current business in the House of Commons.

Frances (Daisy) Countess of Warwick, wife of Francis, 5th Earl of Warwick, of Warwick Castle, made an acute observation in her memoirs on how Jennie handled both her sons:

In those days, people could not see any definite principle behind Jennie Churchill's upbringing of her sons. . . . They did not realize that she was developing in them qualities, which, in the ordinary course, take years to show themselves. She always found time to encourage her boys to express themselves.[29]

WHEN THE NEW session of Parliament convened in January 1893, Randolph was warmly welcomed by the Conservative leaders and invited to sit on the opposition front bench. The new leader, Arthur Balfour, wrote in the friendliest terms to him. At a meeting of the Conservative Party's Carlton Club to discuss resistance to a new Home Rule Bill, Randolph kept quietly in the background until a great clamor went up for him to come forward and speak in the debate. Home Rule was now a serious threat, Gladstone having promised it in his electoral address. Still the expert on Irish affairs, Randolph's experience was needed to help the Tories defeat it.

Afterwards, he embarked upon a demanding series of public speeches all around the country, fiercely denouncing Home Rule, and he was as popular as ever. He was pale, his eyes protuberant, his hair much receded, his beard wild, his hands trembling. Gone was that wonderful memory. He had to read from pages of notes. But his speeches were cogent, closely and carefully reasoned, and full of witticisms. That February, Gladstone introduced the Second Home Rule Bill, and it was passed in the House of Commons on April 21, by 43 votes, but had to go through a third reading before it was approved. The Conservative Party asked Randolph to close the debate on the Welsh Church Suspensory Bill introduced by the Liberals, and which among other things aimed to secularize Church of England schools in Wales.[30] Randolph was in marvelous form. His old vigor restored, he ended by putting aside his notes and excoriating Gladstone in a fierce and sparkling attack that recalled the great days of the eighties. Although his physical health was in decline, there was nothing wrong with his great mind, yet.[31] In May and June that year, he made ten major speeches in ten cities.

Winston's prospects also revived. Captain James was able to report to Randolph on June 19: "Without saying that your son is a certainty I think he ought to pass this time."[32] Jack meanwhile was doing well. Jennie had been to Harrow to see him and heard the highest praise of him from Dr. Welldon. On June 5 a proud father wrote to Jack, "I got a capital report of you today. I will come down Friday, if Mr. Welldon likes I will stay for evening service as I should much like to hear his evening sermon." Jack received a new clock and a new camera as rewards for his good work.

He wrote to his mother about another visit from his father:

I took Papa for a walk on Sunday [June 11], and we had some tea he went to chapel and I think that he liked Welldon's sermon. He told Welldon that Winney had been working very hard and he thought he was going to get through.

That summer, Randolph and Jennie took their holiday together at the German health spas around Gastein. Prince Bismarck called upon them and enjoyed a conversation, in English, about the health resorts, some current foreign news, and how a great country like Britain could be governed by someone as unmanageable as Mr. Gladstone.

Before he left for Germany, Randolph had organized a six-week European holiday for his sons. He engaged a young Eton master, Mr. J. Little, to travel with Winston and Jack, and they left for Switzerland on August 2.[33] There was a good deal of walking in Switzerland, with plenty of opportunity for the young men to improve their language skills. Mr. Little injured his leg in the first week, and the boys were left to themselves for part of the time.

On Friday, August 4,[34] there occurred a most extraordinary incident, which Winston related in *My Early Life*.[35] He wrote that he went boating on a lake with another boy in Switzerland. They got out of the boat for a swim and subsequently got into difficulty when a breeze blew up and the boat began to drift away from them. As the younger boy desperately struggled to stay afloat, Winston, a strong swimmer, struck out for the boat, recovered it, and returned to save the other boy's life. This incident remained a complete secret until *My Early Life* appeared in 1930. From Peregrine Churchill we learned that the "other boy" was Jack.

At the beginning of the holidays in August, Winston received his examination results and learned he had scraped into Sandhurst at his third attempt. However, he had failed to qualify for the infantry, and was consigned to the less-demanding cavalry. From Switzerland, both Winston and Mr. Little wrote to Randolph with the news.

Lord Randolph was not pleased. He wrote to the Dowager Duchess on August 5:

> I cannot think highly of Winston's [result]. He missed the last place in the infantry by about 18 marks, which shows great slovenliness of work in the actual examination. He only made about 200 marks more than last time, I think not so many even as 200. He has gone & got himself into the cavalry who are always 2nd rate performers in the examination and which will cost me £200 [$960] a year more. . . . After all he has got into the army & that is a result which none of his cousins have been able to do.

Randolph's angry reaction on August 9 to Winston's letter of August 6,[36] in which he repeated to his father his exam success, indicates the bitter disappointment of an ailing man, who felt let down by his elder son's poor record and being only able to enter into an inferior arm of the services:

> I am rather surprised at your tone of exultation over your inclusion in the Sandhurst list. There are two ways of winning an examination, one creditable

the other the reverse. You have unfortunately chose the latter method, and appear to be much pleased with your success.

Randolph had addressed Winston man to man for the first time, and it would have the desired effect. At Sandhurst, Winston would do well.

On Winston's return from Switzerland, on August 29, a letter awaited him from the Military Secretary, Sandhurst Royal Military College, offering him a place in the infantry after all, because some candidates, having qualified, then failed to take up their cadetships. Winston sent a telegram and a letter to his father on August 30, telling him the good news. That October, Randolph approached the Duke of Cambridge, onetime commander in chief of the British army, to secure a commission for Winston in the elite 60th Rifles, of which the duke was now colonel in chief.[37]

Seven

SETTLING THE BOYS' FUTURE

1893–1894

In 1893, Gladstone was still the leader of a Liberal government. His Home Rule Bill was due for the third reading in the House of Commons in September. Despite being an old friend of Lord Randolph Churchill, Lord Rosebery (Archibald Primrose, 5th Earl of Rosebery), now an up-and-coming Liberal politician, had supported Gladstone on Home Rule, and helped him achieve success with the bill in the Commons. In March 1894, Rosebery would replace Gladstone as prime minister. Lord Randolph's rapidly failing health would steadily diminish his involvement in politics in the Commons that year.

The third reading of Gladstone's Home Rule Bill took place in the House of Commons on September 1, 1893, and it was passed by 34 votes. It then had to be passed by the House of Lords, where it suffered a massive defeat on September 8, by 419 votes to 41. Lord Randolph's many speeches against it had clearly contributed to its downfall, and he was once again in favor with his party.

Winston was to report to Sandhurst on September 1, 1893, to join the Infantry Class at Sandhurst Royal Military College. His earliest childhood experiences of war were of exploring the huge wall tapestries of cavalry charges on the walls at Blenheim Palace. He much enjoyed riding and secretly yearned to join the cavalry instead, which, at £200/$960 a year more than the infantry (a considerable sum in those days), his father considered too expensive. However, Winston duly wrote to his father that he would take up his commission in the 60th Rifles as Randolph had fondly hoped. He wrote a long and pleading, though carefully reasoned, letter, spelling out the expenses to be incurred at Sandhurst, asking for a quarterly allowance, and promising to account for all his spending.

Winston duly arrived at Sandhurst, and Randolph was pleased to see the mature tone of his letters with their promises of application to the principles of the trade he had committed himself to. The boy-become-man spoke of the lack of comfort and the strict discipline, but expressed interest in the drill and military education he was learning, and expected to improve mentally, morally, and physically. Randolph responded warmly and made him a £10/$48 per month allowance, which Winston professed to be ample. He kept his father fully informed of his daily timetable and the subjects he was studying. However, Winston also made frequent requests for parental written consent to be allowed complete freedom of movement on weekends. Randolph expressed extreme annoyance that Winston would go off to London instead of applying himself to that extra study that would ensure his success.

Winston had left Switzerland before the end of the holiday in August, to take up his cadetship at Sandhurst on time. Mr. Little completed the holiday with Jack, whose French improved after his brother's departure. The latter was always voluble to the extent that Jack seldom found the chance to speak. Jack returned to Harrow School, and his letters home expressed some loneliness and were full of the usual references to being "absolutely broke." He was able to make visits to Winston at Sandhurst and was hugely impressed. Winston was able to return the visits to Harrow and passed on to Lord Randolph the message that Dr. Welldon was anxious to see him to discuss Jack's future.

Randolph and Winston were getting on very well, and Winston settled into his work at Sandhurst. Winston later recalled that his father took him to the Empire Theatre, to the races, and to Lord Rothschild's house at Tring, to join a large gathering of the leaders and rising men in the Conservative Party. The Rothschilds were, and still are, one of the largest names in merchant banking, and those present were the top tier of British society. Nathaniel, Baron Rothschild was a close personal friend of Randolph's. Tring House was his mansion on his country estate in Hertfordshire. Randolph wrote proudly to the Dowager Duchess, on October 23, 1893:

Winston . . . has much smartened up. He holds himself quite upright and he has got steadier. The people at Tring took a great deal of notice of him but [he] was very quiet & nice-mannered. Sandhurst has done wonders for him. Up to now he has had no bad & [only] good conduct [reports] & I trust that it will continue to the end of the term. I paid his mess bill for him, £6 [$28.80], so that his next allowance might not be *empieté* [encroached] upon. I think he deserved it.

Randolph paid for extra riding lessons for Winston from a Life Guards riding master. He also took the time to warn him, from his own personal experience, of the perils of excessive smoking. It was very gratifying for all the family that Winston did splendidly in his end-of-term examinations, coming twentieth in his year, with a fine all-round performance that tempered the slightly negative remark on his conduct, "Good but unpunctual."

DURING THESE MONTHS the Churchills were saving money by living with the Dowager Duchess at her prestigious Grosvenor Square house and renting out their own home, Connaught Place. Randolph had to sell some £500/$2,400 of gold shares, of which £105/$504 had to be sent to Jennie, who was visiting her mother in Paris. Jennie was always very uncomfortable at being beholden to her mother-in-law. This was aggravated by the Dowager Duchess taking advantage of Jennie's absence on a trip to Scotland to dismiss Mrs. Everest from their service, as she was no longer needed to raise the boys and was employed as a housekeeper. Jennie was not able to protest this decision while living under her mother-in-law's roof. She did, however, find new employment for Mrs. Everest as housekeeper to a bishop in Essex, and sent her small sums of money from time to time. Winston wrote a long, impassioned letter to his mother about the "cruel and mean" way Everest had been treated. Mrs. Everest kept up a lively correspondence with both Winston and Jack, reminding them of birthdays and continually monitoring their progress.

That winter, Randolph took another holiday at Monte Carlo. He wrote to Jack at Harrow School on January 30, 1894:

> I am glad to hear you have got your room in order, but I am afraid you must rely on Mama for funds till I return. . . . I have been kept to the house by a bad cough during the last few days but it is getting better and I poked my nose out with the garden today. . . . Mama writes me that the Paddington [Primrose League] Meeting went off very well and that Welldon let you stay [at home] the night for it.

Earlier that month, Jennie had addressed a meeting of the Primrose League in Randolph's Paddington constituency as part of her continual support of her husband's political career and her own interest in political affairs. Randolph also asked Jack if he had begun the army class at Harrow yet. This is the first confirmation that Jack had also decided on a career in the army. Winston was able to report, after a visit to Harrow, that Jack had indeed started with the army class just before his fourteenth birthday.

Jack continued to perform very well at school, always in the top three or four boys in his year. Randolph had arranged to meet Jack at Harrow and introduce him to Lord Roberts, the commander in chief of the army.[1] Having been instrumental in advancing the career of Roberts when he was secretary of state for India, Randolph was now calling in a favor. Randolph had set a date when he was already booked for dinner and was not able to attend. But Jack went ahead and had a long conversation with the great general in Dr. Welldon's drawing room after supper. Jack left no precise record of it, but an army career was clearly now his dearest wish. On April 10, Winston said, after a visit by Jack to Sandhurst, that his brother was looking forward to going there officially.

Meanwhile, on the political scene, Lord Rosebery had, on March 5, 1894, replaced Gladstone as Liberal prime minister.[2] Rosebery had been a lifelong friend of Randolph's from their Eton Public School days. But for Randolph's failing health there can be little doubt that Rosebery, who greatly admired Randolph, would have found a position for him in the government. On March 13, however, there was an unfortunate incident in the House of Commons. Randolph lost control during a debate and screamed abuse at his own benches, along the lines of "You damned fools! You're playing the devil with the Tory Party and making hell of the House of Commons."[3] Members fled from the chamber. This was a clear sign of the relentless decline brought on by a fatal brain tumor. Shortly after this debacle, his doctors advised him to rest and retire from politics.

Whether he was aware of his illness or not, Randolph continued to try to see to family matters. On April 28, he wrote to Jack, "I went to see the Duke of Cambridge yesterday and he put down your name for the 60th Rifles. I gave your name as Jack Spencer Churchill for there was a celebrated Jack Churchill many years ago." Here is a father, proud of the superlative record of his younger son, associating him with England's greatest soldier and one of the great captains of history, the 1st Duke of Marlborough. Randolph arranged a second meeting immediately with Lord Roberts on May 20. First Jack would travel to Roberts's house at Grove Park, Kingsbury, for luncheon. Randolph would join them there on his return from a few days fishing in Scotland. Then they would travel together to Harrow School to hear one of Welldon's fine sermons.

Both Jack and Randolph wrote accounts of the meeting to Winston, regaling him with stories about the wild behavior of an old army horse that Lord Roberts had in harness. Jack wrote on May 23:

> I drove over to Luncheon (only 3½ miles) and there was shown into a very Indianfied room, he [Roberts] was out . . . so I looked around and saw a sort of Butterfly case on the wall. I went for a nearer inspection and found them to be Medals!!!! of every discription [*sic*] under the sun. VC [Victoria Cross] was among them. Then we went to meet Papa. Lord R. got in the little cart and the poney [*sic*] stood on its head, and he sat motionless, then it ran into a wall and smashed all the back of the cart, he seemed rather to like it and at last I got in and we went off alright. Papa missed his train. . . . he did not arrive till the end of Luncheon. Then he came to Harrow. . . . I had supper with Welldon!!!

Randolph wrote to Winston on May 24, clearly very proud of the singular honor done to Jack, a junior boy, by Dr. Welldon, and explained how Lord Roberts's elder daughter, Aileen, had kept the pony quiet when he was being driven over by feeding it lumps of sugar:

> Mr. Welldon insisted on Jack & I having tea in his drawing room alone, as he said he had some hard work to do. I expect thoughts on [the] sermon, which I afterwards heard & thought a very fine one. Jack was greatly honoured on Sunday evening. I told him Mr Welldon would ask him to supper. But he replied that he would only be asked in after supper as Mr. Welldon never asked more out of the school than the two sixth form boys who read the lessons [in chapel]. Sure enough however Mr. Welldon did tell him to come into supper & afterward to sit in the drawing room till I went away at nine o'clock.

Just when things were going so well between Winston and his father, a couple of unfortunate incidents led to a new rupture between them. In February 1894, Randolph had arranged for Winston to lunch with Lord Roberts, who might be very useful in advancing his military career. But Winston had been out on the town the night before, visiting music halls with his cadet friends. He was very late for the luncheon, which was offensive to both his father and the general.

Fearing for Winston's application to his studies, for which he had ample precedent, Randolph wrote to him, on April 13, 1894, "in perfect kindness," a stern lecture on the need for strength of character at this crucial time:

> Now this is your critical time at Sandhurst and you have got to work much harder than in the former term. If you are always running up to town every week on some pretext or other & your mind is distracted from your work besides being an unnecessary expenditure of money. Now I am not [going to] have you this term come to London more than once a month, and I give you credit for not coming to London without my knowledge.
>
> You must remember always that you are a military cadet and not a Harrow schoolboy. Now is the time to work & work hard; when you are in the regiment your work may be slightly relaxed, by the performance of regimental duties. Why do I write all this. Because when you go into the army I wish you to make your one aim the ambition of rising in that profession by showing to your officers superior military knowledge, skill & instinct.

Winston replied a week later, assuring his father that he was working very hard, including the weekends, and attending a voluntary extra class in signaling. Regrettably for him, this letter arrived just as his father discovered a deception on Winston's part. On the tenth anniversary of the death of the 7th Duke of Marlborough (July 1893), Randolph had given his father's treasured gold watch to Winston as a sign of the new respect for him as an adult. Twice Winston had to send the watch to the watch makers for repair. Once it had been knocked from his hand by a running passerby; the second time was more careless. He bent over a stream to pick up a stick, and the watch fell out of his pocket into the water. Having gone to extraordinary lengths to recover it, diving into the pool and failing to find it, he then had it dredged. Finally, he hired a squad of twenty-three infantrymen to completely divert the stream from its course (at a personal cost of £3/$14.40, which he later brought to his father's notice) and recovered it at last. He sent it again for repair in hopes that his father would never know of the mishaps. The broadside he received, dated April 21, must have been a blow:

> I have received your letter of yesterday's date & am glad to learn that you are getting on well in your work. But I heard something about you yesterday which annoyed & vexed me very much. I was at Mr. Dent's about my watch, and he told me of the shameful way in which you had misused the very valu-

able watch which I gave you. He told me that you had sent it to him some time ago, having with the utmost carelessness dropped it on a stone pavement & broken it badly. The repairs of it cost £3 17s., which you will have to pay Mr. Dent. He then told me he had again received the watch the other day and that you told him it had been dropped in the water. He told me that the whole of the works were horribly rusty & that every bit of the watch had had to be taken to pieces.

He concluded: "in all qualities of steadiness taking care of things & never doing stupid things Jack is vastly your superior." When the watch was finally repaired it was given to Jack as a present. However, Jennie was able to write to Winston from Paris, April 22, a comforting note, suggesting that Randolph's annoyance was tempered with a little understanding: "Papa wrote me all about it. . . . However he wrote very kindly about you so you must not be too unhappy. . . . Oh! Winny what a harum scarum fellow you are! You really must give up being so childish." Randolph bought a new, cheaper watch for Winston.

Knowing Randolph would not approve, Winston chose not to tell his father that from January 1894, he had been in negotiation with Colonel Brabazon, of the 4th Hussars at Aldershot Barracks, to join his cavalry regiment when he graduated from Sandhurst. His anxieties at that time were written to his mother during May, who also kept it secret from his father.

That month, Randolph was writing friendly letters to Winston, and was pleased to see him dining out with serving colonels in the army. He would have been less pleased had he seen the letters Winston was writing to Jennie, explaining at great length his desire to join the expensive 4th Hussars, with its posting to India coming up and the faster promotion in the cavalry.

ALSO, DURING THOSE months Randolph's doctors had grown increasingly concerned about his general health and were recommending a withdrawal from public life. Randolph was actually enjoying a slight political revival and was making some excellent speeches at large public meetings with which he continued despite his stammer and having to use notes.

Randolph was very proud of Jack's record at Harrow, and made a point of attending the annual Speech Day, at which the Prince of Wales was guest of honor. After a good win at the Derby, backing Lord Rosebery's horse Ladas, he sent Jack a gift of £2/$9.60.

HIS HEALTH DETERIORATED again, and he was now so ill that his performance in the House of Commons was a subject of public comment when he could not get the words out of what he wanted to say. His great oratory was a thing of the past. His speeches were now sad to behold—halting, forgetful, punctuated by long silences. In late May 1894, he finally accepted medical advice to give up public life, and he said he wanted to go on a world tour. In the beginning Dr. Thomas Buzzard, a specialist in neurological diseases who had attended Lord Randolph some years earlier and whom Randolph had consulted again more recently, agreed to the trip, but then changed his mind, thinking it risky.[4] Randolph countered that he had made all the arrangements and was determined to go.

Having estranged herself from Count Charles Kinsky, Jennie gave up her place in society to accompany her husband on the yearlong world cruise to restore his health. Peregrine said that Kinsky had, somewhat insensitively, asked Jennie to divorce her sick husband and go off to his new posting at Brussels with him, there to be married, and she refused. Kinsky was heavily in debt, and would have been cut off by his father had he gone through with the plan. Jennie, as someone attuned to the importance of social standing in Victorian Britain, knew a divorce was out of the question.

In early June, the Churchills sold their house in Connaught Place, some gold shares, and their share in the great horse L'Abbesse de Jouarre. There were funds enough for what would be an expensive trip when a doctor, maids, and the valet were included. During the last weeks of June, several farewell dinners were held by family and friends in Randolph's honor. The last was at his mother's home on June 26, and Winston received a cable from his father that day to come home for it. At first, permission to leave Sandhurst was refused, but Randolph cabled a personal appeal to the secretary of state for war to obtain a special dispensation. He wished the family to be together to make their farewells. They all drove together to the station the next morning, and Winston recalled that his father patted him on the knee.[5]

Eight

THE LAST JOURNEY

1894–1895

Lord Rosebery continued as Liberal prime minister until June 22, 1895. The Liberal Party had divided into two factions. Lord Rosebery, who had previously been Foreign Secretary, was leader of the Liberal Imperialist faction. Sir William Harcourt, Chancellor of the Exchequer from 1892 to 1895, was leader of the other, more left-wing faction, which opposed Rosebery's imperialism. Rosebery's government was not successful, his designs on such foreign policies as expansion of the British fleet were defeated within the Liberal Party, and his opponent, Sir William Harcourt, emerged as the strongest figure in the Cabinet. The House of Lords stopped the Liberals' domestic legislation.

Randolph and Jennie left for New York on June 27, 1894. Dr. Thomas Keith,[1] a very experienced doctor, accompanied them to attend to Randolph. They were met at New York by Jennie's cousin, William Travers Jerome, and were soon the center of attention in New York society. The *New York Times* reported that at one great banquet Jennie invented a new version of the Manhattan cocktail.[2] Family legend says it was influenced by one of Randolph's many cough medicines.[3] Jennie wrote to Jack on July 10 that they were in Bar Harbor, Maine, relaxing in the bracing New England air:

> It is a most lonely spot right on the Atlantic and great high mountains. The air is wonderful and ought to do Papa a great deal of good. I think we shall stay 3 weeks, of course it is very dull, not a soul or kindred.

On July 17, Jack wrote his mother all the news about school, family, and the holiday in Switzerland. The Prince of Wales had attended Speech Day at Harrow, visited Jack in his room, "and recognized the little tie pin, which he gave me 7 years ago at Cowes." To her sister, Leonie Leslie, living in Ireland, Jennie was more candid about some of the difficulties of the trip. The party had traveled across Canada, and reached Alberta, on August 7:

> R. is not as well as he was at Bar Harbour. Of course the journey has told on him. . . . As soon as he gets a little better from having a rest and being quiet he will be put back by this traveling—and *nothing* will deter him. . . . Keith thinks that R. will eventually get quite well, & I think so too—if only he would give himself a chance. He is very kind & considerate when he feels well—but absolutely *impossible* when he gets X [cross] & excited.

Arriving in California in the third week of August, the Churchills were feted as visiting celebrities. The press hounded them everywhere. It was from there, on August 20, 1894, at the Hotel Delmonte, that Randolph wrote a most interesting letter to Sir Edward Hamilton, Gladstone's private secretary, in reply to his of July 20. It shows the extraordinarily close relationship Randolph had with the leaders of the Liberal Party, and how he freely discussed their policy with them. He even made suggestions about Gladstone's health.

IN THE MEANTIME, the boys had enjoyed another holiday in Switzerland under the care of Mr. Little. Winston had to return to Sandhurst at the end of August, and Jack was back at Harrow in September.

Winston was doing well at Sandhurst and confidently looked forward to his finals. With his parents away he certainly took advantage of every opportunity to get up to London and enjoy himself. The music halls were a great attraction for the Sandhurst cadets, and Winston took to mooning after a musical comedy actress, Miss Mabel Love.

In September, after visiting Japan, Randolph and Jennie had taken a rather risky trip to China, from Hong Kong, upriver to Canton. Jennie wrote to Winston, on October 11:

> I can't imagine how I shall be able to hold out a year! I think Japan has done your Father good—altho' he is not as well as I could wish—I can't tell you how miserable I am, often—so far away from you all.

Randolph was now suffering a transient paralysis of the left arm,[4] but insisted on journeying on, via Singapore to Burma and then to India. In late October at Singapore, despite being told by Dr. Keith that he was very ill, Randolph refused to abandon the trip and set sail for home. It was his idea to bring a lead-lined coffin into the hold of the ship. He said if he died they could bury him at sea.[5]

News that Count Charles Kinsky was engaged to be married had somehow reached Jennie. On October 31, 1894, she wrote a letter to Leonie that shows the extent of her distress and emotional turmoil:

> I do not blame him. I only blame myself for having been such a fool & wanted *l'impossible*. These 4 hard miserable months I have thought incessantly of him & somehow it has kept me going. But there! It is best for me not to write about it all—what is the use. The one thing which stands out . . . is the thought that I have sacrificed to him the one *real* affection I possessed, & that I shall never dare to turn to—for fear of finding that it has gone. . . . Leonie my darling I am ashamed of myself at my age not to be able to bear a blow with more strength of character. I feel *absolutely mad* . . . it hurts me so. I really think I have been paid out for all my iniquities. . . . I know you don't like him but . . . I loved him, I don't think anyone half good enough for him. . . . It is only right & fair that he sh[oul]d have a nice wife— young & without a past—who will give him children & make him happy. . . . From henceforth he is *dead to me*. . . . He has deserted me in my hardest

time in my hour of need & I want to forget him tho' I wish him every joy & luck & happiness in this life.[6]

At the beginning of November, the Churchills were put up in the Government House at Rangoon. It was here that Kinsky's telegram caught up with Jennie confirming the distressing news that he was indeed engaged to be married to an attractive, twenty-one-year-old, wealthy heiress, the Countess Elizabeth Wolff Metternich zur Gracht, a cousin of the beautiful Empress Elizabeth of Austria.[7]

To add to Jennie's troubles it was now obvious to Randolph's doctors that he was dying. Dr. Keith had kept Dr. Robson Roose and Dr. Thomas Buzzard informed of his progress throughout by sending telegrams, and also wrote to Randolph's sister Cornelia, Lady Wimborne, November 22, giving no hope of recovery.[8] The tour was then cut short, and they began their return to England via Egypt and France.

On November 30, Jack wrote to his father: "Here at Harrow we are cursing our founder for having built Harrow on a Hill, because Eton being in a valley is under water and the boys have all gone home, to show what it is like one Eton boy swam the whole of the High Street! . . . This will be the first Christmas when you both have been so far away, one Christmas you were in Russia but that was only a step from here." The ending of his letter made clear the strain this trip brought on the whole family:

> To think I have not been really happy for nearly 6 months since you left. O how I wish I could express my thoughts and soul as regards you and dear Mama but I can't and if I try I only write bad English.

Jennie wrote to Winston on December 1, giving him to understand that his father was not long for this world. But Jennie and Winston withheld from Jack, who was only fourteen years old, the seriousness of his father's situation.

Jack wrote his last letter to his father on December 21:

> We are expecting a telegram any minute from you to say you have arrived at Marseilles. Of course you have heard about Winston coming out 2nd in the Sandhurst riding it is supposed to be a smart thing to do. I think he owes most of it as well as everything else, to you. I will write again to you soon.
>
> Goodbye dear Papa. Lots of love. I remain, Your loving son. Jack S. Churchill.

By December, Jennie had become desperate about Kinsky's impending marriage, and wrote to Leonie:

Oh Leonie darling do you think it is *too late* to stop it? Nothing is impossible you know. Can't you help me—for Heaven sake write to him [Kinsky]. . . . I am frightened of the future alone—& Charles is the only person on earth that c[oul]d start life afresh with—& I have lost him— . . . Leonie darling use all y[ou]r cleverness & all y[ou]r strength & urge him to put off this marriage.[9]

JENNIE AND RANDOLPH arrived back in London on Christmas Eve, 1894, and moved in with the Dowager Duchess at 50 Grosvenor Square. Randolph was, according to Winston, "as weak and helpless in mind and body as a little child."[10] He was nursed constantly by Jennie and several health professionals. He rallied slightly in early January, enough to receive many visitors, with whom he conversed freely. Throughout a dreadfully cold, wet January 1895, the press gave daily coverage to his condition.

It was then that Jennie slipped away and visited Count Kinsky at his flat at Clarges Street, London. She wrote to Leonie on January 3 that they had parted "the best of friends . . . but I care for him as some people like opium or drink."[11] Kinsky married the Countess Elizabeth on January 9, two days after Jennie's forty-first birthday. Jennie felt a sense of betrayal, and Peregrine said she never forgave Kinsky, and burned all his letters.

In his last days, Randolph would have received great comfort from Winston's excellent performance at Sandhurst. A splendid set of marks placed him twentieth in a class of 130 cadets. His conduct had been good, with no hint of the usual lack of punctuality.

In the middle of a snowstorm, in subzero temperatures that froze the Thames, Lord Randolph sank into a coma, and died at 6:15 on the morning of January 24. His wife, his sons, and his mother were all with him at the end. He was three weeks short of his forty-sixth birthday. Winston wrote, "All my dreams" of entering "Parliament at his side" were "ended." But it "remained for me only to pursue his aims and vindicate his memory."[12]

A great funeral was held at Westminster Abbey, with crowds thronging the streets and politicians of all ranks and parties at the service. Lord Randolph's funeral cortege passed through his constituency of South Paddington. He had asked to be buried, not in the crypt at Blenheim Palace, but at Bladon in St. Martin's churchyard with his deceased brothers who had died in infancy. All of Woodstock was there, with large delegations from the Paddington and Birmingham Conservatives and from Ireland. A statue was subsequently erected to his memory at Blenheim Palace and a bust in the House of Commons.

Winston's biography of his father stated that he died of "a rare and ghastly disease."[13] The cause of death, as stated on Lord Randolph's death certificate, was "bronchial pneumonia from paralysis in the brain."

The Dowager Duchess asked Lord Rosebery, Lord Randolph's friend from boyhood days, to write her beloved late son's biography.[14]

Nine

A ROYAL AFFAIR: JENNIE AND THE PRINCE OF WALES

1895–1898

Lord Salisbury took over as Conservative prime minister in June 1895, having formed a coalition with the Liberal Unionist Party led by Spencer Compton Cavendish, known as Lord Hartington,[1] and Joseph Chamberlain. The British Empire was at the height of its extent and power.

At his death, the gross value of Lord Randolph's estate was £75,971/ $364,660 (about £5 million, in today's valuation). A good part of it went to pay his debts. The balance, soundly invested in safe, blue-chip companies like private railways, supported a family trust fund administered by Jennie.[2] She inherited £500/$2,400 a year, which, along with her annual income of £2,000/$9,600 from rental property in America, should have left her quite comfortable.[3] Jennie left it to the family solicitors to sell Lord Randolph's South African gold shares in a bear market at a loss, a move that was unnecessary. All that was required was to raise what was needed to pay her late husband's debts. If she had taken advice from Randolph's friends, the Rothschilds, who were financial and banking experts, or the Churchill's close friend the stockbroker Sir Ernest Cassel, they would have given her advice. She could have sold the shares to reinvest at much greater advantage as they tripled in value the following year.[4]

After his father's death, Winston claimed that Lord Randolph had agreed verbally that he could apply to a cavalry regiment for his first commission. He got Jennie to cable Colonel Brabazon, 4th Hussars, who then gave her the wording for a letter to the Duke of Cambridge. She explained to the duke that there was a vacancy in the regiment, and Brabazon had said that Winston, having passed out ahead of all other candidates for the cavalry, should not be kept idle in London. She felt he should be allowed to fulfill one of Randolph's last wishes. The duke referred the request to the military secretary, and by February 20, 1895, Winston was duly appointed to the 4th Hussars as a second lieutenant.

Jack returned to Harrow, where his work slipped a little as he adjusted to life without his father.

JENNIE WAS THEN forty-one years old, and looking as lovely as ever. The Prince of Wales moved quickly to secure her affection. The first letter of condolence she received, on the day Lord Randolph died, was from the Prince at Sandringham:

My dear Lady Randolph,
The sad news reached me this morning that all is over . . . & I felt that for his and for your sakes it was best so. . . . There was a cloud in our friendship but I am glad to think that it has long been forgotten by both of us.[5]

Jennie might have his sympathy, but she was without a house of her own, and she felt the need to get away from her mother-in-law. She turned to Paris, the city of her youth, where Jack and Leonie Leslie, with their three sons, and Jennie's elder sister, Clara Frewen, were living. In the third week of February, she moved with them into two apartments on the fashionable Avenue Kléber. She proceeded to spend money freely as she redecorated and refurnished her temporary home to the highest standards. The next six weeks would mark a new beginning. If the sudden arrival of Count Kinsky and his young bride at the nearby Hotel Bristol was at all disconcerting to Jennie, she soon found a way to put it from her mind.

In early March, Clara introduced Jennie to a forty-one-year-old millionaire, the charismatic Irish-American lawyer and Democratic senator William Bourke Cockran, who was a friend of Clara's husband, Moreton Frewen. Bourke, as he was always known, had recently become a widower, and he and Jennie embarked on a short but passionate affair. Jennie had "felt a tremor of surprise" when he first walked into the room—tall and broad-shouldered with bright blue eyes that "shone" like "forget-me-nots."[6] Cockran was a fine-looking man, and he was considered one of the best political speakers of his day in the United States. Jennie and he both spoke fluent French and shared a mutual love of horses. She took an instant liking to him, and the Leslie children remembered him as a frequent visitor. Jennie organized lavish dinners for him, and he entertained her and the rest of the family to stories about horse racing in Ireland.[7] They were seen bicycling together, which was very fashionable in Paris, and strolling arm in arm along the tree-lined streets.

From the letters Jennie wrote home to Winston and Jack it was apparent she was having the time of her life. On March 1, she told Jack that Paris was "charming," that she was going ice-skating at the Palais de Glace, and "I find I have not forgotten my various figures—Sea Breeze, etc." Jack replied that he was planning to visit her for Easter, and she advised him to "bring knickerbockers" for bicycling, and "a pair of low shoes." Winston wrote to her on March 2 that he also planned to come to Paris at Easter, "so you must keep a fatted calf for the occasion," and said he was sending her three boxes of her favorite cigarettes, Royal Beauties.

Later in March the Prince of Wales was heading for the Mediterranean in his yacht *Britannia* to practice for a sailing regatta later in the year. He sent Jennie a note (undated) saying that they would meet in the afternoon, "and you shall have your enjoyments."[8] He arranged for Jennie to visit him on board, where their intimate relationship was resumed. He also visited her at the Avenue Kléber. The Leslies' second son, John (Shane), aged nine and a half, remembered the Prince arrived late at night, and he and his elder brother, Norman, were roused from their bed to meet him. The Prince asked the boys what they wanted to be when they grew up, and then gave Shane what he remembered as the "Queen's shilling" (a gold sovereign).[9]

Mrs. Jerome, now up in years, who lived in Tunbridge Wells, Kent, had been ailing for some time, and her elder daughter Clara returned to look after her. At the end of March, she took a turn for the worse, and Jennie and Leonie rushed to her bedside. She died rather suddenly five days later, on April 2. The coffin had to be transported to America for burial, which took some time to arrange.

On April 5, the Prince wrote to Jennie from Marlborough House, extending his sympathy.[10] Later in April, Jennie returned to Paris, and to Bourke, for a final few weeks. Before he returned to America, he asked her to marry him and she refused, but they remained the best of friends for the rest of their lives. In the coming months, Jennie would travel back and forth a good deal to Paris rather than live with her mother-in-law. She was also looking for a new house in London.

The Prince of Wales was still in the process of ending his relationship of several years with a married woman, the rich society hostess Frances (Daisy) Countess of Warwick. In the summer, Jennie was seen out with a handsome, boyish, young officer of the Grenadier Guards, the twenty-seven-year-old Hugh Warrender. She arrived with him at Cowes Week on the Isle of Wight in August. Now out of black mourning, she was fashionably dressed in white from head to toe and wore a straw boater. Warrender was genuinely in love with her and would have married her. There is a group photograph of Jennie, Leonie, Winston, Jack, and Hugh, taken that week. Warrender looks impossibly young.

Daisy Warwick had become a socialist and something of an embarrassment to the Prince in his circle. He was currently keeping the company of another married woman, Georgiana, Countess of Dudley, and left Cowes early with her. This romance did not last, and the Prince wrote to Jennie, on September 8, from Hamburg, saying he hoped she had enjoyed herself at Aix-les-Bains, where she had gone for a rest. Then mixing jest with jealous lust, he chided her about Warrender, wondering "where your next loved victim is?"

In September, Jennie made the major financial commitment to buy a new house, 35A Great Cumberland Place, in West London. She wrote to Clara on October 3, 1895: "I am going to have it all painted from top to toe, electric light, hot water etc. . . . How nice it will be when we are all together again on our 'owns'! The boys are so delighted at the thought of 'ringing their own front door' they can think of nothing else."[11]

The house, of late Georgian design, on seven stories, was relatively modest compared to Connaught Place. But it was only a short distance from Mayfair, and was convenient for the Prince's afternoon visits. Jennie lavished expense on her new house, engaged seven servants, installed her collections of antique furniture, blue and white china, glass and crystal ware, jade ornaments, and her treasured collection of crystal pigs. In November 1895, she moved in, and her exquisitely presented home was once again a social center for entertaining the top tier of society.

It was here, in total privacy, that the sexual relations between Jennie and the Prince of Wales would flourish. In January 1896, the Prince changed his addresses to

Jennie to "*Ma chère.*" From February 1896 until the end of 1897, there was a regular stream of letters and notes from the Prince. Her replies did not survive, as the Prince ordered all his private papers to be burned at his death. His addresses to her followed a pattern he used for all his principal mistresses; they were sent weekly and would read: "Should you wish to see me, I could call at five tomorrow." He would then visit her for dinner or tea and sex.

Bertie, as the Prince was known to his closest friends, was forty-four years old, and had a short, gray, nicotine-stained beard, but was always immaculately dressed and perfumed himself with *eau de Portugal.* His voice was husky from smoking cigars, and he spoke in deep, sexy, guttural tones, rolling the letter *r* with something of his father's Germanic pronunciation. He had a huge appetite for food and was rather portly. Possibly with that in mind, Jennie had a lift installed in the house to the bedrooms. Bertie would later grow very stout from gorging himself with food and drink, and by age fifty-five, his waist measured forty-eight inches. He was, in 1895, still a fine figure of a man. Later films taken of him going riding at Sandringham show that, when he mounted his horse, the poor brute positively shuddered and stumbled under his enormous weight, twenty-two stone, or 308 pounds. Jennie is credited by Leonie with having nicknamed him "Tum Tum." In her bereavements, the Prince came to keep her amused and to comfort her in bed. Bertie had a short fuse and a terrible temper, and Jennie knew how to humor and cajole him and keep him happy.

While being the Prince's current favorite mistress, Jennie also continued an affair with the recently widowed William Waldorf Astor, whose wife, Mary, had also died in 1894. Astor was a severe if distinguished-looking man with an excellent intellect and a keen interest in history. He had rented Landsdowne House, near where Jennie now lived, but had given it up in 1893. Having been born in New York City in 1848, he had studied law and become a financier, and was later a New York state assemblyman and Republican senator. He inherited his father's estate, which provided him with a personal fortune, making him the richest man in the world. Astor now lived permanently in England, and two years earlier had bought a huge country estate, Cliveden House at Taplow, in Buckinghamshire.[12] Jennie also had a nickname for Astor; she called him "Wealthy Willie." Astor's wealth at that time totaled $200 million, and his annual income was $6 million.[13]

The story on the front page of the *New York Times* on February 21, 1896, must have incensed Bertie: "The most interesting bit of society news . . . is the engagement of Lady Randolph Churchill to William Waldorf Astor."[14] It was a completely false report. Astor wanted to marry Jennie, but she would not have him, despite his millions, as she found him too staid a character. Bertie wrote to her on February 27, thanking her for "a charming dinner," but *Town Topics* would not let the matter rest and, on March 12, published a reminder: "Older New Yorkers recall the fact that Mr. Astor admired Lady Randolph before her marriage."[15]

That June, Jennie accompanied the Prince to Epsom racecourse to see his horse Persimmon win the Derby. She wrote to Jack, on June 4: "Winston . . . backed Persimmon. . . . It was a very popular win and the crowd cheered tremendously."

Jennie was a brilliant organizer, and if the Prince wanted a small private party arranged he could rely on her to draw up the guest list and decide the menu. She knew his particular friends and his favorite foods and the kind of music he liked. He showered her with gifts and made her a powerful figure in society. Family letters made continual references to the Prince.

Winston and Jack also visited his homes, and an independent correspondence arose between Winston and the Prince, concerning his army career, in which Bertie took a close interest. Following Cowes Week that August, the Prince was guest of honor at a weekend party given by Duchess Lily at her home,[16] The Deepdene, Dorking, to which Jennie had secured an invitation for Winston. It was a great honor for a second lieutenant, and among the guests was his commanding officer, Colonel Brabazon. But, as ever, Winston could not turn up on time, having missed his train and caught a later one. The superstitious Bertie never sat thirteen at table. To his great annoyance the entire party was left standing about waiting for Winston. When Winston finally arrived, the Prince, in the presence of the colonel, remarked, "Don't they teach you to be punctual in your regiment, Winston?"[17]

All through the autumn that year, Jennie was either the constant companion of the Prince at country house weekends or received a stream of his letters from Sandringham, Windsor, his private club, his yachts, or at stops on his European journeys. In September, Jack had written to her commenting that her dog, a chow, had given birth to puppies, some brown and some black, and Jennie replied on Sandringham notepaper, while staying with the Prince. She had, she said, given one of the puppies to the Prince, who loved dogs, and Bertie had said he was going to name it after him, and call it Black Jack.

From 1896, Jennie gave lavish dinners at Great Cumberland Place for the Prince and her friends, which required a famous wine cellar and necessitated an endless supply of new dresses, usually by the great fashion house of Worth in Paris. All of this Jennie paid for by a spiraling series of loans, the repaying of which was financed by yet more loans. Some of her letters of the time mention that she is either at or going to Monte Carlo, where the gambling casinos were a fashionable haunt of the rich.

The Prince had to balance his visits to Jennie with his duty to matters of state, to which he had to attend, but despite his busy schedule throughout 1897, they still saw a lot of each other. Bertie was obviously taken with Jennie's artistic interest in everything Japanese,[18] and found her at home wearing colorful dresses or a kimono of Japanese silk, which enhanced her dark beauty all the more. On January 4, 1897, he wrote to her from Sandringham, wishing her a happy New Year and asking whether he could visit her for a "Japanese" tea. Two days later, he acknowledged that she had invited him. Other of his letters for February asked if he might come to a "Geisha tea." That April the Prince was visiting France, and wrote to Jennie on April 1, while on the royal yacht *Britannia* in Nice, asking her to recommend French plays that he should see and thanking her for a dinner. The letter was seared with a burn mark, and he apologized, "Forgive my cigarette!" In May, Jennie was staying at William Waldorf Astor's home, with both Astor and the Prince in attendance. How she coped with two ardent lovers under the same roof is best left to the imagination. Cliveden had panoramic views of the Thames, and Astor had furnished it in the most lavish Italianate style, with tapestries and wall paneling. Jennie, however, appeared tired of Astor, and wrote to Jack, on May 31, that it was "rather stiff and cut and dried here." However, William had "a great deal of taste"; she found the "place splendid but impersonal" and "the Prince is in good humour."

On July 2, the Duchess of Devonshire held the season's ball at her London home, Devonshire House in Piccadilly, to celebrate Queen Victoria's Diamond Jubilee. It was a fancy dress affair, and guests had been asked to come attired as a famous person in history. The Prince of Wales came as the Grand Prior of the Order of St. John of Jerusalem, and his wife, Princess Alexandra, came as Marguerite de Valois, complete with attendants of the nobility. Jennie, as ever, went out to upstage every woman there. Wearing the most fabulous costume, she represented the Byzantine empress Theodora. Many column inches in the press described her as the belle of the ball. Jennie's gown was an expensive, flamboyant, heavily embroidered robe, copied from the mosaic portrait in the church in Ravenna. On her head she wore a crown hung with pendants of pearls at the temples and emblazoned with diamonds. From her arms fluttered veils studded with sparkling brilliants. Her neck was covered with pearl chokers, and her long black hair, which she normally wore up, flowed over her shoulders almost to her waist. In one hand she held a giant lily, and in the other the golden orb of power. Reigning supreme, at least for a day, Jennie was Queen in all but name.

In August, at Cowes Week, dubbed by Bertie "the Wild West Show," Jennie was seen in close and friendly harmony with Princess Alexandra. The long-suffering, beautiful Princess, worn out by childbearing, was perfectly used to her husband's serial infidelities. The Prince wrote to Jennie often that autumn, with news of his many overseas visits. He also said he was hearing good things about Winston. Such praise of her elder son was most welcome.

As the Prince's official favorite, Jennie stepped out with him at public functions, for all the world acting as his wife. In a press photograph of 1897, at the time of Queen Victoria's Diamond Jubilee, she is walking with the Prince at the Tower of London.[19]

BY THE BEGINNING of 1898, Jennie was in deep financial trouble and borrowing heavily. The expensive house, the big dinners, and the wine she had provided to the Prince were consuming her estate.

On January 24, the Prince wrote to her from Sandringham, discussing her proposed visit there with Jack, and even which train they should catch. He told her that Maria de Rothschild, the wife of the millionaire banker Leo de Rothschild (whose country home was "Ascot Wing," near Leighton Buzzard, Bedfordshire), was also coming.

In the meantime, Jennie had attracted another young lover, Major Caryl Ramsden, an officer in the Seaforth Highlanders. His name crops up in letters between Jennie and her sons from 1897. "Beauty Ramsden," as he was nicknamed, had been posted to Cairo, where an expedition was being assembled under Horatio Herbert Kitchener, commander in chief of the Egyptian army (1892–98) for the reconquest of the Sudan. Winston was desperate to get transferred to Kitchener's staff in Egypt. Jennie thought she might visit Ramsden in Egypt and lobby Kitchener on Winston's behalf while there. Winston wrote that he was sure her wit, tact, and beauty would overcome all obstacles. He would later describe her in his biography as the woman "who tapped the men and opened the doors" for him.[20]

Jennie stayed with Ramsden at the Continental Hotel, Cairo, and contacted Kitchener. He had brushed aside her request, one of so many he had to deal with of a similar nature. At the end of her stay, she left for Port Said, only to find that her homeward ship had been delayed. Returning to the hotel, where she hoped to spend another night with Ramsden, she entered his room without knocking and found him embracing Lady Maxwell, the wife of General John Maxwell. The row she kicked up was heard throughout the hotel. The incident soon reached the Prince's ears, at Cannes, and he wrote to her: "You had better have stuck to your old friends than gone on your expedition of the Nile! Old friends are best!"

As soon as Jennie arrived home, Leonie called to see her and found her scribbling a reply to the Prince to even the score: "*So* grateful for your sympathy—as your Royal Highness knows exactly *how* it feels, after being jilted by Lady Dudley."[21]

Leonie was concerned that the note would give offense and offered to post it but kept it overnight. Next day, she told Jennie it was "always wise to sleep on such missives."[22] Jennie composed a wittier version and mailed both notes. The Prince sent Jennie an apology from the Grand Hotel, Cannes, on April 8, acknowledging her letters of the fifth and sixth: "*Ma chère Amie* . . . I must ask your pardon if my letter pained. I had no idea *que c'était une affaire si serieuse!* [it was such a serious affair]."

Unbeknown to Jennie, in January 1898, the Prince met the Honorable Mrs. George (Alice) Keppel, a great beauty in her early thirties. Bertie had been invited to a New Year's celebration at Gopsall House, the country home in Warwickshire of George and Georgiana, Lord and Lady Howe, Georgiana being a sister of the late Lord Randolph. Bertie and Alice soon found themselves deeply in love.[23] If Jennie's days as *La Favorite* were coming to an end, she would fight to retain his affections, and in a most ingenious way.

SOMETIME THAT YEAR, Jennie met the twenty-four-year-old, strikingly handsome, George Cornwallis-West, a lieutenant in the Scots Guards. It is likely that they met at the home of General Sir Ian and Jean, Lady Hamilton. Hamilton and Winston had first met in India in the summer of 1897. Hamilton returned to England and became commandant of the army's school of musketry at Hythe, Kent, and the Hamiltons occupied a house in the grounds of the training camp.[24] Jean recorded in her diary that she invited Jennie to dine with her and some of her lady friends, and also invited some "nice boys from the Musketry School."[25] George said in his biography that at the time he met Jennie he was taking a course in musketry there.[26]

VICTORIAN SOCIETY believed George to be the Prince of Wales's illegitimate son because George's mother, Mary (called Patsy in the family), had been his first lover— when she was only sixteen—and the Prince retained a high regard for her.[27] The Cornwallis-Wests lived at Ruthin Castle, Denbighshire, North Wales. Writing of his childhood, George remembered: "The Prince of Wales often came, and was invariably kind to me and always asked to see me. Never a Christmas passed without his sending me some little gift in the shape of a card or a toy."[28]

George attended fishing and deer-stalking parties with the Prince on his estates. The Cornwallis-Wests had little money, but they owned Ruthin Castle; later, 49 Eton Place, Belgravia, London, and Newlands Manor, Lymington, Hampshire, the country home of Patsy's mother, would eventually be theirs. George's two sisters, also believed to have been fathered by the Prince, married men of considerable fortune and status. Daisy married Hugh Grosvenor, 2nd Prince of Pless, and Sheila married the Duke of Westminster.

George's parents and the Prince of Wales did not approve of George's association with Jennie. She was forty-four and still beautiful but probably past childbearing age, meaning that if the relationship became serious, the line would die out without a male heir.

George was fit and active, and very kind, but of no great intellect, and he fell deeply in love with Jennie. One of his letters to her—one of several hundred—was dated July 29, 1898, and was decorated with hearts: "I thought about you all yesterday

& built castles in the air about you & I living together."[29] Jennie soon found herself equally smitten and entertained him at her home, sweeping him off his feet with her beauty, charm, and wit. They spent weekends together at country houses, and then, most conveniently, George's battalion was posted to London, which made it easier for them to see each other.

Ten

FINANCIAL WORRIES AND CAREER DEVELOPMENT

1895–1897

In June 1895, a minor bill that the Liberal government had proposed for an increase in the budget for the purchase of cordite for explosives had brought dissent within the party and had been defeated by a small number of votes. Lord Rosebery, the Liberal prime minister, took it as a vote of no confidence in the government and resigned on June 21. Queen Victoria invited Lord Salisbury to take office. A general election was held from July 13 until August 7, in which the Liberal Unionist Party joined forces with the Conservative Party, and the Liberal Party was heavily defeated. On June 25, Lord Salisbury reemerged as Conservative and Unionist prime minister of the coalition government, continuing throughout 1896–97.

The year 1895 would see yet another death with emotional connotations for the Churchills. Woomany died in July. Mrs. Everest had been a constant feature in their lives for many years, and after she left, Winston and Jack kept up a correspondence with her. They always showed her the greatest respect, and her passing was a great sadness to them. Winston, who was by her bedside at the end, wrote movingly to his mother of her last moments, on July 24: "Her last words were of Jack. . . . Please send a wire to Welldon to ask him to let Jack come up for the funeral—as he is very anxious to do so."[1] Mrs. Everest was buried in the City of London Cemetery, Manor Park, East London. Together, Winston and Jack would see that her grave had a gravestone and was well cared for. It was inscribed "by Winston Spencer Churchill and John Spencer Churchill."

Winston's regiment, the 4th Hussars, were due to go out to India in September 1896 for a lengthy spell. In September 1895, therefore, Winston was granted a long leave and, without consulting Jennie, decided to go with fellow subaltern Reggie Barnes to the Americas to see something of the country and observe the Spanish army in its campaign against rebels in the Cuban War of Independence. He wrote to his mother on October 4, telling her of his intentions. While accepting that he needed to expand his horizons, this new charge on Jennie's finances brought forth the acid comment, on October 11: "Considering that I provide the funds I think instead of saying 'I *have* decided to go,' it may have been nicer and perhaps wiser—to have begun by consulting me."

Still, she made a birthday present of his ticket and was soon contacting friends who could help Winston, notably her former lover, Bourke Cockran. When Winston and Barnes arrived in New York in the first week of November, Bourke met them off the boat and took them to his home, 763 Fifth Avenue, where he had a large library that much impressed Winston. It is likely that at this time Bourke still carried a torch for Jennie, because as of yet neither of them had remarried, and Bourke had been twice widowed. It might explain Bourke taking Winston under his wing in a fatherly role. Whatever was the case, Cockran immediately saw great promise in Winston and encouraged him in a course of reading to further his political ambitions.

Winston praised Bourke highly in his letters home to Jennie and Jack. Bourke, he said, served the best brandy and the finest food. He was a charming host and the most interesting man Winston had ever met.[2] In letters to Jennie on November 10 and 12, 1895, Winston said Bourke had had great discussions with him on subjects ranging from economics to yacht racing. He had shown Winston around the city of New York and introduced him to a luxurious lifestyle and the particular pleasures of a fine cigar. He had also arranged engagements for every meal for the next three days. One was to a big dinner for about twelve members of the New York State judiciary, where Winston met a supreme court judge. Winston also wrote to Jack, on November 10, that Bourke had procured a visit for them to the forts of the harbor and to West Point, the American equivalent of Sandhurst RMC. There he was "greeted like a General."[3] Bourke, a superb orator, greatly influenced Winston's style of speech, and Winston would later freely and generously credit Bourke with teaching him the full use of the English language.[4] Bourke loomed before Winston as a man of enormous wisdom and experience, a great orator, possessing taste and style, much the model of the man Winston himself wanted to be. Here was further encouragement for Winston to enter politics.

Winston and Barnes now prepared for the next adventure. Cuba was under the rule of Spain, and earlier in 1895 the Cuban War of Independence (1895–98) had broken out. Winston and Barnes set off as observers, leaving from Key West, Florida. They arrived in Havana Harbor on November 20. Winston had negotiated a deal with the *Daily Graphic* in London to write letters for them describing his adventures, and for this it would pay him five guineas each. He decided to follow the column of General Valdez, leader of the Spanish army, who was at Sancti Spiritus, and they went there by train.

The next day they set out with Valdez to march to the village of Iguara, which was blockaded by insurgents. They learned (November 29) that 4,000 insurgents under Major General Maximo Gomez, Cuba's commander, was encamped to the east of Iguara. At five o'clock the next morning, Valdez set out from Arroyo Blanco in pursuit of them. Almost immediately, through heavy mist there was firing at the rear of the column, the sound of large-bore rifles, and the sight of flashes and smoke. It was Winston's twenty-first birthday, and he spent it witnessing the fighting between Valdez's men and the insurgents, which lasted for three days. On December 1, Winston and Barnes and some of the officers were bathing in a river. They had just come out of the water and were dressing when a volley of shots began and there was an attack. Winston wrote in an account to the *Daily Graphic* that the bullets were whistling over their heads. Firing by the rebels continued at intervals during the night, and a bullet pierced the hut in which Winston and Barnes were sleeping but missed them. The following day, Valdez conducted the battle of La Reforma, and Winston wrote to his mother, December 6, that rather than taking shelter they stayed by General Valdez all the time and so were in the most dangerous place in the field. The general rewarded them with the medal of the Red Cross, a Spanish decoration given to officers.[5]

On arrival back at Tampa, Winston and Barnes were confronted by reporters. Winston clarified his position to the press, making it clear that he had not been involved in active fighting against the Cubans, which had been assumed on account of his being awarded the Red Cross, and he affirmed that he had been an observer only.

Jennie must have breathed a sigh of relief when, in mid-December, she learned from Winston that they had returned to New York. There he also gave interviews to the press, which was an opportunity to demonstrate both his knowledge as a soldier and his journalistic abilities, telling the press it had always been said that it took 200 bullets to kill a soldier but in the Cuban war 200,000 would be closer to the mark.

Winston and Cockran remained friends and carried on a correspondence after Winston's return home at the end of December. Cockran was in the habit of sending Winston copies of his speeches, and Winston sent Bourke copies of Lord Randolph's speeches.[6] There was one subject, however, on which Winston and Cockran would never agree. Cockran supported Home Rule for Ireland,[7] which must have aroused in Winston memories of his father at the height of his career in politics and the battles he had fought against Charles Stewart Parnell and the Irish Home Rule Party. Winston followed his father's line and was vehemently opposed to Home Rule.

When the press in England learned that Winston had been with the government forces in Cuba, they made scathing comments in their newspapers. The _Newcastle Leader_ wondered "what motive" could "impel a British officer" to become involved in such a "dispute." It continued scathingly: "Spending a holiday in fighting other people's battles is rather an extraordinary proceeding even for a Churchill."[8]

In January 1896, Winston rejoined his regiment at Aldershot. It was during the remainder of the nine months in which he was waiting to set out for India that Jennie and Winston, hugely encouraged by Cockran's continuing praise, finally agreed that he should spend some time in the army to make a name for himself, and then go into politics.

This was in perfect accord with Jennie's great ambition for Winston—that he should pursue a career in his father's footsteps and achieve the great office of prime minister denied to her husband. When Randolph resigned as leader of the House of Commons and Chancellor of the Exchequer in December 1886, the following January, a messenger from Parliament called at the Churchills' home, wanting to buy the official robes that he had worn as chancellor for his successor, George Goschen. Jennie met the messenger at the door and refused to hand over the robes, telling him: "I am saving them for my son."[9] During the months Winston was waiting to be posted to India he pursued political connections.

In September 1896, Winston was obliged to sail with his regiment to India. From Bombay, the regiment moved to Bangalore, where Winston found the climate quite to his liking. He shared a palatial bungalow with two fellow officers, one of whom was

Reggie Barnes, with numerous servants on hand. In India, there was as yet no military action for junior officers, and Winston was bored. He and Reggie had taken to gardening, and Winston resumed an interest in collecting butterflies, and wrote to his mother for flower seeds. Soon they had a flourishing garden, and Winston wrote to his mother that he had 275 rose trees of 70 different kinds.[10]

Before he left home, Jennie had apparently asked Winston to call on a young girl Jennie knew, Pamela Plowden, who lived at Hyderbad. Pamela was the daughter of Trevor John Chichele-Plowden—who was in the Indian Civil Service in the position of Resident at Hyderbad (the equivalent today of governor)—and the late Millicent, daughter of General Sir C. J. Foster. Pamela's mother, having been bitten by a snake, had died in 1892, and her father had remarried in 1895. Winston wrote to his mother on November 4, telling her that after a polo match the previous day he had been introduced to Pamela and that she was the most beautiful girl he had ever seen. They were going to see the city of Hyderbad together on an elephant—the only safe means of travel, as the natives spat at foreigners walking in the street.[11] In Winston's next letter, November 12, he said he had dined with Pamela and her father and stepmother Beatrice at Hyderbad. He and Pamela had completed the trip on the elephant, and Pamela sent "many messages" to Jennie. He had found that, as well as being beautiful, Pamela was also clever.[12] Winston was twenty-one years old, and Pamela, at age twenty-two, was seven months older. From that point Winston would speak privately in his letters to his mother of his love and admiration for Pamela. Of the letters that have survived between Winston and Pamela, little is expressed in the way of romantic feeling. It was not considered proper in those days that such matters should be discussed openly between a young couple who were not engaged to be married. Winston was as yet too young to marry, and he had no money with which to support a wife. Her letters between them speak of family matters, and Winston's letters speak of his intended political career and of army matters. They both, however, possessed a mutual interest in literature, which sustained their interest in each other.

The long and loving letters between Jennie and Winston were a solace during the tedious life of a young subaltern in India. But already on November 18 he was writing to his mother of his frustration with his situation. As an MP he could "get hold of the right people"; as a soldier he vegetated to no purpose. Jennie replied on December 24: "I am looking forward to the time when we shall live together again & all my political ambitions shall be centered in you."

IN FEBRUARY 1896, Jack reached his sixteenth birthday. He wanted to leave Harrow School, believing it was time for him to move on to the next stage of his development. He was intending, on Dr. Welldon's advice, to go to France for a year to study French, which as a modern language was a requirement for Oxford, and at his return, to undergo some further preparation in studying Greek, and then sit the entrance examination. All this Welldon communicated to Jennie. Dr. Welldon discussed Jack's future with him at great length and actively encouraged him to consider following Lord Randolph's course, taking a university degree in history and law, after which a career in the army or at the bar would be open to him. Jack was also invited by Welldon to his home, where they had talks.[13]

With all her hopes for the future tied up in Winston's political advancement, Jennie began to develop a quite different strategy toward Jack. Jack's intentions were misunderstood by both Jennie and Winston because, living with two such strong personalities, he was insufficiently demonstrative. He wanted to join the army, and his father had laid the foundations for his career as a professional soldier. Winston said of Jack, in a letter to his mother in November 1896, that it was very difficult to get at what he really thought. The previous year, Jennie had suggested to Jack the possibility of joining an infantry regiment, where she had contacts and could pull strings. When Jack demurred, she answered, on October 8, 1895: "I do not wish to stand in your way if your heart is not on going into the Army." That is not what Jack had meant at all; he was a natural horseman and yearned for the cavalry.

Jock Colville, Winston's private secretary, later observed: "The character of Jack Churchill was strikingly different [from Winston's]. Loyal, affectionate, scrupulously honorable, he was also endowed with that most endearing of qualities, natural humility. He did not share his brother's restless energy, consuming ambition, gift of eloquence or quickness of mind. He was always proud to be referred to as 'Winston's brother.'"[14]

Winston's attitude to the army would undoubtedly have influenced Jennie's decision about Jack's future. Now eleven months into his service, Winston was disillusioned; he began lobbying for a transfer to a regiment that might be doing something more interesting than serving in India. He described his situation in a letter to his mother on August 4, 1896, as a "useless and unprofitable exile."[15] He was looking for postings in South Africa or Egypt, and soon earned the reputation of a medal hunter.[16]

Jack did make a firm decision about his career, telling his mother in a letter (undated) in November that year: "I have decided I will go to Oxford." In another to Winston, December 11, Jennie discussed Jack's future:

> I have been very busy arranging things for Jack. I went to see Welldon and had a long talk with him as to his future. I am much against his going in the Army. I can't afford to put him in a smart cavalry regiment & in anything else he would be lost & unhappy. I think he might do at the Bar. He has plenty of ability and common sense, a good presence, & with perseverance & influence he ought to get on. The City he hates.

Jack's enthusiasm for the cavalry was under attack—from Jennie's opposition and from Winston's growing disenchantment with his own army career and his preference for politics. Writing to Jack on January 7, 1897, Winston now poured cold water on Jack's idea of becoming a barrister, though he fully supported him in his wish for a university education: "Don't think of drifting languidly and placidly—as your letter apparently suggests to the Bar. . . . I think you have great talents, Jack . . . but I *am* perfectly certain that unless you start full of enthusiasm and keenness, you will never develop your abilities. I shall envy you the enjoyment of a liberal education, and of the power to appreciate the classical works."[17]

Jack was now under pressure from the two people he most adored in the world to give up the one career he truly wanted. Winston, at least, had approved of his going to university, which would have increased his options in life.

Winston was now wavering, somewhat undecided about his own career, and thought he might stick to the army after all. Jennie would not hear of it, and cautioned him, on January 29, 1897:

> How little one hears of any of the Generals in time of peace. There is really very little honor & glory to be got out of the Army. A moderate MP gets better known in the country & has more chance of success than a really clever man in the Army.[18]

AT THE BEGINNING of February 1897, Jennie accompanied Jack to Versailles and installed him with Monsieur Robineau, a French tutor. She stayed for a short while to see him settled in and introduced him to some of her great friends living in France, including Bourke Cockran and Cecil Rhodes, both of whom were visiting Paris at that time. Rhodes was an old friend of Randolph and was a politician in South Africa, and was founder of De Beers diamond company.[19] Dr. Welldon had written to Jack, on February 9, reassuring him that he had written to Magdalen College, Oxford, arranging for him to sit the entrance examination on his return.

In addition to learning French, Jack took piano and dancing lessons, extended his knowledge of music and culture by attending concerts and the opera, and took horse riding lessons. Jennie sent Robineau a check each month for Jack's tuition and board, and she kept her son supplied with money for the other extra lessons and his personal needs, and sent him copies of the *Daily Graphic* to keep him abreast of events in England.

Jennie's letters to Jack in this period were loving and full of gossip. One of the first, on February 18, urged him to learn to speak French: "You must become very talkative. . . . Make the most of it—Do like Winston, talk incessantly!"

Jack wrote to her of his impressions of his new surroundings and the progress he was making. His Romanian riding instructor was "rather dirty," the champagne was so bad that "water is a treat after it," and as for dressing for dinner, M. Robineau "has never seen a tail coat." There was always a reminder of some money that she had forgotten to pay.

While carefully apportioning £3/$14.40 here and £5/$24 there to settle Jack's expenses, Jennie had to cancel a trip to visit him because of Winston's reckless expenditure in India. Despite receiving his £300/$1,440 army pay and an allowance from his mother of £500/$2,400 plus money for letters to the _Daily Telegraph,_ Winston still overspent against his account, and Cox's, the army's bankers, applied to Jennie for these overdrawn amounts. In a letter of February 26 to Jack, Jennie complained bitterly of Winston's behavior.

Throughout 1896–97 there is mention in Jennie's letters that she was in Monte Carlo, where she was undoubtedly frequenting the gambling casinos. There was also mention that she was attending race meetings at home, and backing horses, in a futile bid, it would seem, to improve her income. The rent from the New York house left to her by her father became just an asset against which to make ever-larger borrowings. Just as Winston had left for India, she and her sisters fell victim to a notorious swindler, James Cruikshank. This so-called investment adviser told them he was head of a syndicate investing in American stock. He got them to give him £4,000/$19,200, most of which was from Jennie, and which he was supposed to invest on their behalf, but instead, he spent it on holidays. When the law eventually caught up with him, he was prosecuted in London on November 25, 1897, and sentenced to eight years in prison, but Jennie did not get her money back.[20]

Jack dutifully reported to his mother on his progress in French and music, the concerts he attended, the people he saw. Jennie was overly maternal and protective in her replies, constantly worrying about his spelling, his reading habits, his clothes, his ear infection, the temptations of Paris. Her letters were also full of adulation for Winston's progress, every word of which Jack relished. Jack was soon exploring the countryside energetically on the new bicycle she bought him and writing her letters full of his travel adventures.

In May, Winston left India and started for home on leave, visiting Naples, Pompeii, and Rome along the way. Arriving in Paris, he met up with a delighted Jack. That summer, the family was together for part of the season in London. The Duchess of Devonshire invited Jennie, Winston, and Jack to her annual fancy dress ball. The boys accompanied their mother, and colorful accounts of the ball and the wonderful time they had could still be told by Peregrine. Jack then returned to France to his studies, leaving behind his mother and brother to enjoy the rest of the summer season at the races.

Jack was now approaching his eighteenth birthday, and he knew he had to choose a career. Jennie simply would not treat him as an adult and let him make his own decision about what he wanted to do with his life. Despite her earlier assurances about Oxford, she had been discussing other possibilities in her letters to both Jack and Winston. She thought he might take the Civil Service exams and try for the Foreign Office. She wrote to Winston, undermining Jack's academic credibility, on September 30, 1897: "if he did pass the Exams—but I fear he is not clever enough." Welldon, however, expected him to pass the entry examination for Oxford. Jennie knew from his school reports that Jack had never failed an examination in his life.

Somewhere along the way, Jennie had conceived the idea that Jack would go into the City as a stockbroker, like his American grandfather before him, and make a vast fortune that would solve the whole family's financial problems. She had conveniently forgotten that Jerome had lost his fortune in a spectacular way.

Finally, in November 1897, Jack was preparing to return home from Paris, and he wrote to his mother a long letter regarding his career preferences:

> I have been "going to be" everything under the sun and as you know I have always had a great abhorrence of being a "something in the city" with the chance of becoming nothing. I have been "going into" the army, the city, the army, the bar, the Foreign Office, or diplomacy and now I am to change again to the city. . . . I am nearly eighteen and it must be settled. I am built heart and soul for the army; but you asked me to give it up because it was expensive and not lucrative, because it might leave you alone, and because it was no "career" I began to like the idea of going to Oxford, of going where Winston had not been, and even of plodding away at the Bar. But now you want me to go under the old gas lamp in the city. The life of a cavalry officer appeals to me more; but I will do it if it is necessary and if you want me to. Your letter did not tell me much about your "Serious financial crisis." Have things gone wrong in America? or did they get muddled in England?

Jennie had put all her cards on the table before her younger son. Pleading insoluble financial difficulties, she had induced him to abandon the career he longed for and take on the last thing in the world he would have chosen, to work as clerk to Sir Ernest Cassel in the City of London. Jack was a sensitive boy, and was good at mathematics at school. In the end, he would obey his beloved mother and do nothing to add to her financial difficulties. He accounted to her for the money she sent him and kept a careful record of his spending. He would have realized that the money was not available to send him into the army or to Oxford. But Jack seems never to have uttered a word of rebuke or attributed any blame to either her or to Winston. He was so much younger, his self-esteem was not high, nor was he sufficiently shrewd to see through them. Through her great friendship with Sir Ernst Cassel, a City stockbroker and lifelong friend of the Churchills, or through the Rothschilds, the merchant bankers, Jennie could have invested some money in 1895, the interest of which would have accrued to finance Jack's career. But Jennie lived for the moment; she bought what she wanted and seemed only to awaken to the fact that she had overspent when she had to raise another loan.

Jennie replied to Jack's letter while still on her travels around the country houses of the aristocracy. Having reached Lambton Castle on November 24, she admonished him:

> Your last letter saddened me—but my darling Boy—you can be certain of one thing and that is that your happiness is the one thing I want above all others and that I will make any sacrifice necessary to ensure it—I have never heard you . . . express a real desire to go into the Army. . . . All will come right for you.

Jennie's financial disarray between 1895 and 1897 determined Jack's career. It was a situation of her own making. At one stage it had reached such a crisis that the bailiffs nearly moved in on her.[21] She was constantly preoccupied with how she was going to pay her bills as she got deeper and deeper into debt.

Jack returned to his mother's empty house, 35A Great Cumberland Place in London, on a bleak Friday in December. He wrote to her at the country house where she was staying, telling her he had arrived safely, and he was obviously lonely: "I beg you to come home as soon as you can."

Eleven

FINANCIAL CRISIS AND
A CAREER DENIED

1898–1899

Lord Salisbury continued as Conservative prime minister throughout the period
1898–99. Government expenditure was already high for the financial years 1898
and early 1899, at £117.6 million. In January 1899, the government was facing a
possible deficit of £4 million.[1] Michael Hicks Beach, Chancellor of the Exchequer,
responded by calling for higher taxation, but Lord Salisbury opposed him, so the
deficit grew. There would be wider implications for the growth in expenditure with
the impending Boer War in South Africa, and by 1902 it had reached £295.2 million.[2]

In reply to Jennie's letter of November 1897 saying she was considering sending Jack into the City, Winston had made his opposition clear. He was, he said, prepared to go along with it only on the understanding that Jack would later be allowed to go to university. But with Winston so far from home and unable to assess fully what was taking place between Jennie and Jack, he did not realize that she was in fact forcing his younger brother into the City on a permanent basis. Winston tried to help Jack as much as possible from the other side of the world, and he wrote to Jennie, on January 10, disagreeing with her judgment. He clearly understood Jack's earnest desire for a university education and, in an attempt to help him, even offered to raise a loan in his own name, to be repaid by Jack when he came of age.

When Jennie replied, on January 13, she was clearly furious at being contradicted. She thought she knew best:

> Everyone thinks my plan for him is the best. He will go to Germany for a year, learn bookkeeping & German, & one of these days make a fortune. He is quite reconciled to it now.

Given the prevalent aristocratic disdain for gentlemen going into trade, it is hard to know who "everyone" was. In its day bookkeeping was hardly a proper vocation for a grandson of the Duke of Marlborough, and neither the Marlboroughs nor any of the Churchill relations would have condoned such a move.

While this debate raged between Jennie and Winston, Dr. Welldon, still under the impression that Jack was going to study for a degree, wrote to him, on January 23, saying he had filled in his papers for Oxford.[3]

The amount of money that would have been required to educate Jack was not in fact very great by the standards of the day. Dr. Robin Darwall-Smith, the archivist of Magdalen College, Oxford, at the time of writing, has assisted the authors by producing roughly the costs of living in the university and obtaining a degree. Even allowing for the higher expense bracket, the maximum would have been £339/$1,627.20 per year. Jennie had already estimated that Jack "cost" her something like £300/$1,440 a year.[4]

Toward the end of January, and just prior to taking up his appointment as a clerk to Sir Ernest Cassel, Jennie allowed Jack to satisfy his interest in the army by joining the Oxfordshire Hussars, a part-time Yeomanry Regiment. After a month's training, he could balance the two pursuits, working in the City during the week, and joining his regiment for further service experience at weekends and during holiday periods. Winston had also suggested in his letter of January 10 to his mother that as well as a university education remaining open to Jack, he might still also have the opportunity of going into the army as a professional soldier if he chose. But to this, Jennie made her objections and her annoyance even more clear. Her reply of January 13 continued:

> You talk glibly of Jack going into the Army—but you know he would never pass the medical examination with his eyes—& besides how could I give him an adequate allowance? . . . He has joined the Oxford Yeomanry & will have a month's drill at Aldershot & his 10 days before he goes to Berlin. It will set him up & give him a nice uniform for all requirements. How I am to pay for it I do not know!

Her mention of Jack's eyes referred to an accident when, as a boy, he was shot in the eye by a family friend, John Prescott Hewitt, at The Deepdene. He had experienced some minor eye trouble and wore glasses for reading, but the injury was never considered serious.[5] Jack quite clearly passed the medical examination for the Oxfordshire Hussars, who could, in time of war, be called upon for active service.

FOLLOWING A VISIT to Sir Ernest Cassel on January 20, Jennie was taking Jack a week later to stay with the Prince of Wales at Sandringham.[6] Cassel was looked upon as a financial genius with huge interests in Egypt, South America, and the United States. He was an intimate friend of the Prince and was known in his set as "the King's banker." He was recognized as having invested the Prince's money well, making him a large fortune. Jennie had written to Winston, "The Prince means to be very kind to you both."[7] Jack somewhat reluctantly agreed to work for Cassel, despite the vagueness as to what his job would entail.

Jennie had clearly negotiated a place for Jack in Cassel's employ, hoping perhaps it would strengthen her links with the Prince and set Jack on the path to improving the family finances. There was little hope for Jack now in achieving his own ambitions. Writing to him on January 19, Winston told Jack he was being denied his choice of career because he was not aggressive enough in demanding what he wanted from Jennie: "The whole thing is your own fault for not expressing decided opinions. If you had made up your mind what you wanted—insisted upon it—no one would have stopped you."[8]

During Jack's training in late January and February, he was in a camp near Blenheim Palace, Oxford. Jennie was constantly strapped for cash, and he was reduced to begging her for money to pay to carry out extra exercises. Nevertheless, the relationship between mother and son remained excellent, as always, and Jack urged her (in an undated letter in January) to visit him in camp:

I am going on here very well and am having a splendid time. Can't you come
down to Blenheim next Tuesday and Wednesday. . . . You can come and see
our inspection, which will be very pretty. They are going to ask you to the
mess etc. so do come.

It is unclear whether she actually attended.

On his return home, Jennie did not send Jack to Germany to learn bookkeeping
or improve his German. She was experiencing a deep financial crisis and trying to
raise a loan of £17,000/$81,600.[9] Jack started work around the beginning of March
1898 at Cassel's premises, at Throgmorton, London. He began at a low grade as a
clerk on the basis that he would be trained by Cassel to eventually become a stockbroker, but that was years into the future.[10] Peregrine Churchill was quite adamant
that his father hated the City and the demeaning work he had to undertake there. Although he was engaged as a clerk, he also acted as Cassel's secretary and administra-
tor, and his duties involved working out calculations, writing letters, organizing
business meetings, taking the minutes and letters in shorthand, and typing them up.
He would work long hours in the claustrophobic heat of a City office, and would endure even more harrowing conditions when he traveled many miles overseas with
Cassel on business.

By mid-March, Cassel and Jack had set off to Cairo on a business trip, Jack having taken a crash course in Pitman's shorthand and touch typing. Jack soon discovered he was not able to live on the money Cassel paid him, and there is mention in
both Jennie's and Jack's letters of her sending him a check each month. Indeed it is
not entirely clear whether he received a salary at all in the beginning or was on some
sort of apprenticeship until he got his own place as a stockbroker.[11] Peregrine suspected that, initially, his father had been sent to work for Cassel in lieu of money
Jennie had borrowed from him.

When Jack returned to London around the end of April, he tried to arrange to
continue with his piano lessons in what spare time he had, to provide some respite
from a job he didn't like. Peregrine said Jack was an excellent pianist and went to
classical concerts in London. But his mother and Winston were obviously using him
as their errand boy. Jack was told in letters from Winston to exercise his horses, and
he was expected by Jennie to deal with the family lawyers on her behalf.

While working at his job in the City, Jack was also trying to sort out his
mother's paperwork with Lumley, of Lumleys solicitors, following the granting of
the new loan, and in paying off some old ones. It was the beginning of a life for
Jack of seeing to the Churchills' finances and paperwork. He took solace in his
hobby of photography, and liked taking photographs of his mother. He replied to
her in the height of summer (undated, but circa July/August) from the Bachelors'

Club in Piccadilly, pointedly noting the temperature at an uncomfortable 85 degrees. He explained to her that when Lumley paid up her last loan, he failed to close the insurance policy, which guaranteed the loan, and was still paying the premium on it quite unnecessarily.

Jennie, on her autumn travels around the country houses, replied somewhat insensitively, on September 19, 1898, from Minto House, Hawick, Scotland:

> I hope it is not quite so bad in London. Tell me if you have begun the music [lessons]. I think of you so much my darling alone and dull in London. But good days will come. Are you riding the Arab? [exercising Winston's horse]

In Egypt, Cassel was heavily involved in the project of building the first Aswan Dam, for which he had granted a huge loan to finance its construction. The British began construction of the dam in 1889. The aim was to prevent the rivers from flooding the surrounding areas, as the population who had settled along the edge of the river had increased over the years. Their lands and homes had to be protected and the waters, which were rich in minerals and nutrients, could be used for irrigation purposes on farmlands and cotton fields. When the waters were harnessed they would generate electricity.

Cassel's personal interest in the project was that he owned the Sugar Company of Egypt, cotton factories, and the Daira Saniyeh Co. Ltd.; the headquarters of this last was in London. When Cassel went back to Egypt in January 1899, Jack accompanied him. He had completed another course in shorthand in order to take Cassels's dictation. Jennie knew well that Jack suffered very badly from travel and seasickness. He wrote her an undated letter of his misery, from the train between Passau and Vienna, in the dead of winter, but ever sensitive to her worries he tried to put a brave face on it and soften the effect:

> We are nearing Vienna and I have had very nearly enough of this train, which jolts terribly. We had a very good crossing to Ostend but I did not feel very fit when I started and was sick the whole time. We are doing the journey most comfortably and have a whole sleeping car to ourselves which is rather nice. . . . We are now [a party of] seven with seven servants. We have just been through field after field of deep snow and it is freezing here.

He wrote again, from the Savoy Hotel, Cairo, on Tuesday, February 2, telling her of the Barrage Ceremony, that is, the laying of the foundation stone marking the start of the work of building. It was scheduled to be carried out by the Duke of Connaught, who was delayed because of the weather.

So absorbed was Jennie with George Cornwallis-West that she remained insensitive to Jack's plight. Despite Winston's protests to his mother the previous year about her overspending and borrowing, Jennie was again trying to raise a loan of £3,000/$14,400, possibly the shortfall of the £17,000 she had originally wanted.

Jennie had decided to publish a magazine, the *Anglo-Saxon Review*, and required funds for it, and she had written to Alfred Beit, a wealthy financier and old friend of Randolph's asking him to guarantee her for a loan. Jack wrote to his mother (undated, circa early February) telling her Biet had received the letter. Quite coincidentally, Biet was with the party that included Jack and Cassel, as they proceeded on their business trip, and Beit told Jack about the letter. Jack very gallantly tried to arrange the loan for his mother with Beit, but did not have all the facts to hand, so he arranged for Beit to connect with Lumley in London.

Jack told his mother in a letter (undated) that Cassel and his party were starting up the Nile on February 16, as there was going to be "a sort of inspection of the sugar and cotton factories," also owned by Cassel. Jack's letter continued, "This may be interesting but rather monotonous. . . . They play bridge whenever possible each game takes about three quarters of an hour—1/4 to play & 1/2 to abuse each other afterwards." They were, he said, due to start for home on March 17. He reassured his mother:

> It is rather fun going and ordering two or three special trains and a steamer or two. Mr. Cassel is very kind to me, he has given me his second servant and I have everything I want. . . . Do you know I am nineteen the day after to-morrow [February 4].

Shamefully, Jennie had not remembered his birthday, and he wrote again next day from the Savoy Hotel, clearly disappointed that she had forgotten to send him greetings.

Despite the relentless pressure of work, it had a very interesting side to it that Jack appreciated. He always worked very hard, and he witnessed the initial construction of the Aswan Dam, writing enthusiastically to his mother about it circa late February or early March. He tried to discourage her from going to the gambling casinos: "I don't think I should go to Monte Carlo if I were you—I know what a week there costs." He then complained, "I shall have to come home direct and go back to that horrid City."

THE DOWAGER DUCHESS of Marlborough died at 45 Portman Square, London, on April 16, 1899. Unbeknown to anyone she had cut Jennie out of her will. The only money Jennie inherited was about £2,000/$9,600, which was all that remained of the late duke's money left to Randolph and in his mother's charge until her death. This was the final blow to the Churchills' fortunes, and the end of any chance for Jack to pursue a career of his choice.

During Cowes Week, on August 4, 1899, newspaper headlines blazed out: "British Society Astonished,"[12] as Jennie's engagement to George Cornwallis-West was announced. The following day Winston published a retraction, and the headlines blazed out again: "Lady Randolph Churchill's Son Denies That His Mother Will Marry Young Cornwallis-West."[13]

As to Winston's romantic attachment to Pamela Plowden, there are gaps in the correspondence between them while he was in India, but the threads of their story can be picked up two years into the relationship. Pamela had in the meantime returned to live in England. Writing to her from his mother's home, 35A Great Cumberland Place, November 28, 1898, Winston told her he was going to India on Friday, and that he wanted to come and see her.[14] He was sharing his thoughts with her on the book he was writing, *The River War*, which was about the reconquest of the Sudan by the British army led by Herbert Kitchener. They were now clearly very much in love, but Pamela seems to have grown rather impatient with his aloofness, and had written to him saying he was incapable of affection. His letter continued that he loved her above all others and that nothing would ever change him. Winston still had insufficient money on which to marry, but he was trying to improve his financial prospects as a writer.[15] A substantial and secure income was necessary to maintain a girl like Pamela in the style to which she had been accustomed, though Jean Hamilton commented that Pamela had no money either.[16] Winston wrote to his mother again, May 3, 1899,[17] saying that Pamela was very impressed with the proofs of the first two chapters of *The River War*.

Twelve

JENNIE'S WORK ON THE *ANGLO-SAXON REVIEW* AND THE HOSPITAL SHIP *MAINE* DURING THE BOER WAR

1898–1902

In 1899, British politicians in South Africa engineered a war with the Boer republics, ostensibly to defend the rights of British gold miners living and working there but with a view to acquiring the gold mines for the Empire. In September, British Colonial Secretary Joseph Chamberlain sent an ultimatum to the Boers, demanding full equality of rights for those British residents (uitlanders) in the South African Republic. Paul Kruger, state president of the South African Republic (Transvaal), retaliated with an ultimatum, giving the British forty-eight hours to withdraw all their troops from the border of the Transvaal, failing which, allied with the Orange Free State, the Boers would declare war against the British. The response of the British government was to declare war on October 11.

While Jennie's romance with George Cornwallis-West was blossoming, she needed something of an intellectual nature to fulfill her cultural interests. George Curzon of Kedleston, Conservative cabinet minister and close friend of the Churchills, and his wife, Mary, née Leiter,[1] a beautiful American heiress, daughter of a Chicago millionaire, who was a close personal friend of Jennie's, were due to take up their positions as viceroy and vicereine in India on January 6, 1899. On the eve of their departure from England circa November 1898, the Curzons and Jennie were house guests of the Duke and Duchess of Portland at Welbeck Abbey in Nottinghamshire. Jennie was seated next to George at dinner, and she "bemoaned" to him "the empty life I was leading at that moment." Following that conversation, in which Curzon pointed out the advantages of a single woman, shortly afterward she decided to start a magazine. Jennie "consulted" her "friend Mrs. Pearl Craigie,"[2] who was most encouraging, and decided to publish a prestigious cultural review that would produce articles on literature, art, history, music, politics, and women.[3] Pearl, the daughter of a New York merchant, John Morgan Richards, living in London, was an established writer under the name of John Oliver Hobbes.[4] Pearl was a short, dark woman with fine eyes and a keen intellect, and she was also a well-known novelist and reviewer; her first novel, *Some Emotions and a Moral,* had been an enormous success. Jennie spoke most highly of Pearl, who she said was a "brilliant and clever conversationalist."[5] The two women had a good deal in common with their mutual interest in literature, music, and the theatre, and both were accomplished pianists. They sometimes played together in concerts, one of which had taken place at the Queen's Hall, London, when they made a threesome with Mademoiselle Janotha, a famous Court pianist of the emperor of Germany. Directing Bach's "Concerto in D Minor for three pianos, with an orchestra from the Royal College of Music," the conductor was Sir Walter Parratt,[6] also known as a celebrated organist. Jennie said she "always made a point to go to Mrs. Craigie's plays and we had many discussions about them."[7]

Pearl introduced Jennie to a successful publisher, John Lane, who owned a publishing company, Bodley Head. Jennie had her first business meeting with Lane on December 3, 1898, and he agreed to publish the magazine and take care of paying the writers and arranging and paying for the advertising. Pearl also introduced Jennie to Sidney Low, who had been the editor of the *St. James's Gazette* (1888–97), and was now literary editor of the *Morning Standard,* both well-known British journals. Low would work as Jennie's assistant editor, reading manuscripts and advising her on the selection of ideas for articles so crucial to success. Low suggested that the magazine should be bound in green calf and embossed in gold, and they should use a design and binding that was a replica of one used in the time of King James I. They later decided to use a variety of different period bindings.[8] Jennie consulted Cyril Davenport at the British Museum, an expert in period bookbindings, who agreed to help her choose beautiful covers, "facsimiles of celebrated books of the sixteenth, seventeenth, and eighteenth centuries," which were to be "mostly chosen from examples in the British Museum."[9] Davenport would write an article about the bindings in each issue of the *Review.* The magazine was to be produced in book form, each issue consisting of many pages.

Jennie asked Lionel Cust, an English art historian and director of the National Portrait Gallery, to be responsible for the illustrations. Her idea was to invite people she knew to be of a high literary caliber to write articles for the magazine, and they would be paid. She met up with her old flame Bourke Cockran, who was on a visit to London, and they discussed the financial side of the business. He brought all his cleverness and his great mind to it. They discussed how she would set up a syndicate of six major contributors to supply funds for the first year. She told him of her desire for lots of American talent to write for her. When he returned to the States, Jennie wrote to him (in an undated letter), "You were a tower of strength to me."[10] Presumably he introduced some of the great American writers whose names would appear between the covers in the coming months. All these activities took place during the late months of 1898 and the early months of 1899.

It only remained for Jennie to choose an appropriate title for the magazine. Sir Edgar Vincent, "whose classical and literary education [was] backed by the most admirable common sense[,] suggested 'Anglo-Saxon'."[11] Jennie added the word "Review," and she had a magazine.

The *Review* was intended not only to provide Jennie with a literary interest but also to make money for her. Winston advised her in a letter from Bangalore, on January 1, 1899,[12] that she might make an annual profit of £1,000/$4,800 out of it. Jennie nicknamed the review "Maggie," short for magazine, and priced it at a guinea a copy (today's equivalent of over £73/$35.40).

Writing to Jack on February 24, Jennie told him she was setting up a syndicate of people who would invest in the *Review,* but that it was "anxious work." Among those Jennie is known to have recruited into her syndicate were Bourke Cockran, Ernest Cassel, John Morgan Richards, and the Duchess Lily Beresford, who had formerly been married to the 8th Duke of Marlborough. Winston put in £250/$1,200 for himself and Jack from monies he had invested.[13]

Whatever the fate of the magazine was to be, Jennie's finances were still not in good order. The loan she had raised in 1898 was originally for £17,000/$81,600. In

Egypt Jack obtained Beit's agreement to the loan.[14] He wrote to his mother from the Savoy Hotel, Cairo, on February 2:

> I wired you the other day from here about Beit. I just caught him before he started for Asia Minor. . . . Your letter has been following him slowly and it only caught him a few days ago. . . . He said he was ready to advance the sum himself on the same terms, which Lumley brought forward concerning the last loan.

Winston's disillusionment with the army in India had reached such a state that he was intending to resign his commission. Writing to his grandmother, the Dowager Duchess, on March 26, 1899,[15] about his reasons for leaving, he told her he could live more cheaply at home and earn money by his writing. Winston arrived back in London at the end of April. By May, he was vigorously pursuing a career in politics. He was also helping his mother with writing the preface to the first issue of the *Review*.[16]

Jennie gave a luncheon party "to introduce 'Maggie,' as the *Review* was affectionately called." The "book in its gorgeous cover, the replica of Thevet's '*Vie des Hommes Illustres*,' which was executed about 1604 for James I" was launched.[17]

The first issue of the *Anglo-Saxon Review* was published in June 1899. It contained a lengthy story by the distinguished American writer Henry James, author of such famous novels as *The Turn of the Screw* and *The Golden Bowl*, for which he was paid £40/$192. For a poem on the Battle of the Nile, Algernon Swinburne was paid £15. Pearl Craigie, writing under the name of John Oliver Hobbes, had written a dramatic poem in two acts, *Osbern and Ursyne*, which ran to thirty-three pages; she was paid £40/$192. Professor Oliver Lodge had written an article on wireless telegraphy, and was paid £25/$120.[18] Lodge was a physicist and writer involved in the development of the wireless telegraph. He gained the "syntonic," or tuning, patent from the United States Patent Office in 1898.

Lord Rosebery, Liberal MP and former prime minister (1894–95), had written a twenty-three-page article about Sir Robert Peel, a former Conservative prime minister, known for having started the modern police force. Rosebery, as a friend of the late Lord Randolph Churchill, probably did not accept payment. The Duchess of Devonshire contributed five letters written by Georgiana, Duchess of Devonshire (1757–1806), and was paid £25.[19] Elizabeth Robins,[20] an actress born in Kentucky, who starred in plays by Henrik Ibsen, such as *Hedda Gabler, A Doll's House,* and *The Master Builder*, and was known in Britain as "Ibsen's High Priestess," was paid £31 10s for a twenty-eight-page article titled "A Modern Woman Born 1689," the story of Lady Mary Wortley Montagu, an English aristocrat and writer who lived in the 1700s.

At the time of publication of the first issue, Lane was away for over a month, and Low was off sick, so Jennie had to manage a good deal of the time on her own, though Pearl Craigie provided unfailing support.

The critics got to work on Maggie in both the United Kingdom and the United States. They found fault with the "tone," which was "vaguely aristocratic," and the *Review* "was mocked for having so many contributors from high society."[21] It was considered too expensive, and the binding wasn't real leather. The *Pall Mall Gazette*,[22] however, published a lengthy and very positive review, running to several hundred words:

> Why should not an effort be made to preserve some, at least, of the best work of the day? The United States is represented by Mr. Whitelaw Reid, Mr. Henry James, and Miss Elizabeth Robins. The most interesting contributions, however, and those which may give that abiding interest to the number . . . are those of Lord Rosebery and Mr. Algernon Swinburne. Lord Rosebery's appreciation of the life and character of Sir Robert Peel not only helps to throw new light on the personality of the statesman, but also affords the ex-Premier the opportunity of expressing his own views on the functions and the position of an English Prime Minister. The Duchess of Devonshire contributes some amusing unpublished letters of the beautiful Duchess Georgiana.

In October 1899, what is sometimes referred to as the Second Boer War broke out. Jennie would become involved in war work that would take her to South Africa. Her work on the magazine would for a time be interrupted, but she left Sidney Low in charge while she was away. Low brought out two further issues of Maggie during her absence.

After her return, Jennie resumed work on the *Review* in May 1900. There were pieces about the Treaty of Paris and, of course the Boer War. The names of men of distinction who were contributors included Lord Crewe, Edmund Gosse, and George Bernard Shaw, who submitted an article about Verdi, and whom Jennie described as a "tall, pale, thin, ascetic looking" man "with wonderful, transparent eyes."[23] John Gorst, George Gissing, Maurice Baring, and William Archer appeared in later issues.[24] Frances, Countess of Warwick, whose long affair with the Prince of Wales was at an end, wrote a piece perhaps somewhat aptly titled "Some Minor Miseries of a Book Lover," as it was known she had squandered her great fortune, providing big dinners, parties, and balls for the Prince's entertainment at her husband's home, Warwick Castle. The friendship between Jennie and the Prince of Wales continued amicably, and he had been encouraging to her about the _Review_, but he was now much wrapped up in Alice Keppel and turned down her request to write an article.

John Lane was very much a businessman, interested in making money, whereas Low was more interested in literature for its own sake. From the beginning, Jennie had been quarreling with Lane over a catalogue of irksome errors, one of which was that both their names in the initial masthead were too large. He had gone on a trip to America in May, just prior to the publication of the first issue, scheduled for June 15, leaving her to cope. She would soon grow dissatisfied that "Maggie" was not making money and blamed Lane. Her new husband, George Cornwallis-West, also blamed Lane for the failure and wrote to Jennie from Scotland, on September 28, 1900, imploring her to "get rid" of Lane and that she would never make the _Review_ pay until he was gone.[25] Jennie took his advice, and when the December 1900 issue was released Jennie was the new publisher under her married name of Mrs. Cornwallis-West. She had also engaged two new editors, William Earl Hodgson, former editor of the _National Review and Realm,_ and Charles Whibley, an author of political portraits. At some stage she was of the opinion that the circulation was not increasing, attributed to the green cover of the _Review_ blending too much into the background with other books in bookshops and news agents. Jennie had it changed to bright red, which was more striking and stood out more on the bookshelves.

New articles in the _Review_ included one by the author of the famous _Red Badge of Courage,_ Stephen Crane, "War Memories." He wrote, "War is neither magnificent nor squalid; it is simply life, and an expression of life can always evade us." He died soon afterward, aged only twenty-nine years.

Other issues of the _Review_ had articles about the American Revolution, the American athlete, the great seals of England, the Marlboroughs' ancestral gems, snuff boxes, the absurdity of the critic of music, and celebrated women of recent times. More than one literary critic observed that the problem with the _Review_ was that it covered too wide a range of subjects and so lacked focus.

One issue contained a most embarrassing article titled "The Next Government," which was put in without Jennie's knowledge while she had gone off for a break in Scotland. The article criticized Lord Rosebery, and Jennie had to write and apologize, but Rosebery took it stoically and replied from Edinburgh, September 28, 1901, that he thought it was a great mistake to introduce politics into the _Review_ and that in any event he had not read the article and had no intentions of doing so.[26]

The tenth and final issue of the _Anglo-Saxon Review_ went out in September 1902. The _Review_ had never made a profit. Overall, however, it was considered to have been of high quality. There were just too many other magazines in competition for readers at that time that were a lot less luxurious and less expensive. A journalist, Michael Rhodes, had perhaps the last word on the subject when, in the mid-1970s, he described the *Review* as "unique" and "an international literary review of high quality."[27]

WHEN THE WAR broke out in South Africa in October 1899,[28] Mrs. Jennie Blow, the American wife of the manager of one of South Africa's richest mining syndicates, A. A. Blow, had an idea to provide a hospital ship to care for the wounded from both sides of the fighting. Later that month, Jennie Churchill joined Mrs. Blow and the other ladies in an executive committee[29] working to bring this about, and Jennie became chairman of the U.S. Hospital Ship Fund. The first committee meeting was held at Jennie's house on October 25, 1899. Working enthusiastically during the weeks following, Jennie organized and raised funds for the trip. The task that lay ahead was to send to South Africa "a suitable Hospital Ship, fully equipped with medical stores and provisions, to accommodate 200 people, with a staff of four doctors, five nurses, and 40 commissioned officers and orderlies."[30] Jennie contacted Mrs. Whitelaw Reid in New York, who had excellent connections in the nursing profession through the Mills Training School for nurses, and provided "most efficient doctors, nurses, and orderlies."[31] When the medical staff arrived in London from New York, they received a warm welcome. Hotels offered them accommodation at reduced rates. They were lionized with luncheons and dinner parties. Queen Victoria invited them to view the state apartment rooms at Windsor Castle, and having lunched there, they were formally presented to the Queen.

TO FINANCE the venture the sum of £30,000/$150,000 would be required.[32] It was a tall order, but Jennie was a brilliant organizer, and she knew many wealthy men and women in society. "Concerts, matinees, and entertainments of all sorts and kinds were organized."[33] Soon money and medical supplies poured in. A ship duly appeared in the form of a splendid gift from an American millionaire, Bernard Nadel Baker. Baker, who was founder of the Atlantic Transport Company in Baltimore, gave the British government the use of one of his transport ships, the *Maine*. It had been used for transporting cattle and had to be refitted as a hospital ship, complete with hospital wards. Jennie enlisted the aid of the army to have the ship converted. Already the committee had received £15,000/$72,000 in donations, and Jennie organized a huge fund-raising dinner at Claridge's Hotel in London. Jennie had already decided to travel on the ship to the Cape, and said in an interview to the London *Daily Mail*, on November 9:

> I am not going to do any amateur nursing. . . . I shall superintend the correspondence. . . . When shall I be back? How can I tell you how long the war will last, and I certainly mean to see it through.[34]

For "Sister Jennie," as she would later be addressed by the wounded, the attraction of working for the Red Cross on the hospital ship was that her fiancé, Lieutenant George Cornwallis-West, and Winston had gone out to serve in the war. Jack Churchill, aged only nineteen, followed on January 6, 1900. Although Winston and Jack belonged to the Oxfordshire Hussars regiment, they joined the South African Light Horse as officers, and would soon fight side by side. Winston had gone out in the role of war correspondent for the *Morning Post,* and he would combine his journalistic talents with active fighting. George had sailed with his regiment, the Scots Guards, on a P&O liner, the *Nubia.* He and his fellow officers were reputed to have drunk their way through twenty cases of 1887 Perrier-Jouët, a gift from Alfred de Rothschild of the Rothschild banking family.

Jennie's glamorous fund-raising event at Claridge's, which should have been the highlight of her efforts, was marred when the devastating news reached her that Winston had been captured by the Boers. The train in which he had been traveling had been ambushed. He subsequently escaped, went on the run, and eventually turned up safe and sound.

Jennie prepared to leave with the *Maine* for Cape Town. The launch ceremony was conducted by HRH the Duke of Connaught, younger brother of the Prince of Wales, who hoisted the Union Jack to the band of the Scots Guards playing first "Rule Britannia" and then "Star-Spangled Banner." The *Maine* flew the flags of the United States of America, Great Britain, the Red Cross, and the Admiralty's transport flag. They left Portsmouth Harbor on Saturday, December 23, 1899.

Surgeon Lieutenant Colonel H. F. Hensman, A.M.D, late of the 2nd Life Guards, was the officer in charge of the *Maine,* and Major Julian M. Cabell of the U.S. Army Medical Department was the senior American surgeon on board. Jennie's role was to supervise the medical staff on board, and most particularly to ensure that the wards were ready before they reached South Africa. Miss Mary Eugenie Hibbard, who had been in charge of the Grace Hospital and Nursing School in Detroit, was the professional superintendent of nurses. Such was Nurse Hibbard's professional standing that when she arrived in London she was granted an audience with Queen Victoria and visited Florence Nightingale, who was then eighty years of age. Miss Eleanor Warrender, sister to Jennie's recent boyfriend, Hugh, was acting as Jennie's secretary.

All the nurses on the *Maine* wore simple uniforms: a long white skirt, a short white jacket, a brassard with *Maine* and a red cross embossed on it, and a white cap that peaked in the middle. Jennie wore a nurse's uniform that she had designed herself, a starched white apron and white blouse and an armband with a red cross on it.

The refitting of the ship had been bedeviled with holdups, and as they sailed away the workmen were still on board, hard at it. The ship was well equipped with an operating theater and X-ray room. Jennie had her own room, a photograph of which shows a prestigious, if somewhat cramped space, with her bed in one corner, the only privacy being a curtain. Pictures of her family adorned the pea green walls.

Just prior to leaving, Jennie had received a telegram from George saying he had been invalided out of the army with a bad attack of sunstroke. Her romantic hopes of joining him were dashed, for he was sailing home, and they passed each other somewhere on the high seas. George's parents, William and Mary (Patsy), were vigorously opposing a marriage between Jennie and George, and Jennie received a letter from George, now recovering at home. He was, he said, alone in the house with his father, who was trying to make him give her up. William was dropping hints about the financial difficulties in which the family found themselves, and that they could be easily overcome if he, George, married an heiress.[35]

Winston and Jack were serving together in South Africa under Colonel Julian Byng. It was agreed by Byng that Winston could continue with his work as a war correspondent and participate in the fighting. On January 6, Jennie received a letter from Winston saying that there was to be the greatest battle yet fought, and if he came out of it alive he would run down to Cape Town or she might come to fetch the wounded from Durban.[36]

Meanwhile, the *Maine* ran into a tremendous storm, and there was a good deal of seasickness and things were tossed about. They were on the final leg of their voyage and had taken on fresh supplies at Las Palmas. The ship was still in a mess following the battering it had taken in the storm, and a major cleanup operation was under way. There was conflict throughout the voyage between the American and British staff, and Jennie acted as peacemaker. Miss Hibbard, being a graduate of the first school of nurses in Canada, was very experienced and did not like taking orders from Jennie, who was not even a trained nurse. Jennie's forty-sixth birthday, January 9, passed unnoticed. She wrote to the Prince of Wales from the ship, on January 19, 1900: "We hope to get into Cape Town Sunday morning early [January 21]." Then she told him of the dreadful storm they had experienced at sea:

> We had to "lay to" 48 hrs I never was so buffeted in my life. We are very top heavy—and owing to our large open gangways, most unfitted for high seas.

Referring to the weight distribution in the lower decks of the ship, she continued:

> I understand if we had slipped one or two we would have gone to the bottom.

Jennie suffered from seasickness, and when the *Maine* arrived at Las Palmas, where it stopped to:

re-coal Captain Winty—who commands the *"Furious"* was most civil to me—also the Vice Consul a Mr. Swanston with a pretty wife—they brought me telegraphs and flowers and took me on shore and looked after me generally. . . .

There has been so much to do to get the wards and everything in order—we left in such haste—but the absence of any news is what I find trying.[37]

The *Maine* sailed into Cape Town at 6 A.M. on January 23, where Jack was to have joined his mother. The scene in the harbor was typically one of war: ships full of troops who were disembarking; streets filled with soldiers; but Jack had not arrived. The decision-making instructions for the role of the *Maine* were then taken over by the chief medical officer for Cape Town. He decided to turn the *Maine* into a transport ship. He decreed that they would proceed to Durban on January 25, take on the wounded, and return immediately to England. The ship was never intended for that purpose and was meant as a floating hospital ship, and Jennie was understandably annoyed. The weather was atrocious en route to Durban; there was a terrific storm, lightning flashed, there were "torrents of hailstones" as "large as small plums," a "hurricane" blew up, one of the windows broke, "and water and ice poured in everywhere." The deck was "covered with ice," and they did not reach Durban until the 29th.[38] One thing at least came right: Jack arrived in uniform, wearing a large sombrero tilted to one side, giving him rather the appearance of a cowboy. Winston joined them, and the three Churchills had a brief reunion for two days.

Jennie used all her powers of persuasion to prevent the *Maine* being returned to England and got her way. Winston and Jack left to join their regiment, and Jennie and her staff prepared for the arrival of the wounded from the Battle of Spion Kop, who were already on their way in wagons. When, on February 5, the first ambulance train arrived near the dock at Cape Town, Jennie and Miss Hibbard and the nursing staff were ready to take charge of them. There were sixty-seven injured soldiers, of whom twelve were carried on stretchers and the others were walking wounded. The *Central News of Durban* reported: "Lady Randolph personally superintended their reception, directed berthing, and flitted among the injured as 'an angel of mercy.'"[39]

Part of the reason so much prominence was given to Jennie in the press was Winston's escape from the Boers. He had gone on the run with a price on his head, and the Boers had put out posters for his capture: WANTED DEAD OR ALIVE.[40] Winston was treated as a war hero, and the British press was full of it. But jingoism played a part: Jennie was an American, and openly so, speaking with an American accent, and America was pro-Boer and anti-British, so she was viewed as something of a heroine, flying in the face of her native land.

Jennie comforted the wounded and helped them write letters home to their loved ones, and they called her "Sister Jennie." Her role was necessarily administrative, and, apart from giving help with dressings or bandages where she might be of use, she left nursing to the trained staff.

Jack—whose only experience of soldiering was with his part-time regiment, the Oxfordshire Hussars, at weekends—was now seeing active service for the first time. During a reconnaissance on horseback with Winston, Jack was shot in the leg.[41] True to Jennie's worst nightmare, Jack was one of the early intakes, just nine days after his twentieth birthday.

The bullet that hit Jack was kept as a memento by his younger son, Peregrine, and turned into a medallion on a chain. When Peregrine died in 2002, his widow Yvonne bequeathed it, along with Jack's full-dress uniform, to the National Army Museum in London. Today the bullet is on show in the Churchill Museum, Winston's former Cabinet War Rooms in London.

Jennie wrote to the Prince of Wales again, on March 3, 1900, from Durban:

> Immediately on arriving at Cape Town we were ordered off here [to Durban] and were filled up in hours. Since then we have had various contingents of wounded on and off—as they soon get well and a good many are able to go to the front again. I am glad to say the authorities find us very efficient and are making good use of us.

Jennie went on to tell the Prince of Jack's injury:

> Luckily it was only a flesh wound, but being a spent bullet it made rather a large hole. However he will soon be all right and I am sorry to say able to go up to the front again. He has a troop in the S.A.L.H. [South African Light Horse Regiment] which has been doing a great deal of fighting and doing splendid service.

She then told him of Winston's service:

> Winston is with Lord Dundonald and has been given a commission by Sir R. [Redvers] Buller. He has been a cause of anxiety to me—as they have been fighting for the last 10 days. As you may imagine, Sir, the glorious news of the last week has rejoiced us immensely. One cannot but hope now that the back of the rebellion is broken and that the war will soon be over. . . .
>
> The relief of Ladysmith has been a tremendous task and who knows if Lord Roberts or anyone else could have done it sooner. . . .

The weather is perfect and there is always a breeze on board. We are anchored mid-stream in the Harbour. . . .

Hoping that you are well and asking you to kindly remember me to the Princess [Alexandra].

Believe me as ever

Your Royal Highness's Faithful Servant.

Jennie Spencer Churchill.[42]

Jack had described his injury in a letter to his Aunt Clara Frewen, sent from the *Maine*.[43]

Thank goodness it had turned out to be nothing, but it hurt a good deal at the time. I mounted again as the squadron continued to retire, but after going about a mile, Winston made me get into an ambulance; and so my military career ended rather abruptly. It was very hard luck being hit the first time I was under fire. But I saw a very good day, and while it lasted, I heard as many bullets whiz past as I ever want to.

Listening to Jack's dramatic account of the fighting while he was on board the *Maine* served to increase Jennie's desire to visit the war zone. Another great battle would take place in a few days' time, and she must have gone through torments that Winston, who was so adventuresome and fearless, might get killed.

She wrote to Winston to this effect, and he replied, February 18, that he would arrange for her to come to Chieveley Camp. Winston got a few days' leave and visited his mother and Jack aboard the ship. Also present was Captain Percy Scott, the commander of HMS *Terrible,* who had invented a gun carriage that enabled the 4.7-inch naval gun to be taken up-country to the front. Scott named the gun at Chieveley Camp "the Lady Randolph Churchill," and it was Jennie who historically fired the test round. With the support of Captain Scott, Jennie, accompanied by Eleanor Warrender and Colonel Hensman, went to see the other hospitals at Chieveley. Along the way they passed the mangled, burned-out wreck of the armored train from which Winston had been taken prisoner some weeks earlier, still lying on its side. A few yards away there was a makeshift graveyard where those who had been killed were buried.

The *Maine* was now almost filled with wounded soldiers, and Jennie and her team worked all day and were on duty throughout the night. Both British and Boer wounded men arrived in uniforms torn to shreds and covered with dirt from the field of battle. During this first voyage, twenty operations were performed on board the *Maine,* and there were three deaths. One was from typhoid fever, one suffered an aneurysm, and one died from tuberculosis. The nurses cleaned and dressed the men's wounds and administered what drugs were available to ease the pain, mostly morphine. Where a bullet was lodged, a surgeon performed an operation using ether as an anaesthetic and removed it. Jennie and the nurses helped keep the patients' spirits up. Jennie arranged singing for those who were well enough, and she put on concerts. In the night, men traumatized from the fighting and the severity of their wounds moaned in pain in drugged sleep, and some suffered nightmares and cried out. It was a long and dismal watch for the night staff.

Jennie had for many years, and particularly following Lord Randolph's death, been a close confidante of the Prince of Wales. But all that was changing, as he was fiercely opposed to her marriage to George and took the side of the Cornwallis-Wests against her. Jennie had written again to the Prince, and he replied, on February 16, 1900, from Marlborough House, thanking her for her letter, and saying that he was sorry she had had a difficult journey to Cape Town. He congratulated her on her courageous work with the hospital ship and commented on her disappointment at not seeing George. Jennie replied to the Prince on March 10:

> I am satisfied with the Mission the *Maine* has fulfilled—& if I may say so my connection with it. It has been hard work & sometimes the temptation has been great to fly off in a mail steamer for home—but I am glad I resisted.

On March 29, Jennie was dining with Captain Scott aboard the HMS *Terrible* when the news broke of the relief of Ladysmith. The city of Durban went wild with excitement, and back home in London crowds massed in the streets and sang "Soldiers of the Queen."

When Jack recovered, and after having been photographed for posterity with his mother, he returned to his regiment. He would not allow his prior lack of experience of active service to stand in his way as a soldier.

The *Maine* was laden with wounded being invalided out of the army. They set sail for England, putting in along the way at Madeira for fresh supplies and water. Sergeant Grantham, the tuberculosis patient, died at midnight, while Jennie was off the ship. She organized Grantham's funeral at Funchal.

The *Maine* arrived back at Southampton in April 1900 carrying over 350 wounded soldiers. The press reported that as the ship sailed into the dock, Jennie stood on the deck looking radiantly healthy. She wore a blue serge dress and the *Maine* badge over her left breast. Round her neck was a red cravat (neck band) pinned with a Red Cross broach. The blue silk ribbons, embossed with the American flag, fluttered in the breeze on her white straw boater. She had brought back with her a lizard, a chameleon.[44]

The *Maine* would sail again only nine days later, but Jennie would not be on board. The reason given was "political," in that the United States did not support the war. But that stance had not deterred her going out in the first place.

On her return home she faced financial problems. The *Anglo-Saxon Review* was failing to make money, and the funds provided by the syndicate were fast running out along with those she had borrowed to set it up.[45] Perhaps a piece in the December 1900 issue of the *Review* titled "Impressions and Opinions" told better Jennie's reasons for not going out again with the *Maine:*

> The fight is not for victory but for conquest. We do not ask for our beaten foes to make terms; we require an unconditional submission and the surrender of their territory. There is no question of treating for peace. . . . Nothing can be more cowardly than to say to a general: Do what you think proper. Burn farms, starve women, lay waste land, shoot, hang and plunder. But for Heaven's sake don't tell *us* anything about it.[46]

It summed up the opposition that already existed to the war in the United States, and the revulsion that was building in the United Kingdom, as stories filtered back from South Africa that the Boer women and children had been forced out of their homes and farms and herded into the first known concentration camps, where thousands were dying of illness, disease, and malnutrition.

Jennie did not go out again on the next voyage, but she continued for a time with her administrative work for the *Maine.*

Thirteen

BROTHERS IN ARMS:
WAR IN SOUTH AFRICA

1899–1900

After suffering several early defeats in battle, the ponderous weight of the British army drove the Boers back and captured their capital cities. Before they would surrender on May 31, 1902, the Boers, fighting in fast-moving and hard-hitting commandos, humiliated the British in a long and costly guerrilla war.

In the summer of 1899, both Winston and Jack were living at home with their mother at 35A Great Cumberland Place in London. Winston, having prepared for publication his new book, *The River War*[1] (mentioned previously), which also told the story of his service in the Sudan, was now vigorously pursuing a career in politics. He was on the lookout for a political opportunity. It came his way somewhat unexpectedly. He had been invited to speak on Conservative policy at a public meeting of the Conservative Party branch of the Oldham parliamentary constituency in Manchester on June 15. On June 17, Oldham's senior MP died, and Winston was asked to stand for election for the vacant seat. Oldham was a large borough and in those days had two seats. The member for the other seat resigned, meaning both seats were up for election.

On June 20, Winston wrote to Pamela Plowden, saying he was beginning his speaking engagements that night at Oldham in the buildup to the election.[2] On June 26, he wrote to his mother asking her to come and campaign for him. He told her that if she brought Pamela there would be no room for either of their maids. If she (Jennie) could not do without her maid, she was to put Pamela off.[3]

Winston had a throat infection, and Dr. Robson Roose had promised to send him down a special spray. On June 28, Winston wrote to Pamela that his meeting the previous night had been a great success and he had spoken for fifty minutes, but that his throat was no worse. He had, he said, arranged for copies of all the local newspapers, which contained excellent reports of his speeches, to be sent to her. He said he was sorry that she had not been able to come to Oldham and that he had asked his mother to give her an account of the meetings.[4]

He wrote to her again on July 2,[5] saying he would not attempt to forecast the result of the election. He was unsure how the trades unions would vote. The stumbling block was the Clerical Tithes Bill. And again on July 2,[6] he told Pamela that he had made eight speeches to packed halls. Pamela had given him a lucky charm, and he said he was wearing it and that he had had her in his mind more than ever that week. There can be little doubt that Winston was building up to propose marriage if he won the election. Members of Parliament were not paid unless they were cabinet ministers, but with his increased status as member for Oldham, he would have been given paid speaking engagements around the country, and the publicity would have increased the sales of his forthcoming book. He concluded his letter by saying that he was glad to think that when it was all over they would meet up at Blenheim Palace on July 15 for "another quiet Sunday," which gives the impression they were in the habit of meeting there away from society's gaze.

The election was to take place on July 6, and Winston wrote to his mother again, on July 2, saying he would like her to come down and help him and that his campaign was going well.[7] Jennie set out with confidence, as she had formerly campaigned for his father in Oldham. Before she arrived, Winston made the tactical blunder in the week of the election of attacking the government and Tory Party's position over a minor Clerical Tithes Bill, which was intended to benefit the clergy of the Church of England and its schools, referring in his election address to "lawlessness in the Church."[8] When the election results were made public on the evening of July 6, Winston had been beaten into third place by the two successful Radical candidates.[9] Despite Winston's defeat, he was encouraged by his mother and the Conservative Party leader, Arthur Balfour, to try again.

Winston then went to the quiet of Blenheim Palace (where he got on very well with Sunny Marlborough, the 9th duke), to continue with his writing. In a letter to his mother of August 13, he said he was working on proofs of *The River War,* and he was looking forward to Pamela coming to join him on Wednesday, August 15.[10]

OVER A NUMBER of years in South Africa, the high commissioner of Cape Colony, Alfred Milner, wanted to gain the gold mines in the Dutch Boer republics of Transvaal and the Orange Free State for the British Empire. He also wanted to create a Cape-to-Cairo confederation of British colonies to dominate the African continent, and he wanted to rule over it.

In 1899 a crisis had arisen between the Boer republics and the British government over the lack of voting rights for the huge numbers of non-Boer (mostly British) workers in the goldfields (the Uitlanders). The British government ordered extra troops to South Africa from India as the crisis deepened. In September, Winston secured a position as war correspondent in South Africa with the *Morning Post.*

The Second Boer War between the Boers and the British broke out on October 11. On October 14, Winston sailed for Cape Town on the SS *Dunottar Castle.* By coincidence, on the same ship was General Sir Redvers Buller, going out to take command of the army in South Africa, and specifically that month as commander of the Natal field force. Expecting to take up an old offer Buller had made previously to be found a place on his staff, Winston, keen to be in the actual fighting as a soldier, pulled what strings he could to secure a regimental commission, but to no avail.

With the Boers launching a quick offensive before the British were really prepared for war, Winston's greatest fear was that the war would be over before he got to the front. With two other journalists, Winston left the ship at Cape Town and used rail and boat to get into Natal four days ahead of Buller. He immediately set off for Ladysmith, having hired a special train, but got no farther than Estcourt, for the Boers had blocked the line.

It was at the suggestion of Captain Aylmer Haldane, 2nd Gordon Highlanders, a friend from army days in India, that Winston was taken along on an armored train carrying Haldane's troops, which was making a reconnaissance for the army, out toward the Boer position at Colenso on the Tugela River in Northern Natal. The force set off on November 15, 1899. On its way back the same day, the Boers ambushed the train, and three cars were derailed, one of them blocking the line and preventing the safe passage of the engine, tender, and two other train cars. Captain Haldane commanded the infantry on board in its efforts to suppress the enemy fire, while "Mr. Churchill, the special correspondent of the *Morning Post*" (as the British press would later describe him), endeavored to clear the line. Winston displayed great personal courage under fire while encouraging soldiers to manhandle the derailed coach out of the way so that the engine, carrying a number of wounded men, could escape.

Having seen the engine safely away, Winston returned to the fray, and, as the Boers closed in, he was made prisoner with two officers and fifty soldiers. They were taken to the States Schools prison at Pretoria. All eyewitnesses agreed that, if he had been a serving soldier at the time, he would have merited a Victoria Cross, which is the highest military decoration awarded to members of the armed forces for valor in the face of the enemy. For Winston the incident was a huge boost to his fame and glory, and he was taken into captivity at Pretoria on a perverse wave of British press euphoria.

The news flew around the world by cable; his mother knew of his capture the next day, and Jack cabled her on November 17, assuring her that he had heard Winston was not wounded and had been splendidly brave.

Winston wrote to Pamela on November 18 from the State Model School, Pretoria, where he was being held prisoner.[11] He told her he thought of her often. He was, he said, hoping to be released as he had been taken unarmed and had his credentials as a press correspondent, proving he was not on active service.

Winston wrote to his mother on the same day, suggesting that, since he was only a press correspondent, the Boers might not keep him captive.[12] By the time that letter reached London on New Year's Day 1900, he had already escaped.

When Pamela received news of Winston's escape, she sent his mother a telegram containing just two words: "Thank God."[13]

In a story made famous by Winston himself, and more recently told in vivid and immaculate detail by his granddaughter Celia Sandys,[14] he escaped prison on the night of December 11 by climbing over a wall into a garden while the sentry was lighting his pipe. Other prisoners were meant to join him, and he waited in the bushes about one and a half hours for them. When they did not appear, Winston decided to strike out on his own for the nearest railway line, with a plan to "jump" a train to get away to Portuguese East Africa. With the greatest good fortune, at the first house he approached with an unlikely story of being a doctor who had fallen from a train, he fell in with the thoroughly loyal British manager of the Transvaal and Delagoa Bay Collieries, Mr. John Howard. By December 18, the Boers had posted Winston's description, with a £25/$120 reward for his capture, "dead or alive." Next day Howard and his friends smuggled Winston on board a train bound for Lourenço Marques, capital of Mozambique, situated on the north bank of the Espirito Santo River. Once inside neutral Portuguese East Africa, Winston passed through the British consulate and sailed for Durban in South Africa. On December 23, 1899, he landed there to a hero's welcome. But Winston wanted to return to the seat of the war immediately and took a train for Pietermaritzburg, intending to join Buller's forces. On Christmas Eve, he rested just a few hundred yards from the spot where he had been captured on November 15.

It is known in the Churchill family that Winston and Pamela became secretly engaged that Christmas.[15] Since Winston did not return home for some months, the proposal must have been made by letter. The engagement had been kept secret because, as yet, Winston did not have sufficient income with which to marry. Couples were expected to marry within a month and certainly within three months of their engagement.

At the beginning of January 1900 Buller granted Winston, of whom he wrote "He really is a fine fellow,"[16] a commission as lieutenant in the South African Light Horse regiment.[17] To Winston's great delight and good fortune, Buller did not require him to give up his paid employment as a press correspondent. Winston would repay his generosity by writing an impassioned appeal in the *Morning Post* for more Englishmen to come forward and join the South African Light Horse.

THERE WAS SOMETHING for Jack too, when Winston cabled him that Lieutenant Colonel Julian Byng, commander of the 1st South African Light Horse, was offering Jack the command of a troop in the regiment.[18] Jack sent his acceptance by return, and was on his way in the first week of January.

The whole Churchill family was rallying to the British cause in its hour of need. As has been seen in the previous chapter, Jennie was on her way to Cape Town on the hospital ship *Maine*. Jack was able to meet up with her there and join the ship and accompany her to Durban, which they reached at the end of January 1900. He told Jennie, somewhat jovially, that she was arousing some "jealousy," for her sister-in-law, Georgiana Curzon, Lady Howe, was trying to organize a Yeomanry ambulance medical unit for service in South Africa. Winston's and Jack's cousin Sunny, 9th Duke of Marlborough, was going out as a Yeomanry officer to take up a staff appointment; his young son John, aged two years, was the only Churchill male not in uniform.

On January 10, Winston wrote to Pamela from Chieveley, Natal.[19] He said he had received her letter in which she told him her half-brother Rupert was critically ill. Rupert was a son by the second marriage of Pamela's father to her stepmother. Winston's reply was full of descriptions of how the Boer War was being conducted. He was, he said, afraid that Ladysmith would fall and all his friends led off again by the Boers into captivity. Writing again on January 28, Winston told Pamela he had received five letters she had written him in a week, so clearly her concern had intensified.[20] He told her they had lost in battle 70 officers and 1,500 men. He would not, however, comply with her wish to return home. His mother and Jack were arriving that day at Durban on the hospital ship *Maine,* and he asked her why she had not come out as a secretary, providing an opportunity for them to be together. The scenes on Spion Kop, he said, were among the most terrible he had ever witnessed. The *Maine* would take 200 men to be nursed. He had been five days under shellfire.

Jack, just nineteen years old, and only two days in the country, rode out with his brother with the South African Light Horse, who were attempting to relieve Ladysmith, which was besieged by the Boers. On February 12, with a patrol mission accomplished, the Light Horse was riding back to camp. Winston, with that second sight that came with experience of patrolling on the North-West Frontier and on the veldt, suddenly felt the situation to be dangerous and warned his men accordingly. Immediately they came under very heavy Mauser fire, and the regiment dashed over a crest some two hundred yards off before dismounting and returning fire.

In the ensuing firefight Jack, who was crouching on a slope in the line beside Winston, gave a sudden jump and wriggled back down the slope. He had been shot in the calf by a Mauser bullet that Winston said (because of his crouching position) had narrowly missed his head.[21] Winston helped Jack back to an ambulance wagon and, after the skirmish was over, visited him in the field hospital. Winston then ensured that Jack was placed in an ambulance and sent a letter with him to their mother, dated February 13, saying the field doctors had told him Jack's wound would take a month to heal. A number of works state that Jack was the first wounded man on the *Maine,* but other enlisted men had been treated earlier. But by an extraordinary coincidence the first wounded officer received by Jennie on the *Maine* was her son Jack.

While Jack convalesced, Winston rejoined the South African Light Horse (SALH) for the relief of Ladysmith. Lord Douglas Dundonald was in command of the South Natal Field Force and took command of the 2nd Cavalry Brigade, which, on February 28, entered Ladysmith. On February 26, Lord Dundonald had walked over from his brigade headquarters to the bivouac of the SALH, where he found Colonel Julian Byng laughing. "I must tell you what Winston said this evening," Colonel Byng went on: "Winston said he wanted to get the DSO [Distinguished Service Order], as it would look so nice on the Robes of the Chancellor of the Exchequer." He added, "I told him he must first get into Parliament, if he could get any constituency to have him!"[22]

Byng could not have known that Winston was now so famous in England that the Southport Conservative Association, in a seaside town on Merseyside (near Liverpool), had already cabled asking him to stand as their next parliamentary candidate in an election. With commendable loyalty he replied that he felt obliged to contest Oldham again at the next opportunity.

That February, Winston's romantic novel, *Savrola,* was published by Longmans. It is full of gunfights, heroism, and danger. The hero Savrola, who is obviously meant to be Winston, is a democrat who leads the fight against a dictator, Molara. There are complications when Savrola, however, falls in love with Molara's wife. Leonie Leslie had written letters to Winston in which she helped him with the love scenes.[23] There were reviews in the press in both New York and London, and it was described as "brilliant," "witty," and an "exciting political tale."[24]

On February 21, Winston replied to two letters from Pamela.[25] She had told him that Rupert, aged four years, had died. His reply begins "My Pamela," which would tend to confirm that they had got engaged, as previously he addressed her mostly as "Miss Pamela." Winston was about to face the biggest battle, and his letter continued that with God's help they would relieve Ladysmith the following day. He was, however, not sympathetic about the death of Rupert, saying she shouldn't suffer for other people's trouble. He felt the deaths of babies were the least sad of partings, and that women felt them most. He considered the loss of a strong man, meaning a soldier in battle, more important. Continuing the letter on February 25, he plunged into a description of the horrors of the fighting and that his regiment was struggling toward Ladysmith.

Buller's army remained relatively inactive and in early April Winston was able to obtain an extended leave of absence from his regiment. Field Marshal Sir Frederick Roberts (who, it will be recalled, was promoted to commander in chief, India, by Winston's father when he was secretary of state for India) was in command of troops relieving Kimberley. The *Morning Post* applied for Winston to join Lord Roberts's main army as it prepared to march on the Boer capitals of Bloemfontein and Pretoria. Winston found himself cooling his heels at Cape Town without the necessary accreditation (the army's permission to act as a war correspondent). He applied to two friends on Roberts's staff, Ian Hamilton and William Nicholson, to help him, and they had to tell him that some of his writings had greatly upset Lord Roberts. His friends were able to patiently win their chief over, and Winston at last received the press accreditation. Colonel Neville Chamberlain wrote to Winston, on April 11, that Lord Roberts was willing to have him as a press correspondent "for your father's sake."[26] Winston attached himself to Ian Hamilton's fighting command as it protected the flank of the main army in its relentless northward advance. The dispatches Winston wrote at this time were later published in book form as *Ian Hamilton's*

March and did much to add luster to that popular general's name.[27] Hamilton later asked Winston to carry his dispatches back to Lord Roberts, and he was able to tell Roberts that Johannesburg was taken. In the long talks about this, they restored their previously friendly relationship, which dated from the time Winston's father had introduced them in 1894.

JACK, HAVING LONG since recovered from his wound, had rejoined the 1st South African Light Horse in February. On April 3, he wrote to his mother of the dreary service in and around Ladysmith:

> We are still here in this camp [Chieveley] to which you came to tea, and the life is becoming very monotonous. Winston has gone off to the other side to join Lord Roberts, and although he has left his ponies and a good deal of his kit here, I doubt whether we shall see him again. At present there is no attempt at a move on this side, and it is getting very tiring. . . . But the health of the regiment is good and I feel as fit as a fiddle.[28]

Jennie wrote to Winston, May 20, and she clearly wanted Winston home from the fighting and married:[29]

> You know what you are to me and how you can *now* and *always* count on me—I am intensely proud of you and apart from this—my heart goes out to you and I understand you as no other woman ever will—Pamela is devoted to you and if your love has grown as hers—I have no doubt it is only a question of time for you 2 to marry—what a comfort it will be to you to settle down in comparative comfort—I am sure you are sick of the war and its horrors—you will be able to make a decent living out of your writings and your political career will lead you to high things—Probably if you married an heiress you would not work half so well.

By the end of April, Jack was wondering why he had not heard a word from his mother since he last saw her on March 17, before she sailed for home on the *Maine*. By June, with still no word from any of his family, Jack was feeling really neglected, for he did not know that his mother was not to be aboard the *Maine* when it returned to South Africa. He wrote to her on June 2:

> I am beginning to feel like the prodigal son who is sent away to these horrible colonies with instructions never to be seen or heard of again. I have not heard one word of you or about you since you sailed away from Durban

nearly 3 months ago. I picked up an old *Vanity Fair* the other day and found that you were probably not coming out again. That and a little paragraph in some Natal paper saying that the *Maine* had sailed again for Cape Town [on its second voyage] is all I have heard or seen since you left. I expect I shall find a lot of letters waiting for me somewhere—but my squadron has been detached from the regiment and we have been roaming about on our own for some time.[30]

Jack regretted not applying to rejoin the Yeomanry cavalry that was serving with Roberts's principal field army as it advanced on Pretoria, which would have meant he would have been with Winston. He had, however, vowed to himself that he would stick with the SALH until the end of its service. In common with most soldiers at the time he thought the end for the Boers was not far off and hoped to be home by August. As the nights grew colder and he often camped out with just a blanket, he was critical of the cautious approach of General Buller. The nastier side of the war was intruding itself by now, and he wrote to his mother:

We have been doing a little Rebel hunting round here. It is very sickening to find these devils smiling in their comfortable farms when all the loyal farmers have had their places sacked and often burnt. However we have packed a good many off to prison. Some of them are almost pure English and they meet you at the doors of their farms with beaming faces saying they have waited so long for our troops. And then when the evidence comes along you find they have been shooting at you for the last 6 months.[31]

On June 26, Jack finally heard from his mother. She had been writing to Winston, telling him to send her letters on to Jack, which he had failed to do. Jennie had been wondering why she got no reply.

Soon after her return from South Africa, Jennie heard that the Prince of Wales's mistress, Alice Keppel, was about to deliver a child, widely believed to be fathered by the Prince.[32] Jennie immediately arranged her marriage to George Cornwallis-West. She asked Jack to come home for the wedding, but he could not leave his regiment. She was also rather desperate to get him back into the employ of Sir Ernest Cassel, lest he renege on their arrangements and take on someone else. Before long, Winston was also writing to advise Jack to chuck the regiment and get back home to work. They were already seeking financial advice from Jack, and clearly wanted him home for that purpose.

Jack, with a new sense of confidence born of active service, was not to be put upon quite so easily. His squadron had rejoined the regiment, and they had been very busy. In an exciting week they had played a leading part in a major move by Buller to turn the Boers out of formidably strong positions.

Jack heard that Winston was leaving South Africa for home on July 4 and had a twinge of regret that he was not joining him. In his next letter home, Jack pointedly remarked that one letter from his mother and one cable from Winston (saying he was leaving) was the sum total of his mailbag to date. He skirmished with the enemy on a daily basis. He noted that nearly all the war correspondents were going home and deduced from this that the war must soon finish. He hoped so, for "the novelty has worn off, and even a little fight does not seem to exercise the men much."[33]

His next letter to Winston, on July 10, described some very significant fighting, but opened with a gibe against having only City of London work to return to: "although I am very sick of all this here, I should feel very unhappy if I were home before it is all over. The quills of the City can I think wait a little while and so can the arms of the ladies."

JENNIE AND GEORGE were married in St. Paul's Church, Knightsbridge, on July 28. She was beautiful and George adored her, and she was again seizing the headlines in society. The bride wore a gown of pale blue chiffon, with real lace and ostrich feathers in her toque. She was given away by the Duke of Marlborough (Sunny), and the best man was a friend of George's from the Scots Guards, Lieutenant H. C. Elwes. The guests were the best of society, including the American Ambassador Choate.[34] The Prince of Wales called on her before the wedding and gave her a wedding present of a little gold pig set in jewels. Instead of bringing a dowry she brought a raft of unpaid bills for George to settle.

A short letter of August 5 acknowledged a wire to Jack from his mother, who was still trying to get him to come home. He said he would like to do so, but had no intentions of leaving the regiment while there was work to be done. Buller was just starting a major sweep toward the frontiers of Portuguese East Africa, and Jack expected the SALH would "have the fun" if there was any. Jack wrote to Winston, on September 12, 1900, about his increasing annoyance at the general abuse directed toward Buller, mainly by the men of Lord Roberts's army, for Buller's slowness in relieving the siege of Ladysmith. He reminded him of some of the fierce fighting in the broad sweeping operations against the Boers.

In one particular action, to prevent the escape of a Boer wagon train, Jack's troop was ordered by Colonel Byng to lead a charge over very steep ground. Obeying instantly, Jack found himself under increasingly heavy fire. Then, his letter continued,

> finding that I only had about 5 men left I jumped . . . into a donga (a dry
> water gulley). I crawled back to the regiment & was very glad to find that

only one man had been hit, the rest had taken cover earlier. The Colonel said he was very sorry I had gone & that he had tried to stop me etc. . . . But why 15 mounted infantry should be ordered to charge Boers in position on a mountain road I don't know. The order was cancelled almost as soon as given but I had started. It was a very exciting ride but rather unhealthy.[35]

Jack surely deserved a gallantry award for this display of courage and leadership. Perhaps his colonel realized that he had made a serious error of judgment in ordering the charge and did not wish to draw attention to the matter.

Jack's last two letters to Jennie and Winston from South Africa, dated October 3, display a maturity that had been building over these months of active service. Campaigning was as tough as ever. The rainy season had set in, and they were saturated all the time.

This battle-hardened twenty-year-old could now stand up very firmly for his Natal army when it was routinely abused by Lord Roberts's men. His vocabulary was no doubt improving all the time, and to Winston he wrote on October 3:

The ill-feeling here between our Natal Army and "the other side" is growing more and more. It is such a pity. But it drove me mad in Pretoria hearing everybody abusing Buller. I went on a 40 mile trek the other day as escort to a convoy to Nelspruit. We were received by a staff officer who asked what he could do for the "jam army." Did we want more jam? Really we ate an awful lot. We told him we thought him very unkind to grudge us food considering we did all the fighting for him. We also mentioned his impudence in uncomplimentary terms and he went away his red collar and face blazing.[36]

He also stood up to his elder brother in a very firm manner. "I am very glad now that I did not chuck the regiment at Standerton. It would have been very uncomfortable coming home for no reason whatever while the fighting was still going on. I wonder that you advised me to do so. They are not saying nice things about those who have gone home just because they are sick of it." Having stuck it out, Jack could take his leave of South Africa confident that he had done his duty and had enriched his life beyond imagining.

By the autumn of 1900 many believed the fall of the Boer capital cities, Pretoria and Bloemfontein,[37] signified the end of the war, and Jack took the opportunity to return to the United Kingdom. Before he left, Julian Byng wrote this high commendation to Winston:

Volkerust 23.X. [1900]

My dear Winston

I am sending Jack home now as to all appearances the war as a war is over though I am afraid there is a lot of dirty work still to be done but I cannot let Jack go without sending you a line to say how well he has done. Of course I always knew he would, but still I thought I would let you know how all his good work has been appreciated by me.

Since Ladysmith the Regt. has always been at it—with scarcely a week's rest anywhere—and had some exceedingly hard work and heavy losses. Jack has always done his share with the greatest keenness—he is most gallant in action, and most trustworthy and hard working in camp. In fact I am very sorry to lose him. . . .

I don't know what is to become of us but it looks very bad for getting home for some time. . . . But Jack will tell you the situation better than I can write it and will also narrate all our doing since you left.

Ever yours

J. Byng.[38]

His Grace the 7th Duke of Marlborough, John Winston Spencer-Churchill of Blenheim Palace (the father of Lord Randolph Spencer-Churchill), when he was Viceroy of Ireland, taken circa 1877.

Her Grace the Duchess of Marlborough, Frances Spencer-Churchill (née Vane), the daughter of Lord Londonderry, when she was Vicereine of Ireland, taken circa 1877.

Lord Randolph Churchill as a rising political star in the Conservative Party, circa 1880.

Lady Randolph Churchill (Jennie) in riding habit in Ireland, 1877, photographed on the steps of the Viceregal Lodge, Phoenix Park, Dublin, during the time the 7th Duke of Marlborough was Viceroy of Ireland.

Left to right: John (Jack) Spencer-Churchill aged seven years; Lady Randolph Spencer-Churchill (Jennie) aged thirty-three; Winston Spencer-Churchill aged thirteen years, photographed at Blenheim Palace, 1887.

Winston and John (Jack) Spencer-Churchill wearing their South African Light Horse Regiment uniforms as soldiers during the Second Boer War, 1900. During the early part of the war they served together side by side.

The wedding of Captain John (Jack) Spencer-Churchill, aged twenty-eight years, and Lady Gwendeline Bertie, aged twenty-three years, taken outside the bride's family home, Wytham Abbey, Oxfordshire, August 8, 1908. Winston was best man. Jack's regiment, the Oxfordshire Hussars (in the background) formed a guard of honor outside the Church of St. Aloysius, at Oxford. Photograph provided by the kind permission of His Grace the 11th Duke of Marlborough.

Captain John (Jack) and Lady Gwendeline (Goonie) Spencer-Churchill on holiday on a cruise ship later in the year of their marriage, 1908.

Lieutenant George Cornwallis-West, Jennie's second husband, at the time of his marriage, 1900.

Left to right: Colonel the 9th Duke of Marlborough, KG, PC (Charles "Sunny" Spencer-Churchill); Major Viscount Churchill, GCVO (Victor Spencer); Major Winston Spencer Churchill, MP; and Major John (Jack) Spencer-Churchill; taken on a training exercise with their regiment, the Oxfordshire Hussars, circa 1912.

The Churchill family, 1914, taken at Admiralty House when Winston was First Lord of the Admiralty. Left to right: Winston Spencer-Churchill; his eldest daughter, Diana; seated, his wife, Clementine (Clemmie), with baby Sarah on her lap; his son Randolph; his mother, Jennie; seated, Lady Gwendeline Spencer-Churchill (Goonie), with her younger son Peregrine, aged one year, on her lap; standing, her elder son Johnny, aged five years; standing, Major John (Jack) Spencer-Churchill.

The staff of the hospital ship Maine, taken below deck in the wards, 1900. Left to right: seated, Sister Ruth (Miss) Manly; Lady Randolph Spencer-Churchill ("Sister" Jennie); Miss Eleanor Warrender; Sister Sarah (Miss) McVean. Standing: Dr. Weber; Sister Virginia (Miss) Ludekins; Colonel H. F. Jensman, in command of the ship; Captain Stone; Dr. Dodge; Sister Margaret (Miss) McPherson.

Blenheim Palace, Woodstock, Oxfordshire, 1934 (the seat of their Graces the 7th Duke and Duchess of Marlborough, the parents of Lord Randolph Spencer-Churchill), looking much as it did when Jennie (née Jerome), Lady Randolph Spencer-Churchill first arrived as a bride to live there in May 1874.

Fourteen

GETTING ON

1900–1906

Lord Salisbury continued as Queen Victoria's favorite Conservative prime minister. But in January 1901 the British nation was plunged into mourning when Queen Victoria died. The following day, the Prince of Wales was crowned King Edward VII. On July 11, 1902, in failing health, Lord Salisbury resigned as prime minister. His nephew Arthur Balfour became the new prime minister. His administration lasted until December 1905 when the Liberal Henry Campbell-Bannerman became prime minister of a minority government. He called a general election for January 12– February 8 1906, in which the Liberals won a large majority.

Winston had written to his mother from Pretoria on June 9, 1900, saying he was anxious to return to politics and Pamela.[1] He arrived home from South Africa on July 20. Sometime after that date the relationship between Winston and Pamela broke down, but it is unclear what went wrong or why Pamela went off him. Pamela was now twenty-six years old, and Winston had kept her waiting for over three years. He had been either preoccupied with his political career or out of England in the army. Meanwhile, Pamela was at home and meeting other eligible young bachelors at dinner parties and balls. That their engagement had been kept a secret meant that other men would ask her to marry them. Jennie had written to Jack, who was still serving in the Boer War, that Winston had been neglecting Pamela. On June 23 she wrote: "I can't think what he is about—I hear he has not written to Pamela for 8 weeks."[2]

When Jennie married George Cornwallis-West that July, he moved into 35A Great Cumberland Place with her. Luckily for the happy couple, George's father did not disinherit him, and his allowance, though not very great, supplemented in the short term what little money he had of his own.

In October, having done his duty faithfully to his country in the Boer War, Jack returned home from South Africa a mature young man to a familial landscape that had changed dramatically. His mother presented him with a stepfather not much older than himself. Churchill family recollections are, however, that George got on well with his two stepsons. Jennie was wrapped up in her new husband, and Winston had moved out of the house into a flat, 105 Mount Street, London. There was no further mention of Jack pursuing a career other than working for Cassel, and he was obliged to return to work he openly despised in the City of London.

Also that October Jack confided to George that he had heard gossip in town that Pamela was engaged to two other men.[3] The news was a dreadful blow to Winston. Leonie, who was Winston's favorite aunt, was over from Ireland holidaying with Jennie and George. Winston told her about the situation, and Leonie went to see Pamela. Pamela told Leonie she did not want to hurt those who had proposed to her by refusing them.[4] Jean Hamilton, who was a friend of Pamela's from the time they lived in Simla, India, had a different angle on the story, and wrote in her diary:

> I remembered the little scene she [Pamela] had told me about, with such bitter tears, when in a ballroom he [Winston] had gone up to her, and brutally asked her "if she had no pride, because he had heard she was going about saying that Winston had treated her badly."[5]

In terms of finances, Jennie was as extravagant as ever. George had been obliged to resign his commission in the army over hostility in his regiment to his marriage and now had to find work. His commanding officer, Colonel Dalrymple Hamilton, had told him that if he married Lady Randolph Churchill he would have to leave the regiment.[6] Jennie once again sought the assistance of Ernest Cassel, who knew of a vacancy with the engineering company British Thomson-Houston, contractors for the Central London Railway. Initially, when he started work, circa November 1900, George became one of the unpaid members of the company's staff in Glasgow, in order to learn the business.[7] He would stick to the work and eventually, within the year, become chairman of the company,[8] and later of several others, and did really well. He was working in Scotland five days a week and living there while Jennie was in London working on the *Anglo-Saxon Review.* They met only at weekends when he arrived back in London.

As the widow of a former cabinet minister and titled lord, Jennie had enjoyed privilege of entrée, which meant she was invited to private teas by Queen Victoria in her drawing room. When she remarried, it was withdrawn, and no reason was given. Other titled aristocratic women had remarried and had not been treated in this way. A defiant Jennie eventually dropped the title Lady Randolph Churchill and called herself Mrs. George Cornwallis-West.[9] On August 10, 1901, while staying at Blenheim Palace, she had signed herself in the guest book as "Jennie Cornwallis-West."

The couple made a brave show of things, and when George came home from work from Scotland at weekends their time together was filled with endless rounds of parties and visits to country houses.

Winston had returned home on July 20, and was soon drawn into the election campaign in Oldham. The returning hero was well received by the Conservative Party and the press. His mother again campaigned for him in September. On October 1, Winston achieved a narrow victory by just over two hundred votes. The Conservative Party was back in government, with a majority of 134 seats. With an eye to his financial requirements, Winston, on October 30, embarked on a well-organized lecture tour of the United Kingdom, which netted him a profit of £3,782/$18,153. He had adopted much of Bourke Cockran's style of oratory and public debate, both on the platform and in the House of Commons: simple, honest, direct, eloquent, sharp, and to the point.[10]

Rather than take up his seat in Parliament, he left on December 1, 1900, for a lecture tour of America and Canada. On December 8, Winston arrived in New York, where he was met by Bourke Cockran. Despite his own strong opposition to the Boer War, Bourke gave Winston a warm welcome and organized a dinner for him at the Waldorf Hotel. Winston met President McKinley, and received an invitation to dine with Theodore Roosevelt, who was related to Jennie. Roosevelt, who was at this time governor of the state of New York and vice president elect of the United States, would eventually take office on March 4, 1901.

The lecture tour was in the hands of a Major J. B. Pond, who did not make much of a success of it in the United States. Pond did not organize very many talks, which meant Winston did not make as much money as he expected. Moving on to Canada, Winston had Christmas dinner with Earl Minto, governor general of Canada, another friend of his mother's. Winston grew disenchanted with Pond, and in a letter to his mother, on January 1, 1901, described him as "a vulgar Yankee impresario."[11] Apart from some success with speaking engagements in Canada, Winston was disappointed. Still, he made a profit of £1,600/$7,680 over two months, which, when added to his successful books and speaking engagements, meant he could boast to his mother in a letter on January 1 from Toronto of having made £10,000/$48,000 in two years, entirely by his own efforts. He wisely put most of the money in the safe hands of Ernest Cassel for investment.

On the day Winston completed his trip to America and set sail for home, January 22, 1901, Queen Victoria died. The next day the Prince of Wales was proclaimed King Edward VII. Winston wrote to his mother wondering, jokingly, if "the Keppel," as they called Alice, would be named "First Lady of the Bedchamber." The family had good cause to resent the powerful hold Alice now had over the former Prince of Wales. As king, Edward was privy to British cabinet papers and secrets that had previously been made known only to his mother. Jennie no longer had easy access to Bertie to further promote Winston's political career, at a time when it would have been most beneficial to him.

Winston took his seat in the House of Commons on February 14, 1901, and four days later made his maiden speech during a debate on a political settlement in South Africa. It was a good speech, arguing for a moderate approach to the Boers, to secure their early surrender and future friendship.

His next major intervention, in May, was in a debate over army estimates, in which he took up the tattered flag his father had fought under many years before. He took strong objection to an increase in army expenditure of some £5 million/$24 million a year, while accepting that the Royal Navy needed all the money spent upon it.

Although he annoyed many Conservatives with this stand, he caught the attention of the Liberal opposition, just as his father had done. Winston paid handsome tributes to Lord Rosebery, a great friend of Lord Randolph's. Winston even hoped for a while that he might create a new, centrist party. Like his father before him, he seemed to sit uneasily in the Tory ranks.

A RECONCILIATION BETWEEN Winston and Pamela did not take place, and Pamela married the "other man" in her life, Victor, 2nd Earl of Lytton, on April 3, 1902, at St. Margaret's Church, Westminster.[12] It was a beautiful society wedding, her father gave her away, and there were five bridesmaids and five pageboys.[13] Winston and Pamela would, however, remain friends.

Jack, meanwhile, had resumed his weekend duties with the Oxfordshire Hussars, and his recent combat experience was greatly appreciated within the regiment. In May, he attended a course of instruction at Aldershot, preparing him for promotion to captain and the command of a squadron. Jack would make a fine squadron commander. His horsemanship was superb, and he won the regimental cup for riding.[14]

At this time Winston set to work on a biography of his father, a project suggested by one of his publishers. He asked Jack to sort his father's papers for him. On August 15, 1902, Winston wrote to Jennie, saying that Jack was "very busy" with all the letters belonging to Lord Randolph, and how he had reduced them to good order. Jack had sorted and transcribed hundreds of letters and speeches to help Winston with the book. Jack may have undertaken this work to give him something interesting to do to relieve the tedium of a City office, as in his letter to his mother he complained how stuffy and hot it was in the office throughout the summer.

After all the inspection work Jack had done in Egypt for Cassel, it was Winston who, as a British MP, was invited by Cassel to be one of his special guests to attend the opening ceremony of the Aswan Dam, which was to take place on December 10, 1902. Cassel would have been aware that Winston was an up-and-coming member of Parliament, and he was also liberal in granting loans to Winston so that in the future they might mutually assist each other. On October 9, Winston wrote to Jack with this news, asking him to exercise his horses while he was away, and suggesting that he might speak to Cassel and get Jack a month off work in order to rest quietly at Blenheim Palace. It was at least partial recognition of how hard Jack was working on the book while holding his full-time job in the City. Winston thanked him for arranging "all the letters and scrapbooks."

A TRUCE HAD obviously now been called between King Edward VII and Jennie over his opposition to her marriage to George. Writing on March 23, 1902, the King told her he had made arrangements for her ticket to attend the coronation. On August 8, Edward and Alexandra were crowned King and Queen at Westminster Abbey. The King had invited several of his mistresses to the coronation, making available to them his personal box at the Abbey. The Earl of Crawford, who was the acting deputy marshal at the coronation, and something of a wit, dubbed it "the King's loose box," meaning a horse box.[15]

What Jennie said in private to Winston about Alice did not reflect her attitude to her when she met her at house parties, and no word of reproach ever passed between them. Jennie had deliberately made a friend in Alice Keppel, and they were often seen chatting together at social events. They were photographed together seated in the back of Bertie's first car, with him in the front. Bertie and Alice and Jennie and George dined together quite often. But Jean, Lady Hamilton revealed in her diary the bitterness simmering below the surface when they were part of a large gathering during a New Year's party at the house of Jennie's sister-in-law's Georgiana, Lady Howe:

> Mrs. George West and family departed to-day—an interesting, dominating woman; yesterday when she and I walked back together from skating, she told me that the other day she had said something about Fiscal Policy, and that Lady Howe and Co. had seemed so bored that she, Mrs. West, had flown into a rage, and said, "Oh, I forgot, nothing must be mentioned in this house but golf and bridge," and flounced out of the room. . . . Alice Keppel, she declared, seemed very anxious to be well informed, and to pass for a clever woman. . . . It was shocking how initiated [her daughter] little Violet Keppel is, and that on Xmas morning Mrs. West said to her, "What a lovely brooch—is it a Xmas present? Who gave it to you?" Violet looked carefully all round the room, then whispered "The King."[16]

FROM 1903, WINSTON had been increasingly disturbed by the swing in the Conservative Party toward protectionism—a tariff reform measure that would favor the produce of the British Empire by putting higher tariffs on foreign goods. The Conservatives were heading for electoral defeat, and Winston was anticipating a change of party as a shrewd move.

Like his father's, Winston's public speeches were radical, often in defense of workers' rights and against capitalist interests. In November 1903, in a speech at Halifax he had exclaimed, "Thank God for the Liberal Party." By January 1904, he was threatened with the loss of the position of party whip by the leader of the Conservative Party as a punishment for his being so at odds with the party on so many issues. Given that he was researching his father's stormy parliamentary career at this time, it must have seemed like life imitating art. On entering the House of Commons on May 31, 1904, Winston paused and looked about, before crossing the floor to sit beside a Liberal member from Wales, David Lloyd-George,[17] who was a friend of his. He had cast his lot with the Liberals—a step further than his father had taken.

In yet another parallel with his father's career, Winston now felt the full force of Tory rage, expressed both through their domination of the press and through the icy reaction of Tory society closing its doors to him. Of course, the Liberal grandees opened their doors to him, and he was marked out by them as a young man of great promise.

In the summer of 1904, Winston attended a ball given by Lord and Lady Crewe at their house in Curzon Street, London W1. Winston was intrigued by a beauty there, and asked his mother who she was. Jennie arranged an introduction and discovered that this beautiful girl was Clementine (Clemmie), the daughter of her old friend Lady Blanche Hozier. Clemmie recalled that Winston had stood and stared at her, but had not asked her to dance, and someone else whisked her off. He appeared to have lost all confidence with women and was far from over the loss of Pamela. Clemmie was only nineteen, and he was thirty, and he may have thought he was too old for her.

Following reports of his heroism in the Boer War in the press, Winston's books sold well, and he was now a very successful author.[18] On October 30, 1905, he was able to secure a very healthy advance of £8,000/$38,400 from Macmillan, his London publisher, for his forthcoming book, which was a major study of his father's political career that he had begun in 1902.[19]

In December 1905, the Tories, sensing imminent defeat, resigned as the governing party, and the Liberals were invited to form an administration until an election could be held. Henry Campbell-Bannerman became Liberal prime minister. Winston was immediately recognized by both the Liberal Party and the press, as his father had been before him, as a "coming man," meaning he was going to rise higher as a successful politician.[20] The Liberals offered Winston the post of financial secretary to the Treasury, a stepping-stone to the cabinet, but he knew that he was too new to politics to shine as a deputy to Herbert Asquith (Chancellor of the Exchequer, 1905–08). He had also been offered the position of under secretary to the colonies, and he accepted this position, knowing that he would handle all the department's work in the Commons, for the colonial secretary, Lord Elgin, sat in the House of Lords, and would therefore be unable to conduct business in the Commons.

The general election of January 1906 was a landslide victory for the Liberals. Winston won his seat as part of a Liberal-Labour clean sweep in Manchester. He was confirmed in his new post and worked hard at the Colonial Office, where Lord Elgin did not always enjoy his flamboyant style. Winston was often in a hurry, and as he was very ambitious, people sometimes found him arrogant.

JENNIE AND GEORGE were doing well financially, and Jennie wanted a house in the country. She decided to sell 35A Great Cumberland Place and buy a lease on a country home, Salisbury Hall, near St. Alban's, Hertfordshire. Although not a stately home, it had royal connotations of a saucy nature, as it was there, in 1669, that King Charles II set up his mistress, Nell Gwynne, who had been something of a comic actress and amused him. Jennie spent months refurbishing her new house, decorating it to a high standard, and buying new furniture and more antiques. In late 1905, she and George moved in. They had been happily married for just over four years.

George, who loved shooting, now had his own estate for pheasant shoots, and Jennie had taken up golf instead of riding.

A home in the country allowed Jennie to entertain the King and her other friends well away from the prying eyes of London society. Cordial relations now existed between her and the King and Alice Keppel. Her house book bears testament to the signatures of those who spent adulterous weekends there, as well as those making normal, social visits.[21] When Jennie selected Salisbury Hall as her new home, she clearly had it in mind to create a microcosm of the King's Marlborough House set. Here under her roof, in total privacy, married couples might sleep with other partners. A downstairs drawing room was specially converted for the King en suite, and she installed a four-poster bed specially for him for when he came to stay.[22] How could Bertie resist an invitation to an autumn shoot with his "son" George, followed by a fine dinner laid on by Jennie? Alice came with him. Their signatures appear in the house book on October 20, 1905, and May 26 and October 13, 1906.

George Cornwallis-West matured during the years of his marriage to Jennie. In addition to their enjoyment of hunting, shooting, and fishing, they took to the new thrill of motoring. The Wests were the first family in their circle to buy a motorcar. From around 1904, George had spent four years with the British Electric Traction Company, while earning a good income from his directorships, consultancy fees, and investments. In 1906, however, George got into financial difficulties when a lawyer swindled him out of £8,000. His brother-in-law, the Duke of Westminster, wrote to Winston that August, concerning George's financial problems, and offered to help him. To spare George any embarrassment, the duke sent immediately a check for £3,000/$14,400 to Winston, with whom he secretly agreed that the money should be paid into George's bank account under another pretext. Unfortunately, the economic boom did not last, and George lost out again in the stock market crash of 1907 when the value of his shares tumbled.

Jack was finding it too far to travel into the City of London each day by train from his mother's home in Hertfordshire, and he moved in with Winston for a time at his house, 12 Bolton Street, London, and sometimes spent weekends at the Duchess Lily's house at Dorking in Surrey. Jack's career had moved upward, and he was working as a stockbroker with the firm Nelke, Phillips and Company in the City. The exact date he started there is not known, but he was there in 1905, and had taken rooms at Throgmorton Street. He applied himself to the work but could never be said to have enjoyed it. In his approach to financial affairs he was essentially cautious, and was a constant source of steady advice to his brother. In 1906, he was made a partner in the firm. On August 23,[23] Jack wrote a long letter to Winston (who was staying at Ernest Cassel's house the Villa Cassel, in Riederfurka, Switzerland), relating to sharp movements on the stock exchange that had caught many dealers short; Jack was negotiating his way through carefully.

In 1906, Winston's two-volume biography of his father was published; it sold some 11,000 copies in three years. It is a magisterial work, which demonstrates what a great reforming parliamentarian Randolph was. There is, however, not one word of acknowledgment in the book to thank Jack for the huge amount of work he did.

IN MAY 1907, Winston was appointed a privy councilor. A Privy Council is a body that advises the head of state on how to exercise executive authority. The Liberal government was already finding much of its reforming legislation being blocked by the House of Lords, where 355 diehard Tories easily dominated the 124 Liberal Unionist and 88 Liberal peers. A powerful campaign developed to confront this problem, and the speeches got very radical indeed. Winston was very much associated with this movement, and was an ally of the fiery Liberal David Lloyd-George, who in 1906 was made president of the Board of Trade.

Jack was now of great use to his mother in respect of her complicated financial affairs. Lumleys, her solicitors, had still not finalized Lord Randolph's estate, twelve years after his death. Jennie wrote to Winston, on August 27, 1907, that Jack was "quite competent" to manage such matters. Jack's great joy was his weekends with the Oxfordshire Hussars, and his photography.

On the other hand, George Cornwallis-West's finances never recovered from the crash of 1907, and Jennie and George were in deep financial trouble. George, who had worked hard for years and done well, had to watch it rapidly disintegrate before his eyes between 1906 and 1907. His problems had been further compounded in 1907 by losses on the stock exchange caused by the financial panic in New York. It was very painful to him and he was taken ill with worry, and the doctor advised him to go on holiday. He went to St. Moritz by himself as they both could not afford to go. Jennie wrote to Winston, on November 21, "George hasn't been able to draw one penny from his business this year—so we have no nest egg to fall back on. It preys dreadfully on poor George, who is getting quite ill over it all."

From 1906, in a calculated attempt to make money, Jennie had been writing her autobiography, *The Reminiscences of Lady Randolph Churchill*. Winston helped her by proofreading some of the chapters. With an eye to the American market for the book, Jennie painted a view of her life as if she had been the queen of British society from the day she married. It was not an accurate depiction of her early married life and actually detracted from her better qualities displayed at that time. Future biographers would interpret her supposedly never-ending, glamorous lifestyle as being inconsistent with a caring mother. It was in this way that the myth grew up that Jennie neglected Winston. The colorful volume was published in 1907, and again in 1908, under the name of Mrs. George Cornwallis-West. It was a bestseller in America.

Fifteen

TWO BRIDES FOR
TWO BROTHERS

1907–1908

Henry Campbell-Bannerman remained prime minister until April 3, 1908. Herbert Henry Asquith, having served as Chancellor of the Exchequer since 1905, had acceded as Liberal prime minister on April 5, 1908. Asquith immediately made Winston Churchill president of the Board of Trade.

B y 1907 the Churchill brothers had matured into two very good-looking young men. Winston, at five feet eight inches tall, with red hair and pale skin and a high color in his cheeks, was slightly smaller than his younger brother. Jack always looked tanned from his outdoor pursuits, and was well developed physically from his horse-riding activities with the Oxfordshire Hussars at the weekends, though his black hair was somewhat sparse at age twenty-seven.

From the time he joined the regiment in 1898, Jack's duties meant he was often in camp near Blenheim Palace. A neighboring estate, Wytham Abbey, was owned by Montagu Arthur Bertie, the 7th Earl of Abingdon.[1] The Berties, a family of ancient, noble lineage, had known the Churchills for many years. Letters extant from 1890 show a ten-year-old Jack reporting that members of the Bertie family had been asking after his well-being.

Sometime in 1906–07, Jack found himself falling in love with the lovely Lady Gwendeline ("Goonie" as she was known in the family[2]), a daughter of the earl by his second marriage. Born on November 20, 1885, Goonie had been educated at home by a governess, which was usual for ladies of the aristocracy. She was tall, with a good figure, dark hair, clear, blue eyes, and pale complexion, and there was something of an air of innocence about her. Goonie was "not considered beautiful in the conventional sense of the word," but she was described as lovely, and was "adored by all who knew her."[3] It was her "atmosphere and charm"[4] that lent her a unique kind of inward beauty. She was a good conversationalist, and of a kind and understanding disposition, but witty, with a great sense of humor, and was very artistic, painting scenes in oils.

Jack and Goonie had been introduced by her same relative, Frank Bertie, who had introduced Randolph to Jennie in 1873.[5] From 1906, Jack became a frequent visitor to Wytham Abbey.

Their romance began in earnest in the early summer of 1907.[6] But as Jack had little in the way of money, and no title, they could not, for the time being, let her parents know about their romance. Jack used to make the seven-mile ride on horseback, from Blenheim to Wytham Woods, where Goonie would be waiting on horseback, and they met in secret. Meanwhile, Jack tried to improve his financial prospects sufficiently that he could approach her father for permission to marry her.

Jack wrote to Winston, who was in Africa for several months from October, in his role as under secretary to the colonies, November 14, 1907, that he was in love with Goonie, and that he had declared himself to her:

I am writing to tell you that a very wonderful thing has happened. Goonie loves me. I have loved her for a long time— *This is absolutely secret.* Only my mother and George know about it. Her parents know nothing. Nor must they— *until I can come with some proposition.*

Winston responded graciously. He would later write to his mother that Jack had a very much better understanding of women than he did, that he easily "got in touch" with them, and greatly depended on feminine influence "for the peace and harmony of his soul." Winston freely confessed to being "stupid and clumsy" in that respect.

Goonie's father, Montagu Arthur Bertie, was a severe man, though he was himself feckless with money, losing heavily at the races. He had converted to Roman Catholicism with his first wife, and though Goonie was by his second wife, the children were all brought up in the Catholic faith.[7] The young couple feared telling him of their romance lest he put a stop to it, for Jack as yet had not a great income that would keep a wife.

Due to panic selling of shares on New York's Wall Street that October, which affected Jack's income as a stockbroker, his income was not likely to increase immediately. But the faithful Goonie vowed to Jack that she would wait and wait, until he could come and claim her. There were serious problems with the copper market, and the price had slumped. Jack discussed this and his love life in a series of letters to Winston of 1907–08.[8] Jack's letter of November 14 continued: "I have only seen Goonie for two minutes at a Railway Station! Was there ever such a way of making love." But he had, he said, spoken to his employer, Mr. Paul Nelke, a senior partner in Nelke, Phillips and Company, the stockbrokers, about his financial prospects.

In December, Goonie plucked up her courage and told her mother of their love for each other, who then forbade her to see Jack. Hidden away in her old schoolroom in Wytham Abbey, she wrote in secret to Winston, December 16, pouring her heart out: "Jack and I are so happy, but, Winston is it not cruel that I am not allowed to see him & even writing is forbidden, though I do write all the same."

In Jack's next letter to Winston, January 2, 1908, he said Nelke would not guarantee him £1,000/$4,800 a year, but he would allow him £500/$2,400, a modest sum for a family of the Churchill- Bertie status, plus one percent of the profits of the firm. "Many people," he said, "marry on less." Goonie, he said, would "have something given to her," by way of a dowry, possibly £200/$960. "I am looking forward very much to your return in order to have your advice and your help." At that time, Jack had been able to bring some of Nathaniel Rothschild's business into Nelke Phillips, and he continued: "This has been a feather in my cap—and I have rubbed it in."

In June 1908, Jack approached Goonie's father, and he gave his consent to the marriage. The engagement ring was a family heirloom, a sapphire and diamond ring, that Randolph had given to Jennie—it was one of three. It had been his wish that one each would be passed down to his sons' intended brides. Jennie's house book for her country home, Salisbury Hall, shows that Goonie and Jack visited on July 3. Underneath Goonie's signature is Jack's, and a drawing of a heart with an arrow through the center.

Jack had agreed to be married in the Catholic Church, but in accordance with the law Catholics had also to register a civil marriage. Winston was to be the witness at the registry office, and best man at the church service. He came to stay for the wedding with his cousin, Captain Freddie Guest, and his wife, at a rented house, Burley Hall, near Oakham. After a jolly, and somewhat liquid, evening meal, they all went to bed. In the early hours of the morning of August 6, a fire started and everyone fled from the house, some still in their pajamas. The fire brigade arrived, and Winston, donning a fireman's helmet and taking control, proceeded to direct the operations of the firemen. An eyewitness later related how, in heroic style, Winston climbed a ladder onto the roof with a fire hose in his hand and tried to put out the blaze all by himself.[9]

On August 7, the registry office marriage took place as a formality only to satisfy the requirements of the state. On August 8, the lovely twenty-three-year-old Gwendeline was escorted down the aisle on her father's arm. Her wedding gown was of ivory satin charmeuse; the under sleeves were delicately ornamented with silver. She wore a wreath of myrtle, and a veil of white tulle, and carried a huge bouquet of roses and lilies. Her betrothed, Captain John Strange Spencer-Churchill, wore a morning suit in tails, as did Winston as best man. Goonie was served by five bridesmaids: her sister, Lady Elizabeth (Betty) Bertie; the Misses Doris and Olivia Harcourt, cousins of the bride; and the Misses Iris and Daphne Grenfell, cousins of the bridegroom. They wore dresses of white muslin over silk, tied with soft satin sashes of pale blue; on their heads they wore white lace caps. The pageboy was dressed in Directoire costume, a style inspired by the French Revolution, of white nankeen trousers and a blue satin coat. The Woodstock Squadron of the Queen's Own Oxfordshire Hussars, Jack's men, formed a guard of honor outside the church, making an arch of crossed swords.

The reception was hosted by the Earl and Countess at Wytham Abbey, and a sumptuous feast was provided for family and friends.

When the reception was over, the happy couple left by motorcar for Highgrove, Pinner, a house owned by Jennie's old flame from 1895, Hugh Warrender, which he had kindly lent them for the honeymoon. The men of the Oxford Yeomanry insisted on pulling the car some distance along the road. The presence of Winston, now a rising star in politics, ensured full press coverage of the wedding.

THE CHURCHILL FAMILY motto on their coat of arms, "Faithful But Unfortunate," was an apt description of Winston's romances to date. The thought of his political career and a life in the public eye, together with his lack of fortune and his adventures in war, was too daunting a prospect for most young ladies to whom Winston proposed. He and Pamela, now the Countess of Lytton, were on the best of terms. When he had left the previous October to go to Africa, Pamela had contacted him and had seen him off on the ship. They communicated by letter while he was away.

But a new love was about to enter Winston's life. He had met Clementine Hozier again in March 1908 when her great-aunt, Lady St. Helier, gave a dinner party at her London home. Clemmie was the daughter of Sir Henry Montague Hozier and Lady Blanche (née Airlie). Clemmie was also of noble and ancient lineage on her mother's side as her grandparents were the Earl and Countess of Airlie, who lived at Castle Airlie in Scotland. Henry had died in 1907, but Clemmie hardly knew her father. Her parents never got on and had lived apart from her childhood. Many years later, there were wild stories about who may or may not have fathered all the four Hozier children. There seems little doubt that Henry fathered Clementine and her elder sister Katharine (Kitty), who died young, aged fifteen, of typhoid fever. But there was a question mark over the twins born later, William (Bill) and Margaret (Nellie), whom Henry refused to recognize.[10]

Be that as it may, at Lady St. Helier's dinner party, Winston, having turned up late, seated himself in the chair next to Clemmie, with whom he had been partnered. On this occasion, he finally got up the courage to engage her in conversation. Now aged twenty-two, Clemmie had matured into a radiant, beautiful redhead, with a fine complexion and sparkling, green-hazel eyes. She possessed a natural charm and great intelligence, having been an excellent academic at school. Clemmie had been head girl at Berkhampstead School, where she excelled in French and German. When she left school, her mother was so hard up financially that Clemmie made a small living of her own, giving French lessons for payment. A firm Liberal, she had witnessed Winston in action in the Commons and was impressed by his speeches and admired him. He was taken by her beauty, charm, and intelligence, and they had something in common in their interest in politics. Clemmie was a no-nonsense type of girl, with her feet firmly on the ground, and was, without a doubt, the best girl in the world for Winston. Winston spent the rest of the evening in Clemmie's company. He asked her if she had read his recent biography of his father, and when she told him she had not, he offered to send her a copy, but true to Winston, he forgot to do so.

Herbert Henry Asquith, having served as Chancellor of the Exchequer since 1905, had acceded as Liberal prime minister on April 5, 1908. He and his wife, Margot, were friends of Jennie and Winston. Asquith immediately made Winston president of the Board of Trade. Winston's elevated political status and the salary that went with a cabinet minister's post meant that he had enough money on which to marry and provide for a wife. He asked his mother to invite Clemmie to spend the weekend of April 11 at Salisbury Hall. Their signatures appear in Jennie's house book. Clemmie wrote to Jennie, on Monday, April 13, thanking her for the weekend:

> At this moment your whole mind must be filled with joy & triumph for Mr. Churchill, but you were so kind to me that you made me feel as if I had known you always. I feel no one can know him, even as little as I do, without being dominated by his charm and brilliancy.

Unfortunately for the couple, Clemmie had to leave right away to accompany her mother to Germany, where her younger sister Nellie was being discharged from a clinic where she had been cured of tuberculosis, and Blanche was going to bring her home.

As a newly appointed cabinet minister, Winston was obliged to stand again in a by-election to retain his parliamentary seat of North-West Manchester, so a long and arduous campaign lay ahead for him during the time his beloved was away. The Hoziers were not due to return until the end of May as they were taking a holiday, so the separation between Winston and Clemmie was to last for six weeks. Absence duly made the heart grow fonder, and love was blossoming on both sides. Winston had found the woman he wanted to make his future wife, and he wrote to her frequently. In his first letter he told her, on April 16, 1908, that he took "comfort and pleasure" from meeting "a girl with so much intellectual quality & such strong reserves of noble sentiment."

Winston was narrowly defeated in the Manchester by-election of April 24, which was something of a blow.

Meanwhile, Jennie did everything she could to further the relationship, and when Clemmie returned, she was again invited to Salisbury Hall. On May 28 her signature is recorded in Jennie's house book.

Winston had to undergo the entire, exhausting process over again, this time for a seat in the working-class constituency of Dundee in Scotland, where, by a stroke of luck, a parliamentary seat had become vacant. In Scotland, his humor and wit in speech making obviously went down well, and he entertained the crowds, pouring scorn and ridicule on the Tories, telling them that the Conservative Party was

> filled with old, doddering peers, cute financial magnates, clever wire-pullers, big brewers with bulbous noses. All the enemies of progress are there— weaklings, sleek, smug, comfortable, self-important individuals.[11]

The working-class crowds loved this grandson of the 7th Duke of Marlborough for attacking his own social class, in language that even they probably would not have dared use. Clemmie, who possessed a keen sense of humor, must have been in raptures when she read the reports of his speeches in the newspapers. Winston had stepped into his late father's political shoes with a vengeance, and on May 9 he won an overwhelming victory in Dundee by a majority of nearly three thousand votes, confirming him in his cabinet post as president of the Board of Trade.[12]

Winston's life as a cabinet minister was packed with engagements. In accordance with the social restrictions of the times, Clemmie could not be seen alone with Winston in public. Blanche was so badly off financially she could not pay for a maid for her daughter. Clemmie was therefore reliant on her mother or Jennie to escort her when in company with Winston. Consequently, the young couple only managed to see each other at intervals over the intervening weeks. However, Jack and Goonie, and Winston and Clemmie, met at the Oxfordshire Hussars' maneuvers in late May 1908, and were photographed together for posterity. At the beginning of August, Clemmie had to accompany her mother to Cowes Week and so missed the marriage of Jack and Goonie. In his letters, Winston combined his wish to see Clemmie again with somewhat hilarious accounts of Jack's wedding and the fire.

Winston wrote to Clemmie, on August 8, inviting her to Blenheim Palace. Despite being the granddaughter of an earl and a countess, she felt shy about going to the overpowering ancestral Marlborough home. Her family had little money, and she had so few clothes that she was down to her last starched dress. Her mother could not accompany her, so in the afternoon of August 10, Jennie went with Clemmie, and they spent the night there. On the morning of August 11, she presented herself at breakfast on time, but Winston did not appear. She nearly went home. Sunny had to send up a note to get Winston out of bed.[13]

In the afternoon, Winston took Clemmie for a walk in the garden, but the unpredictable British weather put a damper on his romantic plan to show her the lovely gardens and the roses. The heavens suddenly opened when a torrential rainstorm blew up, and they had to take refuge in the ornamental Greek temple overlooking the lake. Winston dithered and dithered, and did not pop the question, and Clemmie saw an insect crawling across the stone floor toward a crack. She said to herself that if he did not propose before the beetle reached the crack, he never would. But Winston's declared his love for her, and asked her to marry him, and she accepted.[14]

For once in Winston's life everything was going right for him. The betrothal was supposed to be kept a secret for the moment, but Winston was so excited that he got completely carried away and ran across the lawn and told the others the news. He wrote a letter to Clemmie's mother, on August 12, telling her he felt Clemmie's love would give him the strength to take on the "great and sacred responsibility" of giving her the happiness "worthy of her beauty and her virtues."[15]

Clemmie wrote to her sister, Nellie, telling her of the engagement:

I have the most lovely ring—a fat ruby with 2 diamonds—Lord Randolph gave her [Jennie] 3 lovely rings—I have the twin ruby—Lord Randolph said they were for his sons to give their wives.[16]

Winston also wrote, on August 12, to his old love, Pamela, asking that they continue to remain "best friends," just as she had written to him when she married Victor. Winston and Clemmie, and Pamela and Victor, Earl of Lytton, would remain friends for the rest of their lives. Clemmie's grandmother, the Countess of Airlie, wrote to both Jennie and Winston of her joy at the match. To Winston she said: "A good son is a good husband."[17] It was undoubtedly one of the best compliments anyone had ever paid him.

The official announcement of the engagement appeared in *The Times*, on Saturday, August 15. King Edward VII telegraphed his good wishes from Marienbad.

In the midst of trying to find a wedding dress, Clemmie wrote to Winston, on August 22, "My darling . . . I feel there is no room for anyone but you in my heart—you fill every corner." And later: "how I have lived 23 years without you. Everything that happened before about 5 months ago seems unreal." Winston replied: "There are no words . . . to convey to you the feelings of love & joy by which my being is possessed. May God who has given me so much more than I ever knew how to ask keep you safe & sound."[18]

ON THE WEDDING day, September 12, 1908, the bride and groom passed through the City of London, and were cheered by large crowds assembled in Parliament Square. The wedding took place at 2:00 P.M., in St. Margaret's Church, Westminster, the church of the House of Commons. It overflowed with family, friends, and political dignitaries. Clemmie was given away by her brother, William (Bill), who was a sublieutenant in the Royal Navy. She was a dream of loveliness, wearing a shimmering ivory satin gown, with flowing veil of soft white tulle, held in place by a coronet of white American orange blossoms. Her bouquet was of white tuberoses; she was a religious woman, and she carried a prayer book bound in white parchment, a gift from her godfather, Sir John Leslie, 2nd Baronet. Her only jewels were diamond earrings, a gift from Winston. She was served by five bridesmaids: Nellie, her sister; her cousins Venetia Stanley and Madeleine Whyte; Winston's cousin, Clare Frewen; and Horatia Seymour, a friend of Clemmie's. They wore gowns of biscuit-colored satin, and large black picture hats wreathed in roses and camellias, and carried bouquets of pink roses. Winston's old headmaster from Harrow Public School, now Bishop Welldon, Dean of Manchester, gave a most appropriate address:

There must be in the statesman's life many times when he depends upon the love, the insight, the penetrating sympathy, and devotion of his wife.

The influence which the wives of our statesmen have exercised for good upon their husbands' lives is an unwritten chapter of English history, too sacred perhaps to be written in full.[19]

Winston's best man was a great friend of his, Lord Hugh Cecil, Conservative member for Greenwich in South East London.[20] The only flaw in the otherwise immaculate turnout was Winston's suit, reported by the *Tailor and Cutter* as having something of a "flung together at the last minute" appearance about it, "neither fish, flesh, nor fowl . . . one of the greatest failures as a wedding garment we have ever seen, giving the wearer a sort of glorified coachman appearance."

While the newlyweds celebrated their marital vows, the marriage of George and Jennie was not on the best of terms. George's business had failed. It was said in the Churchill family that an urgent business appointment kept him from attending the wedding. So it was Jack who escorted his mother down the aisle. Ethel, Lady Desborough, one of the great society hostesses of her day, was a wedding guest, and she spotted George (who was suffering with his nerves at that time) crying in the church.[21] Although Jennie was immaculately and expensively dressed, and was glamorous for a woman of fifty-four years, photographs show she had a double chin and a big bottom and looked plump and middle-aged. As Clemmie was unknown to the press, they endeavored to build the story of the wedding round Jennie. A report in *Current Literature*, in December, would have its readers believe that Jennie stole the show, providing a greatly inflated description of her. Another report said: "It seems too cruel to say, his mother seemed the junior of the bride by at least two years."[22]

The wedding reception, a modest affair for family and a few friends, was held at the house of Clemmie's aunt, Lady St. Hilier, in Portland Place, London. The young couple left immediately afterward for Woodstock in Oxfordshire to begin the first two nights of their honeymoon in the splendid surroundings of Blenheim Palace. Among the jolly crowd cheering them on their way, when they stepped out of the door of Portland Place, were the East End Pearly Kings and Queens. These were a group of street market traders who were costermongers. They wore a black costume covered with pearl buttons the size of a penny, and were a dazzling sight.[23] In his work for the Board of Trade, Winston had helped protect the rights of costermongers to street trading, hence the couple's popularity. When Winston and Clemmie arrived at Woodstock, there was another crowd waiting to cheer them, and the bells of the church of St. Mary Magdalene rang out.

Winston wrote to his mother on September 13 of his wedded bliss, and the marvelous honeymoon they were looking forward to in Italy for two weeks. Jennie would soon be a grandmother twice over.

Sixteen

LIBERAL BRITAIN

1909–1914

With a Liberal Government now firmly in power, a period of change in legislation would take place. A political battle ensued between the House of Commons and the House of Lords, which was an unelected body of hereditary peers who had the power to pass or reject bills sent to them from the Commons. The Lords tried to block legislation put forward by the Commons by refusing to approve it. There were moves in particular by the Liberals to curb the sale of alcohol and spirits, which caused alcoholism and violence amongst the lower orders. Peers in the House of Lords with financial interests in the brewing companies would not approve the bill. David Lloyd George, who had become Chancellor of the Exchequer in 1908, produced the first People's Budget in an attempt to tax the wealthier classes of society.

J ack and Goonie had a modest honeymoon of just a couple of days. Their first home had to be as the guests of Jennie and George at Salisbury Hall. They signed the house book on August 10, 1908, for the first time as husband and wife. Goonie, as the daughter of an earl, retained her title as Lady Gwendeline Spencer Churchill. She was grateful to Jennie for providing a home for them until they could set up on their own. Goonie was initially fond of Jennie, and was soon calling her *Belle-Mère* (beautiul mother), as she sometimes signed her letters to her boys. But Goonie would have difficulty reconciling the somewhat easy virtue existing in Jennie's household with her own strict Catholic upbringing.

On return from their honeymoon at the end of September, Winston was immersed in his duties at the Board of Trade. His predecessor, David Lloyd George, had put it in such good order that Winston found he had little more to do. In characteristic style, he looked for other parliamentary work to keep him busy. He strongly backed the provision for old-age pensions in the 1908 budget, fulfilling promises he had made to himself that he would not see elderly folk, like his beloved Woomany, suffer indignities in their old age through poverty. Like his father before him, he supported legislation aimed at curbing the power of the great brewing companies. For instance, a shareholder in a brewing company could sit as a justice of the licensing at licensing sessions and there was a move to preclude him. Drunkenness and alcoholism were enormous problems among the lower classes in the poverty-stricken parts of the big cities in the United Kingdom. A penny could buy a tankard of ale or a glass of gin. It led to crime and prostitution, and there were domestic violence, fights, stabbings, and murders. Gin palaces were infamous in places like White Chapel in the East End of London. Winston and other like-minded Liberals wanted the sale of alcohol to children and young people curbed, and the price increased to make it less easily accessible to the poorer classes.

WHEN THEY RETURNED from their honeymoon, Winston and Clemmie lived in Winston's former bachelor house, 12 Bolton Street, London, while a larger house, 33 Eccleston Square, was being prepared for them. From the outset, the four younger Churchills got on well together. Clemmie was particularly fond of kind, easygoing Jack, and Goonie was a kind and understanding person to family and friends. In early May 1909, Winston and Clemmie moved into their new home, with an eighteen-year lease, at £195/$323 per year.

Life at Salisbury Hall was proving a strain for Jack and Goonie as it was too far for Jack to travel to his job in the City. It didn't help that the Cornwallis-Wests' marriage was in difficulties over financial losses. George was ill and thought the house was haunted; he claimed to have seen in the hallway the ghost of its sixteenth-century occupant, Eleanor (Nell) Gwynne, whom King Charles II had installed there as his mistress.[1] Within six months of their marriage, by which time Goonie was expecting a baby, the newlyweds beat a retreat. By February 1909, with his usual thrift and good order, Jack had managed to buy a modest house of their own, 10 Talbot Square, Hyde Park, in reasonably fashionable London W2. Whatever Goonie made of it all at Salisbury Hall, she never complained. Those who knew her spoke of her as kind and sincere and not one to pass harsh judgments upon others. George West later said of her, "One had not got to know her long without realizing what a truly loveable character she was. I can never remember her ever saying an unkind word about anyone, and there are precious few women one can say that about."[2] In an endeavor to economize, Jennie and George gave up Salisbury Hall later that year, and moved to live in London, though they still on occasion rented the house for weekends.

Goonie gave birth to John George (known in the family as Johnny) on May 31, 1909, with Jack present throughout, which was unheard of in their day. Winston wrote to Clemmie from Camp Goring, giving her some encouragement as they, too, were expecting a child, which they affectionately referred to in their letters as P.K. (Puppy Kitten). According to Winston, Jack was like a "little turkey-cock with satisfaction," exuding an "alone I did it sort of air."

On July 11 it was Clemmie's turn, and she gave birth at home to a daughter, Diana. Clemmie and Winston were overjoyed with their new baby, and when Winston was out of town and writing to Clemmie, he would include in his letters: "Kiss especially the beautiful P.K. for me." His own father had never concluded a letter to Jennie without a message to "kiss the baby." Clemmie suffered from postpartum depression,[3] though that medical term had not yet been coined. The pregnancy left her exhausted and low in spirits, and soon afterward she went on vacation to Brighton, and was joined by her sister Nellie. Diana was left at home, and the nurse and Winston minded the baby. In another reprise of his father's life,[4] Winston wrote loving reports to Clemmie of how Puppy Kitten was progressing.[5]

After the traditional family get-together on Christmas Day 1909, and the New Year's celebrations at Blenheim Palace, Winston and Clemmie immediately set off to campaign in Winston's parliamentary seat, Dundee in Scotland, for the coming general election. In January 1910, Winston won his seat handsomely, but the Liberal Party, while holding on to power, lost a lot of seats. On February 19, Asquith made Winston Home Secretary.

JUST PRIOR TO the election, British politics had entered an extraordinary phase in which the language used made it seem like a bloody social revolution was in the offing. Despite the urgent need for a considerable increase in tax revenue to fund the

new welfare provisions and pay for a major reequipment of the Royal Navy, the cabinet emasculated Lloyd George's first People's Budget to reduce its impact on the
wealthier classes of society. Still the House of Lords flung it out and began a series
of battles with the House of Commons that would end with the Parliament Act of
1911, which greatly reduced the powers of the Lords, by then under the threat of
the Liberals to create enough peers of their own to destroy the natural Tory supremacy there. In the meantime, another general election had been forced in December 1910, but still the Liberal Party clung to power.

As Home Secretary, Winston was a proponent of less harsh prison conditions
and a reluctant supporter of the death penalty. He commuted twenty-one of the
forty-three capital sentences that crossed his desk for confirmation. Jean Hamilton
revealed something of Winston's deep compassion for a troubled society in a record
of a dinner conversation with him on February 21, 1910. He confided that he had
signed "a death warrant for the first time . . . and it weighed on me. A man who took
a little child up a side street and brutally cut her throat." Jean replied cheerfully:
"That would not weigh on my mind." "Think," he said rather savagely, "of a Society
that forces a man to do that."[6]

After a short illness, King Edward VII died suddenly on May 6, 1910, and political life was suspended during the week of his lying in state and his funeral. His successor, King George V, was not long enthroned before Winston sent him a long
memorandum on prison reform, making arguments for reducing the number of in-
mates sent down for trivial offenses that could have come straight from the debates
in our own times.

JACK'S JOB as a stockbroker in the City carried a lot of responsibility. While constantly monitoring the rise and fall of stocks and shares, he gave financial advice to
Jennie, George, and Winston. He provided a comfortable income for himself and
Goonie, though they would never be rich. He inherited a great love of classical music
and the opera from his mother, which he shared with Goonie, and they went frequently together to the Covent Garden Opera House.

Goonie was not educated in the strictly academic sense, in the way that Clemmie
had been, and joked about the gaps in her education. But she had a taste for literature
and drama and kept herself abreast of modern literary developments by reading reviews and books on the topical subjects of the day and going to see plays at the theatre. She was a keen artist, and her artistic talent, and interest in literature, gained her
many intellectual friends, like the artists William Orpen and Sir John Lavery, who
were both Irish and were official British war artists during the First World War. Hazel,
Lady Lavery was from Chicago and was a renowned sketch artist. She was considered
a great beauty, and her likeness as an Irish colleen was used by the Irish on their bank-

notes in the twentieth century. Another of Goonie's friends was J. M. Barrie, the Scottish playwright and novelist, whose most famous play was *Peter Pan*. Goonie was a Liberal and close friend of Herbert Asquith and his wife, Margot. Goonie's friends adored her, she could light up any party with her wit and humor. Jean Hamilton and Pamela Lytton described her as a gorgeous creature. Others spoke of her great kindness and ability to understand everyone else's troubles, and she was a good listener.

On the other hand, the Cornwallis-Wests' marriage had never really recovered from George's financial crisis in 1906. To make matters worse, he seemed to have gradually tired of his bossy, maternal wife, and had developed a roving eye for other women. He also wanted the son and heir that Jennie could not provide. In 1909, Jennie had written and staged a play in which the famous actress Mrs. Patrick Campbell (Stella) had the leading role. Mrs. Pat, as she was known, met George, who was engaged in a minor role in the play, and they fell head over heels in love. Unbeknown to him she was, like Jennie, past childbearing age. Stella was a widow, her husband having been killed in the Boer War.

The Wests' financial difficulties, and George's flirtations, were taking their toll on Jennie. However, she seemed to have an endless aptitude for reinventing herself, and she promptly hit on a new plan in the spring of 1909, probably suggested by Sir Ernest Cassel. Entering into the property market, she first bought the house of a friend, Madame Melba, who had been a neighbor in Great Cumberland Place. Having restored it to a high standard, she rented it out to tenants. Winston wrote to her on August 4, congratulating her on developments after just two or three months' work.[7] Developing her skills further, she moved on to buying old, run-down Victorian houses, refurbishing them, and selling them at a substantial profit.

So it was not until the spring of 1911 that Jennie wired Jack to let him and Winston know of her predicament with George.

When he first fell for Stella Campbell, George had moved out of the family home and was living apart from Jennie. Then he had regrets and asked to come back, and Jennie wrote to him from her latest home, 2 Norfolk Street, Mayfair, on April 19, 1911: "Certainly come back to your own home — & with God's help we shall start afresh." The quarrel was patched up, and they got back together again.

On May 28, Clemmie gave birth to Winston's only son, Randolph, at their home in London. Military duty called Winston away with his Yeomanry regiment, the Oxfordshire Hussars, within days of the birth, and the daily letters between parted husband and wife were full of a deep love and joy. Randolph was referred to as "the Chumbolly," a name possibly derived from a beautiful flower that grows in northwest India.[8]

On hearing that Clemmie was somewhat weak after the birth and felt unable to attend his coronation on June 22, and out of his high regard for Winston, King

George V went to great lengths to arrange a special carriage for her that would deliver her for the ceremony itself and then get her home quietly, avoiding all the crowds and waiting about.

IN OCTOBER 1911, Winston was appointed First Lord of the Admiralty, a post he had been expecting after some heavy hints, and one that ideally suited his temperament and talents for organizing in case of war. Clemmie had grown accustomed to appearing with her husband in public, and participating in official duties. She launched the battleship *Centurion* at Devonport on November 18. Their official government home was to be the large and prestigious Admiralty House.

Winston was working with the First Sea Lord, Admiral Sir John (Jacky) Fisher, at a time when the Royal Navy had increased its power enormously through the introduction of the Dreadnought class of battleship. Winston fully understood the importance of the Royal Navy in any future conflict, and was anxious that it should be able to deploy its full power, immediately, in the event of hostilities. Like many others, he had watched the German buildup of military and naval power under Kaiser William II, and expected a war. With Europe divided into two great armed camps by a system of military alliances, it would take a fairly minor political crisis to plunge the continent into war.

Winston settled into his job as First Lord of the Admiralty, which he would hold until May 1915. Meanwhile, Winston and Clementine and Jack and Goonie with all the children went on holiday together for breaks to the seaside. For important calendar events, like Easter and Christmas, they met up at Blenheim Palace. Clemmie and Goonie got on really well together and were rearing their children side by side as often as time and occasion permitted.

By the autumn of 1912, Goonie was again pregnant. She gave birth to their second son on May 25, 1913. The christening took place in Westminster Cathedral, with Winston as godfather, and there emerged a good story that Peregrine liked to tell. Goonie went to the front of the church to pray, and the priest came out to baptize the baby, and asked: "What name is this child to be given?" Someone said "Henry," then Winston suggested "Winston." Goonie had not heard this exchange, and by the time she came to the baptismal font the priest had poured the water over the infant's head, and named him Henry Winston. Goonie had intended giving him the name Peregrine, which had been in the Bertie family since 1570. She did not approve of the improvised change, and insisted on calling him Peregrine, by which name he would be known throughout his life. Peregrine's brother Johnny, aged four at the time, could not pronounce it and called him "Pebin," an affectionate nickname by which he was known to all the family.

In early April 1913, the situation between Jennie and George had reached the point of no return. He was again besotted with the famous actress Mrs. Patrick

Campbell, and if Jennie had not agreed to divorce him, she would have had to suffer the humiliation in society that he would have started divorce proceedings against her. Jennie was a society hostess, the former daughter-in-law of the Duke of Marlborough, and the mother of a senior cabinet minister. The shame of this second husband divorcing her on the grounds that the marriage had irretrievably broken down would have been unbearable. Their divorce was granted on the grounds of his infidelity in July, but George was legally obliged to wait another nine months before he could marry Mrs. Patrick Campbell. Once again it was Jack who had to sort out the incredible tangle into which the finances of his mother and stepfather had descended.

Family relationships would come under their greatest strain when, in early February 1914, Jack made the remarkable discovery that their mother had been deceiving the two brothers for many years over the exact nature of Lord Randolph's will. He had left his estate in a trust fund for the benefit of his wife while she lived, and for his two sons and their children after her death. But he had inserted a clause that said:

> after the decease or second marriage of my said wife whichever shall first happen to advance . . . any part not exceeding in the whole one half of the presumptive share of any child or issue in the said trust fund towards his or her advancement in the world.[9]

Entirely unknown to them, Winston and Jack could have had a claim on their father's estate since Jennie's second marriage in 1900.[10] In a long letter to his mother of February 14, Jack unburdened himself, giving full vent to the exasperation he felt:

> We had always thought that Papa was very wrong in not making any provision for us during your life. We thought the will left us in the possible position of being for many years without a penny while you were in receipt of over £5,000 [$24,000] a year. This did in actual fact happen & you were unable to give us any allowance. It now appears that there is a clause in the will providing that while in the event of your remarrying the trustees could demand on our behalf or on behalf of our children, should we be dead. . . . Winston and I are now making our own living and as long as we do so of course nothing will be claimed—although I believe that at the present moment we could each demand about £600 [$2,880] a year. But supposing I found myself in a state of penury with a wife and family—I might have to ask for the money—I am only—I hope—thinking of remote possibilities. Again if I or Winston die before you—our wives will be left very badly off. There is nothing for them to bring up the children on except our insurances . . . and in that case there is no doubt that our children's trustees would demand the

money for their keep and education. . . . It makes a considerable difference finding that Papa's will was not made—as we were always led to suppose—carelessly and without any consideration for us. It is quite clear that he never thought that while you were single you would be unable to pay us an allowance, and the clause in the will covered the situation—which did actually arise—of your remarriage.[11]

For nearly twenty years Winston and Jack had thought their father had made no useful provision for them in his will; for nearly fourteen years their mother had denied them a half share of their full inheritance. If Jack, returning from the Boer War a combat veteran, had received his £600/$2,880 a year from 1901, he could easily have become a professional soldier. His inheritance would have supplemented his army pay, and he could have pursued his preferred career and lived very comfortably.

Jennie's response to Jack's letter, if she sent one, has not survived. Undeterred, in the spring of that year, she wrote to Jack from Monte Carlo, where despite all the warnings from her family, she was back at the gambling casinos. She was in a depressed state and complaining somewhat pathetically about feeling unwanted by her family.

On April 16, the decree absolute was granted, and on the same day, two hours later, George married Mrs. Patrick Campbell.[12] He left with her for a tour of America, where she was starring in George Bernard Shaw's play *Pygmalion,* in which he played a minor role as Alfred Doolittle, the dustman, father of Eliza Doolittle.

The painful last days of her marriage to George behind her, romance was in the air again for Jennie. She attended the wedding of her sister Clara's son in Rome, and at a ball was introduced to the wealthy, thirty-seven-year-old Montagu Porch, who fell in love with her at first sight. Porch was serving in the Colonial Service in Nigeria, and was very handsome, with a slim figure and hair that was prematurely white. Porch would write love letters to her and pursue her in the coming months.

DARK WAR CLOUDS would soon, however, gather over Europe. On June 28, 1914, the Archduke Franz Ferdinand of Austria-Hungary and his wife were assassinated at Sarajevo in Bosnia. Austria suspected Serbia of colluding in the assassination, and the harsh demands it made upon that little country led Russia to mobilize in support of its Slavic ally. Mobilizations followed in Germany, France, and Britain, and the "inevitable" slide into war began.

Jack, ever watchful of his family's finances, sounded warnings to them regarding the effects war could have on their investments. Writing to his mother in July, he told her: "The world has gone mad—the whole financial system has completely broken down. . . . Be careful with what you have got—Gold will soon be unobtainable."

Winston at the Admiralty kept his family informed of the risks, which Jennie wrote about from her latest home, 72 Brook Street, London, to her sister Leonie in Ireland, on August 1:

W. [Winston] tells me [Raymond] Poincaré [president of France] has written an impassioned letter to the King imploring his aid. The [British] fleet will be mobilized today probably—Germany is holding up English vessels & has mobilized & massed troops on the French frontier.[13]

Germany asked Britain to remain neutral in any future conflict, and they refused. On August 2, Germany declared war on Russia, and the following day declared war on France and Belgium. German troops invaded Belgium, and on August 4 Britain asked Germany to withdraw. Germany did not respond. Britain, now forced into the position of having to maintain the balance of power in Europe, declared war on Germany.

Clemmie and Goonie had each rented a cottage by the sea for their summer holidays for the months of July and August, in the village of Overstrand near Cromer, in Norfolk. Winston spent "several Sundays" with them, playing with the children on the beach, while carrying on with his job and living in London. He also kept closely in touch by telephone, ringing Clemmie every night, and they wrote each other long letters. Jack, too, went at weekends and had some scheduled holidays from work, which he spent with his family. Clemmie, Goonie, Jack, and the children were still at Overstrand when war was declared. Clemmie was expecting their third child in eight weeks' time. Her immediate concern was that her mother was living in Dieppe, France, and had to be fetched back to England by her sister Nellie, as it was not safe for her to remain there; she joined them at Overstrand. What had begun as a happy, family holiday in the sunshine and sea air now rapidly turned into a nightmare. As soon as war was declared, Jack left and joined his regiment, the Oxfordshire Yeomanry, to train for active war service. He had expressed a decided wish to go and fight at the front, and for Goonie this prospect was frightening beyond belief. The British fleet was put on a war footing, and Winston, as First Lord of the Admiralty, had huge responsibilities for the fleet in wartime. Once again the Churchill family was off to the wars.

Seventeen

A WORLD AT WAR:
FROM THE WESTERN
FRONT TO GALLIPOLI

1914–1915

On August 4, 1914, Liberal prime minister Henry Herbert Asquith declared war on Germany. Britain joined France, Russia, Belgium, and Serbia in a war against Germany and Austria-Hungary. After stalemate developed along the main front in France and Belgium, Turkey joined the war on the side of Germany. The Western Allies took the opportunity, early in 1915, to open a new front in the Dardanelles, aimed at knocking Turkey out of the war.

As First Lord of the Admiralty, Winston read the developing crisis in masterly fashion and quietly began to prepare the Royal Navy for war. It has to be said that he was exhilarated by the turn of events; the excitement of war suited him, and he shared a good deal of the enthusiasm for war that swept most of Europe in the summer of 1914. While Clemmie and the children stayed at Overstrand, he worked hard at the Admiralty. On questions of naval and military strategy he dominated his political colleagues in the cabinet, who were wholly lacking in military experience or expertise, and he was the equal of the political novice, the new secretary of state for war, Herbert, Earl Kitchener of Khartoum, who had led the Egyptian army in the reconquest of the Sudan (1896–98).

On August 4, 1914, the Oxfordshire Hussars were mobilized for war. Jack reported to his squadron at its camp near Blenheim Palace. In common with the whole Territorial Force, their first duty was the defense of the United Kingdom, but many were anxious that the fighting in France would be all over by Christmas and they might miss the chance to get into action. In this respect a regiment with such powerful social connections as the Oxfordshire Hussars was well placed. Having the brother of the First Lord of the Admiralty in its ranks was an added bonus.

On August 24, Winston wrote to Jack from the Admiralty to convey the serious news of the Battle of Mons, where the British army stood up well to the enemy but had to retreat. Already Winston was opining that if Britain did not win, he had no wish to live. "But," he wrote, "win we will." He was still lobbying on behalf of Jack and the regiment to get them employed at the earliest opportunity.

After a number of naval losses that autumn, Winston, in his role as First Lord of the Admiralty, came in for some personal criticism, but he retained the confidence of Prime Minister Herbert Asquith, who admired his combative spirit. In his exuberant desire to engage the enemy more closely, Winston took a keen interest in the military campaign, and he looked for every opportunity to commit naval forces to support the land forces engaged against the German armies in Belgium and France. An opportunity soon presented itself that, while his critics seized upon it as grist to their mill, in reality had a profound effect on the long-term development of the war in Europe. In late September 1914 the Germans suddenly threatened the early capture of the Belgian port of Antwerp, which would have had the direst consequences for the British Expeditionary Force (BEF) fighting in Belgium. It would have put German armies on their flank, threatening their lines of communication to Britain. Winston took the urgent step of sending everything he could by way of military force to support the city garrison.

As part of this effort, Winston was also finally able to persuade Lord Kitchener to release the Oxfordshire Hussars as divisional cavalry for the Royal Naval Division (RND). The regiment left for France on September 19; some of its latest recruits were still in civilian clothes. Jack, with no real knowledge of where they were off to, only that Winston had cabled promising a "really good show," fired off a message to his brother with a long list of demands for stores and equipment his men needed. His D Squadron was the first across the English Channel, ahead of the rest of the regiment. On September 28, Jack wrote to Jennie, asking her to look after Goonie: "I am afraid she feels my going very much—but I know she would have hated me to have stayed behind."

At a crisis meeting of the cabinet Winston learned of the Belgian decision to evacuate Antwerp, a move that would have released major German formations for action against the hard-pressed BEF. On October 3, with Kitchener's blessing, Winston proceeded at once to Antwerp, promised the Belgians that his new Royal Naval Division would join them, and, at his persuasive best, got them to promise to hold on for ten more days as new British formations would be arriving in Belgium by then.

For four days Winston was in his element, witnessing the frontline fighting under enemy fire and directing a stream of telegrams back to the Admiralty. He even asked Asquith if he could resign as First Lord and take an army commission as commander of the Antwerp garrison. Kitchener would have made him a lieutenant general; it took Asquith to point out that promoting a former lieutenant of Hussars to lieutenant general, a leap of seven ranks over a number of major generals, brigadiers, and colonels, was asking for trouble. In truth, Asquith needed Winston in both the Admiralty and the cabinet.

That Antwerp fell after seven days, and that the wretchedly inexperienced Royal Naval Division lost so heavily, is all held against Winston. He accepted much of the criticism and later wrote that he would have done things differently with hindsight. Even Clemmie, clearly annoyed that he had dashed off to war just as she was about to give birth to their daughter Sarah, thought he had lost his sense of proportion.[1]

But this courageous and imaginative stroke did have an extraordinary effect on the campaign. That extra five days of resistance at Antwerp by the Belgians and British early in October tied up German formations and allowed the main Belgian army to fall back along the coast toward its British and French Allies, keeping it in the field and allowing the savage fighting around the small Belgian city of Ypres to run its course and halt the German offensive for the year 1914. Depriving Germany of victory in the short term condemned it to ultimate defeat in a long war of attrition it could never really hope to win.

THE OXFORDSHIRE HUSSARS became attached to general headquarters to provide a daily guard there. The crisis of the First Battle of Ypres, as the Germans threw huge, fresh forces at the weary British defenders, changed all that. The regiment was ordered to join Beauvoir De Lisle's 1st Cavalry Division, then locked in battle along the Messines Ridge. On October 29 Jack was appointed second in command of the regiment. Within twenty-four hours they were in place behind the ridge, tired and very wet, and about to intervene at a critical time. Jack was ordered to take half the regiment to reinforce the hard-pressed 1st Cavalry Brigade. Jack dismounted his men and led them forward for a quarter of a mile up onto the ridge, selected a well-covered position, and supported the cavalry fighting in the village of Messines. He deployed his men just below the crest of the ridge and then advanced the whole line up to the top, where they took post along the thick hedges bordering the road. The rest of the regiment soon joined them, and they held their ground under heavy fire. When, in the late afternoon of October 30, the fire increased dramatically, Jack got his men to fall back to the covered position just below the crest. He was able to keep casualties down to just seven men wounded. The British were forced to abandon the Messines Ridge, and the Oxfordshire Hussars covered the withdrawal of the defenders. The regiment had been moving and fighting for sixty hours without any real break for sleep.

When the 1st Cavalry Division in which they were serving was finally relieved, Jack's regiment made its way to safety in the rear and found that Major Churchill and one of his subalterns had made excellent arrangements for their accommodation and the distribution of hot food and mail from home. Jack again showed his excellent organizational skills when put in charge of the regiment's horse lines. The headquarters of the BEF was desperate for good, reliable officers to serve in a number of important staff roles, and so it came to pass that, on November 19, Jack was ordered to report for duty as the camp commandant of a new training center for Territorial Force units near St. Omer.

When Winston heard from Jack that Sir John French, commander in chief of the BEF, had personally asked for him to take up a staff appointment, he understood immediately that Jack would feel a great wrench at having to leave the regiment, but wrote to his brother:

> It is very clearly your duty to go where you can be most use. I expect you will do this work very well and as more and more Territorials arrive its importance will grow. Your brains and business training should be useful and will find a wider scope. You will know more of what is going on. . . . In your position you will have lots of opportunities of helping the regiment and the Territorial interests in general. There will be plenty of chances of being shot at before the end is reached.[2]

Winston wrote that Goonie, who had been "very good and brave" while Jack was serving with the regiment in action, was "enchanted at the news." Jack did indeed relay his feelings about the new job to his mother: "Goonie will tell you that I have been ordered back here for some staff job—I am out of the firing line for the time being—I don't mind that one bit—but I do not like leaving the others in it."[3]

Winston was also keeping Jack informed of the important new operations against the Turks in the Dardanelles. When an appeal came early in January 1915 from Britain's Russian Allies for some action against Turkey to take the pressure off the Russian armies in the Caucasus, Winston responded immediately and generously with an offer to use the strength of the Royal Navy in that capacity. He asked Admiral Sackville Carden, commanding the Royal Navy at the Dardanelles, to work out a plan for the bombardment and reduction of the forts guarding the straits and the Gallipoli Peninsula. Passing warships through this historically vital waterway would pose a direct threat to the great Turkish city of Constantinople, destroy the arsenals there, and, it was hoped, force Turkey out of the war entirely. Some early success in battering the outer forts guarding the straits into silence was soon frustrated by the inability of British minesweepers to clear the way for the capital ships. They were always under heavy fire from mobile batteries of Turkish artillery operating from the Gallipoli Peninsula itself. It was this problem that finally determined the need for troops to land on and clear the peninsula, to enable the fleet to batter its way through to Constantinople.

In something of a rush, General Sir Ian Hamilton was appointed on March 13 to command a hastily assembled Mediterranean Expeditionary Force (MEF) that was largely unprepared and certainly inadequate in strength for the heavy responsibility it carried.

THE WINTER OF 1914–15 was a hard one, and the BEF struggled to make itself comfortable as its strength increased by leaps and bounds. Jack's good humor shines through in a typical soldier's story he told his mother. "I must try and pay a visit to Boulogne I think and see the *hors de combat*—I hear the place is full of lovely ladies—ready to bandage anyone anywhere. We call it the Remount Depot!"[4]

As the BEF prepared for its first offensive action on the Western Front in March 1915, Jack was beginning to find the life of a staff officer at St. Omer "a bit of a bore." On March 12, he was feeling at loose ends as most of the general staff went off to the front to observe the progress of the Battle of Neuve Chappelle, when Winston suddenly rang at noon and asked if he would like a posting elsewhere. "Would I not!" he recorded in his diary, especially as it involved working with their old friend General Sir Ian Hamilton, who was putting together his staff for the Gallipoli campaign.

Jack was in London by March 13, with just enough time to see Goonie and pick up some items of kit. Hamilton and his staff left that very day for the Mediterranean. Sir Ian wrote to Winston the next day, as their train raced through France heading for Marseilles. He said what a lift it was for them to be seen off by so many well-wishers, and that Jack seemed cheery and fit. He thought he would be a great addition to "our little band of adventurers." Indeed, Sir Ian had asked for Jack, not just out of friendship with the family, but because he was the only one of his staff officers with practical combat experience in the current war.

Sir Ian Hamilton met the new admiral, John De Robeck (Carden had retired sick), and learned of the major naval attack due to take place the very next day. On March 18 Jack accompanied Sir Ian and the French general, Albert D'Amade, on a reconnaissance by destroyer along the west coast of the Gallipoli Peninsula.

The party returned to the entrance of the Dardanelles straits and witnessed the climax of the great naval attack of March 18. They watched in awe as the guns of the British and French battleships battered the Turkish forts; and then they saw six battleships lost to enemy mines, three sunk, and three severely damaged, before their eyes. The attack was broken off, a disappointing failure. The Royal Navy would not be rushing the Dardanelles. Troops would be needed to storm the Gallipoli Peninsula, and clear the way for the warships to close upon and destroy the forts at the Narrows.

The whole expeditionary force would have to be reorganized back at the major port facilities of Alexandria.

From March 28 Ian Hamilton's staff settled down in a new venue, and the hard work began. Jack had been appointed camp commandant at Hamilton's general headquarters, an unglamorous post but vital to the smooth running of the headquarters and so to the well-being of the campaign. He had to scour Alexandria to lay in hard-to-find office furniture and supplies to enable the general staff to get on with its work. He had such a difficult time galvanizing Egyptian government officials into activity that, as he describes it in his diary, he "went into business" on his own account and negotiated privately with a "rich old Turk" for the exclusive use of a large empty hotel.

Just as he had got the Alexandria staff offices working smoothly by early April, they were all back on ships heading for Lemnos again. The general headquarters had to work from the battleship _Queen Elizabeth_. Once again the camp commandant had to make all the work go smoothly. "There is a good deal of difficulty in trying to fit up the ship as an office," Jack wrote in his diary. "Everyone comes to me for everything."[5] Jack accompanied Sir Ian Hamilton on a reconnaissance of the Gallipoli coast on April 12. They were confident that the landings could be effected but expected heavy casualties in the process.

As there was no official post of camp commandant, Jack was delighted when he was appointed a deputy assistant adjutant general on the staff, at a useful salary of £550/$2,640 per annum. He was constantly in liaison with all manner of officers, of the assault formations, the navy, the French, and so he leaves us a very valuable record of how the operation was planned and executed from a unique perspective. There had never before in history been an assault landing against a coastline defended by an alert enemy armed with such terrible weapons as machine guns, quick-firing artillery, and magazine rifles.

On April 20, Jack wrote to his mother to bemoan the chaotic state of the postal service, and hinted that, before she heard from him again, she would hear of great happenings in the news. Presumably this letter passed the censor after the landings had taken place or it would never have been delivered.

Finally the great day arrived. On April 25, 1915, Jack spent the whole day on board the *Queen Elizabeth* with Sir Ian Hamilton and his general staff. In fifty-seven timed entries in his diary, he recorded the confusing picture of the assault landings against the Turkish-held beaches on the Gallipoli Peninsula based on the messages received on the headquarters ship. They first watched the Australians go ashore above Gaba Tepe on the west coast of the peninsula and then steamed south, past Y Beach, where things appeared to be going well. At Cape Helles, on the southern tip of the peninsula, they could see that the infantry was having a torrid time against a very determined defense. The *Queen Elizabeth* lent support with her huge 15-inch guns and 6-inch ordnance. Only slowly did they realize that things had not gone so well at Y Beach[6] and that the Australians and New Zealanders in the north were so stiffly resisted that they even considered evacuating the beaches completely. Hamilton encouraged them to dig until they were safe, and over the next two days Jack's detailed diary tells us how the army gradually secured its toeholds on the peninsula, exhausting itself in the process.

Jack often went with Sir Ian when he visited the front lines on the peninsula. In the confines of the severely restricted bridgeheads at Gallipoli, this was always a dangerous venture. Snipers and artillery observers were quick to spot any unusual movement, and large groups of army and navy officers would always attract unwelcome attention. The Western Front veteran could write with feeling, "I disliked walking about trenches with people in red caps and men in white cap covers!"[7] German submarines arrived in the eastern Mediterranean and began sinking British ships with impunity. The entire fleet had to shelter in Mudros Bay on the nearby island of Lemnos, and the army was left feeling terribly vulnerable on shore.

BACK AT THE Admiralty Winston had been finding himself increasingly at odds with Admiral Sir John Fisher, the First Sea Lord and service chief of the Royal Navy. He delighted in writing memoranda of the most intricate detail that were tantamount to orders for the Royal Navy, and had brushed aside Fisher's doubts about the viability of the Dardanelles expedition. Famously Fisher thundered in one memo to Winston, "Damn the Dardanelles! They'll be our grave!" One night Winston fired off his usual detailed orders to the Board of Admiralty for reinforcing the fleet at Gallipoli and to one document added the ill-considered words "First Sea Lord to see after action." He might have thought this was a routine matter that shouldn't have taken up the First Sea Lord's time, but, for Fisher, it was a last straw, and he sent a letter of resignation on October 30, 1915, and promptly absented himself.[8]

Fisher's resignation, at a time when the war was not going well in general, created a political crisis in the House of Commons. The Conservatives were ready to withdraw their support for the government, and Asquith was obliged to accept the notion of a national government to include ministers from all the principal parties. One of the conditions for Tory support for the new government was that Winston, whom the Tories still hated as a "turncoat," must leave the Admiralty.

All this came as a terrible blow to the embattled soldiers and sailors at Gallipoli. Jack recorded that Sir Ian was very upset at the loss of their staunchest ally in London; the naval commanders wrote very kindly to Jack, saying they were going to miss Winston at the Admiralty very much. Jack was glad that Winston's family was able to move into his house with Goonie. Winston's ministerial salary, £4,360/$20,928 per year, would mean that both families would manage financially.

FROM MAY 1915 German submarines began to take a toll on British ships, and so it was finally decided that running the campaign headquarters of the MEF from on board the *Arcadian* was no longer safe or practical. Jack was involved in selecting a permanent campsite on the nearby island of Imbros. When Hamilton landed there on June 1, the camp was running smoothly. Jack's new responsibilities kept him away from the front line now, and he only reported the next battles, without witnessing them. The weather had turned very hot, the plague of flies was frightful, and the arrival or nonarrival of the post from home became a constant theme in Jack's diaries and letters.

Jack carefully observed the fighting on the peninsula, which showed a number of tactical victories toward the end of June but at a terrible continuous drain on the divisions in the line. A regular refrain in his letters to his mother was the growing admiration of the army for their Turkish enemy: "The Turks are very brave at this particular kind of warfare. They seem to behave fairly well as regards wounded etc. The prisoners say they do not like fighting England, but that as we have attacked their country—they have no choice."[9]

In July 1915 came news that massive reinforcements were on their way from Britain for a final push to victory. While busy with his normal staff work, Jack had the unenviable opportunity to watch the new offensive out of the Anzac area, in the north of the peninsula, go horribly wrong. The new troops put ashore at Suvla Bay on August 6 were keen enough but were very badly led and, before long, were thrown into confusion and passivity. The mainly veteran forces attacking out of Anzac were defeated by the terrain, their own exhaustion, and another brilliant battlefield performance by the Turkish commander, Mustapha Kemal. Jack went ashore at Suvla Bay on August 8 with Lieutenant Colonel Aspinall of the general staff and saw at first hand the appalling incompetence of the Suvla generals. On October 16 came the bombshell of Sir Ian Hamilton's dismissal as commander for his failure to achieve victory at Gallipoli. In letters home Jack would deplore the fact that the continuous efforts of his companions were held to no account by people who knew little or nothing of the extraordinary difficulties under which they labored.[10]

In the short term Jack was cut adrift, and he expected to be sent to his regiment in France. After Hamilton's dismissal, Sir William Birdwood became the temporary commander in chief, and all the staff were kept very busy coping with the many changes.

Birdwood took kindly to Jack, retained him as camp commandant, and asked him to prepare encampments on Imbros for anything up to sixteen thousand men. Jack was busy on this, and nursing an injured ankle, when Kitchener made his one and only visit to the Dardanelles. He was sufficiently shocked at the conditions the troops had endured there for so long that he saw evacuation as the only real choice.

By Sunday, January 9, 1916, the last Allied soldier had left the Gallipoli Peninsula, most heading straight for Egypt. Jack moved to the small Greek port of Mudros on the Mediterranean island of Lemnos with Birdwood, who had offered him a posting on the staff of the Australian and New Zealand forces. Jack was eager to get home on leave to see Goonie and the children. He often wondered if little Peregrine was talking yet; he was only just walking when he last saw him. He was greatly heartened to receive two honors—a mention in Sir Ian Hamilton's final dispatch, and from the French, the medal of the Legion of Honor. This was a personal commendation from the French commander in gratitude for all the liaison work Jack had done with the French forces.

Back in Cairo in January 1916, Jack's money worries were heightened by the news that his employer, Paul Nelke, the senior partner in Nelke Phillips & Co., the stockbroking firm for whom he worked in London, was obliged to reduce the retainer salary he was paying him to £250/$1,200, and if he were sent back to his regiment in France he would lose another £200/$960 a year. Jack wrote home that he "had not spent a fiver since March last!" and all his pay went to Goonie.

Eighteen

SEEING IT THROUGH

1914–1918

At the outbreak of war between Britain and Germany in 1914, women were needed on a scale never before experienced to carry out war work. They rapidly took up nursing services for the wounded in hospitals and took over men's jobs in the munitions factories. In 1915, when it was apparent it was to be a long war, the Liberal and Conservative Parties formed a coalition government under the leadership of the Liberal Herbert Asquith. In 1916, Asquith was replaced as prime minister and leader of the coalition by David Lloyd George.

The Churchill womenfolk, in common with women around the world in wartime, got on with their lives as best they could. Jennie, buoyed up by the love of Montagu Porch, had soon after the outbreak of war joined the opera singer Maud Warrender. Ever the accomplished pianist, Jennie accompanied Maud on a series of morale-boosting concerts. Before long Jennie was also engaged in hospital work.

Goonie's high-strung nerves made her very fearful as the war started. She unburdened herself in a letter to Jennie in August 1914 of her dread of Jack's being injured or killed and wondered how she would cope now that his income was so drastically reduced. His employer, Nelke, Phillips and Company, had put him on half pay. While she was proud that Jack was serving his country well, she confessed that "we have not a 'bob' left in the world and I do not know what the future holds in store for us."

By the end of August 1914, the sisters-in-law had returned home from their holiday by the sea in Norfolk.

Jennie persuaded Mr. Paris Singer, son of Isaac of the Singer Sewing Machine Company, to offer his large residence, Oldway Mansion, Paignton, Devonshire, for military use, and it became a perfectly equipped 250-bed hospital with an operating room. Wounded soldiers were transported to the hospital in ambulance trains. Jennie also helped organize buffets at railroad stations for the thousands of traveling troops.

Throwing herself into fund-raising for the American Women's War Relief Fund, she became chairman of its executive committee. The funds provided motor ambulances for the front, clothes for refugees, famine relief for Belgium, and employment for women.[1]

In September, Goonie wrote to Jack of her work for All Saints Hospital, where she was to assist in the preparation of a small ward for seriously wounded officers. "I am going to organize and arrange, and feel quite competent, cool, collected and confident that it will be done beautifully, and I think I shall be made a Lady of Jerusalem."[2] Her financial situation was now quite difficult due to Jack's obvious loss of yearly bonus, plus the loss of income from stocks and shares brought about by the larger financial crisis. At their home, 41 Cromwell Road, Goonie would later that year have to dismiss three of her six servants, retaining only the cook, the nanny, and one other.

In the midst of all these war troubles Clemmie gave birth to another daughter, Sarah, on October 7 at Admiralty House. Winston's private secretary, Edward (Eddy)

Marsh, stood sponsor for her at baptism. Clemmie was exhausted after the birth and in November went to stay at a friend's house, Belcaire, Lympne, in the Kent countryside. Goonie joined her there. On a cold and snowy winter's day, November 19, the two women comforted each other. Jack had been in the trenches with the 2nd Division during an action on Tuesday of that week, and Goonie was very worried about him. Winston rang to assure them that Jack was safe and that he had been transferred from active fighting to a staff job with Sir John French, commander in chief of the British Expeditionary Force (BEF) in France.

Goonie was now obliged to move out of her home and rent it out to provide more money for the family to live on. Meanwhile, she and her children lived in houses loaned to them in London by friends who had a country home where they no doubt felt safer. The 9th Duke of Marlborough, Sunny, gave over a room at Blenheim Palace to the Royal Red Cross to be used as a military hospital. Some of the time Goonie was staying at Blenheim with the children and helping with the hospital.

Because it was a war situation, the Liberals and Conservatives pooled their political resources, and a coalition government was formed on May 26, 1915, under the leadership of the Liberal prime minister Herbert Asquith. Winston lost his job at the Admiralty in the coalition reshuffle over the defeat at Gallipoli, which had been Winston's idea and which he had supported in the Commons. As a consequence, the Churchills also lost the official residence, Admiralty House, that went with the job. With their own London home, Eccleston Square, leased out, they had to move temporarily into the London house of Winston's aunt, Lady Wimborne, at 21 Arlington Street. The reduction in Jack's pay from his employer meant that Goonie had to economize further, and she and her children moved in also. With two households, including five children and their nannies, under one roof, it was cramped. Winston promptly moved out to live with his mother. By October 1915, they had all moved together into Goonie and Jack's home, 41 Cromwell Road. Jennie would eventually join them there, and was able to contribute to the upkeep of the chaotic and noisy ménage.

In June, Clemmie took up important war work by joining the Munitions Workers' Auxiliary Committee formed by the YMCA. Lloyd George headed the new Ministry of Munitions, and women flocked to the arms factories to take up posts vacated by men going into the armed services. To maximize production, canteens were provided to feed the workforce. Clemmie became responsible for opening, staffing, and running nine canteens in the north and northeastern metropolitan area of London, each one providing meals for up to five hundred workers. Her job was to tour the areas and enlist ninety unpaid volunteer helpers, and to serve as liaison with, and obtain the cooperation of, factory managers.

Winston missed having a decisive role in the higher direction of the war. He suffered from low moments, which he called his "black dogs." In the late summer of

1915 he took up painting in oils to reflect and find solace. Goonie had helped in starting this interest when they were on holiday that summer at a rented house, Hoe Farm, in Surrey, when he came upon her painting in the garden.

Winston was so eager to be doing something active that he wanted to go back into the army and resigned from the cabinet on October 30. He vainly sought command of British forces in East Africa, and got a hint that Sir John French might get him a brigade command in France. In November he decided to rejoin the Oxfordshire Hussars in France. Sir F. E. Smith, the attorney general and a great friend of the Churchills, was present in their house the morning Winston left. He recalled how anxious Jennie was for Winston's safety, and her telling him:

> Please be sensible. . . . I think you ought to take the trenches in small doses, after 10 years of more or less sedentary life—but I'm sure you won't "play the fool"—Remember you are destined for greater things. . . . I am a great believer in your star.[3]

In December, Sir Douglas Haig replaced Sir John French as commander in chief of the BEF in France, and he told Winston that, with no vacancies for a brigade command at present, he would have to make do with a battalion. Thus Winston found himself, as of January 5, 1916, a lieutenant colonel commanding the 6th Royal Scots Fusiliers. This battle-hardened battalion was not certain what to make of its political colonel, but by dint of hard work and attention to military detail, Winston won their trust. That month, they went into the line at Ploegsteert Wood (known to the British Tommies as Plugstreet), situated on a sector of the Western Front in Flanders, Belgium.[4] It was a quiet sector, and the winter months saw no great actions. Winston worked his men hard improving their defenses, but was never a ferocious disciplinarian. He was once criticized from higher command for undue leniency. He never shirked danger, and did his share of frontline duty and patrolling. But by March 1916 he was anxious to return to the House of Commons, where he thought he could make a more meaningful contribution to winning the war.

That March, also, Jack had sailed with the Anzacs from Egypt to France, landing at Marseilles and moving by train to the front. After some training, they went into the line in the Armentières sector. This was just a few miles south of where Winston was serving, and Jack had the opportunity of dining with him on occasion. Jack was responsible for the smooth running of corps headquarters and was content with his job, if sometimes anxious for his wife and family at home.

Presumably Winston had voiced his dissatisfaction to his brother, and Jack's letters to his mother from April 1916 speak of what a waste it was to keep Winston in a dugout when he could be doing more important work at home. In May, on hearing that his under-strength battalion was due to merge with another, Winston resigned his commission and returned to England.

Jennie, now deeply immersed in war work, was interviewed in June by a *New York Times* reporter about the role of women in wartime. She emphasized women's understanding of the human values that were at stake and which must not be lost to "brutal foreign forces," presumably meaning German aggression. She saw the contribution of women to war work and their acceptance of responsibility in it as advancing their position in society and an aid to the suffrage movement. She believed that many women would be unwilling to return to "a sense of uselessness" or to "pleasure-loving" pursuits when the war was over. There had been, she said, a sea change in the attitude of the British government to women's war work. At the outset, there was reluctance to allow women even to set up canteens. But women had demonstrated their competence in many fields, leading to their general acceptance. She quoted as an example a woman at Woolwich Arsenal who had taken charge of the motor pool there. Jennie forecast that this transformation in attitudes to the role of women would guarantee them the vote after the war: "Dozens of men who in the past opposed the idea agree with me upon this subject." Jennie concluded by saying she hoped that the war would bring about closer relations between Great Britain and the United States of America.[5]

THOUGH OUT OF the cabinet, Winston still retained his parliamentary seat and wanted to be promoted again, but found himself unpopular in the House of Commons, with no effort being made to bring him back into useful governmental employment. For months the newspapers were full of adverse press publicity blaming Churchill and General Sir Ian Hamilton for the failure at Gallipoli. Winston was for the moment out of favor with the Liberal-led administration.

Jack, on the other hand, was busy in France, and in July, the Anzacs moved south to the battlefields of the Somme, and once again, he had to oversee the upheaval of moving the great concern that was a corps headquarters and see them all settled in a new camp. The Australians were plunged into the savage fighting around Pozières. He wrote to Jennie on August 16:

> The offensive continues slowly and there seems to be no idea of stopping yet. Worn out troops are relieved & sent off to recover and be reinforced—then back they come and again "go in." All the time the artillery never stops day or night. The supply of munitions is quite wonderful & there does not appear to be any falling off yet, in spite of the enormous amount used in the last 6 weeks.
>
> The Anzacs have done very well—as fighting men they are hard to beat. The awful shell fire was a surprise to them—but they have gone on making

frequent attacks, nearly all of which have been successful. The German resistance is wonderful, but they are without doubt hard pressed. . . . The letters found on prisoners give very gloomy accounts of life in Germany—all
are longing for peace, but the majority are still convinced that they are winning and will, in the end, win a complete victory.[6]

In the midst of all the fighting, Jack, to the great good fortune of the Churchill family, kept a close eye on their finances, and changes in the regulations, and his letter
concluded:

I wrote some time ago to Winston & told him that he should look after the
American securities which are at Parr's Bank. I hope they have been ex-
changed. If not, they should be as soon as possible, otherwise the extra tax
on the dividends will have to be paid.

That summer Jack got leave, and was delighted to meet Goonie in Paris and spend
more time with her than he had in the previous two years. In a letter in September,
he told Jennie, "Goonie seems to be going a round of visits & if I get home I shall try
to join her wherever she is for the week. Best love Your Jacky." He was referring to
Goonie's propensity for living the life of a nomad, constantly on the move, staying
with her many friends in London and around the country. It was a means of escape
from the terrible crush at 41 Cromwell Road. An added bonus was the separation of
the sons of Jack and Winston, Johnny and Randolph, who, when allowed to go about
together, were as mischievous as possible for two small boys to be.

IN NOVEMBER 1916, a letter from Jack to Jennie showed what a strain the constant
fighting was on officers and men. He wrote of the "indescribable mud" of that winter, and of men getting stuck fast and needing to be hauled out, and of some drown-
ing in shell holes. Jack said he was "in a paradise compared to the poor people in the
so called trenches & dug outs."[7]

When the corps headquarters was in a fixed location for a long period, Jack's duties became fairly routine. He was then used as a sort of public relations officer, receiving visitors, and escorting General Birdwood (who was in command of the 1st
ANZAC Corps from March 1916), on some of his trips. In April 1917, he was tasked
with showing visiting Australian journalists the battlefields where the Corps had seen
severe fighting around Bullecourt. The Australian newspapers carried a report that
included this description of Jack: "Sir William Birdwood had caused Major Churchill,
younger brother of Mr. Winston Churchill, who is a very winsome and brotherly kind
of man, and wholly without 'side,' to conduct us along some of the more historic por-
tions of the front."[8]

At home, domestic arrangements continued to cause concern. In the spring of that year, Paul Nelke, the senior partner in Nelke Phillips & Co., died, and Jack was worried that his place at the firm would not be kept open. He envisaged the war ending and finding himself without any job or regular income. From his letters to his mother we see that Jennie was being very kind to his family. She had moved back into her own house, and Johnny was so happy staying there that he refused to move back to Cromwell Road. Jennie also paid for summer holidays for Goonie and the children, renting apartments for them.

FROM THE TIME the Liberal-Tory coalition government was set up in 1915, the Tories had been demanding more power. Compromises were made, and when the coalition was reformed on December 7, 1916, the new prime minister was the Liberal David Lloyd George. Lloyd George had been minister for munitions in 1915, and war secretary in 1916, and had a good working relationship with the Tories. He was also a good friend of Winston's, but, because of his unpopularity over Gallipoli, he could not for the moment give him a cabinet post, but Winston knew his chance would come.

Meanwhile, Clemmie and Winston had moved back to their own home, 33 Eccleston Square, and in the spring of 1917, Winston bought a country home, Lullenden Farm, at East Grinstead, Sussex. It cost £6,000/$28,000—a considerable sum in those days, and he paid for it by selling £5,000/$24,000 worth of Pennsylvania railroad stock and £1,000/$4,800 of Exchequer war bonds. Lullenden was a beautiful, half-timbered Elizabethan house with a great hall and a solar room, set in picturesque countryside. It provided a safe refuge for the family from the London bombings, and was the ideal location for Winston's new hobby, painting. There were extensive gardens, which Clemmie enjoyed landscaping. Attached to the house were a hundred-acre working farm where livestock was bred, and a barn that they converted into a nursery, where the children lived with their nanny.

With his friend Lloyd George well settled in as prime minister, Winston might have expected a return to government duties sooner rather than later. Winston apparently did not fully understand the bitter resentment felt toward him by the powerful Tory hold on the coalition government. The Tories' deep dislike of Winston was still partly because he had left the party and joined the Liberals in 1904. He was heavily blamed by both the Tories and the Liberals for the disaster at Gallipoli in 1915, led by his friend General Sir Ian Hamilton, which operation had been abandoned, with the loss of many lives. The amphibious attack on the Gallipoli Peninsula in April that year had been Winston's idea, and he had promoted it as a government minister.[9]

After Clementine and family moved out of her house, Goonie rented out 41 Cromwell Road on a three-year lease, and continued to either rent more cheaply for herself and the children or stay in the homes of friends or at Blenheim Palace. The furniture was stored at the Duke of Westminster's stables and the surplus sold at a good price. Johnny and Randolph were at school, and the younger children when together were less trouble to care for. It was probably during the war years in time of worry and anxiety that Goonie became a heavy smoker.

Jack's letters home to his mother from the Western Front give an interesting commentary on the conduct of the war as seen by the men engaged in it. America's joining the war in April 1917 was a lift, though by July, he notes sardonically, in Paris, "England is quite forgotten & everything is American now. I met several American officers. They have got a great deal to learn and I am afraid they will do this learning in a very hard school."

It was not until July of that year that Winston's old radical ally felt secure enough to appoint Winston to a ministry. Lloyd George gave him his old role as minister for munitions. The restoration of a ministerial salary was good news for Clemmie and the family. This was very important work for the successful prosecution of the war, and Winston was as vigorous and demanding as ever in seeing the work was done well. In a diary that is usually filled with invective against politicians, Sir Douglas Haig recorded the visits of Winston to the armies in France most cordially, complimenting him on "excellent work," and on his enthusiasm to concentrate all resources on winning the war on the Western Front "by August 1918."

IN SEPTEMBER 1917, Jack reported to his mother on the victories in battle that form the middle part of the Third Ypres campaign and which were fought to gain control of the ridges in West Flanders, so often forgotten because of the costly battles for Passchendaele that followed. "The Bosche's[10] great defensive schemes have been defeated." He had, he said, been able to show Winston some of the scenes: "I saw W[inston] & Eddie [Marsh] over here for a moment on their way to Paris." But by November the tone of the outlook of the war had darkened again, with the onset of atrocious winter weather, and more bad news from the East as Russia was taken out of the war by the October Revolution.

The spring of 1918 opened with a series of huge German offensives, as the enemy tried to force a decision in battle before the Americans arrived in sufficient numbers to tip the balance against Germany. The Anzacs were not engaged in March, but by late April had made decisive interventions to stem the German advance. Writing to his mother on April 21, Jack summed up the situation with an expert eye: "The Germans must be disappointed with the result of their two great attacks. They achieved a great deal and captured much ground and great booty. But they did not do anything decisive, and the line remains intact." It was understood in the family that although Jack wrote to Jennie, as had been the family tradition since childhood, his letters would be passed around to other family members.

MONTAGU PORCH got home on leave in March 1918, and he and Jennie went to Castle Leslie in Ireland for a holiday, from March 28 until April 15.[11] It was there, in April, that he proposed to her and she accepted. Once again, Winston and Jack were presented with a stepfather a few years older than Winston. On May 25, Jack's reply to the announcement, sounding more like that of a parent to an errant child, says it all:

> What a surprise! Your letter has just been forwarded to me. Whenever I go to a war you do these things!
> I feel sure that you have thought it all out carefully and that you are certain that you are acting wisely. I know that the last few years must have been lonely for you. With both of us married it was inevitable that you should be alone. I do not remember hearing you talk of him and I have never met him. If he makes you happy we shall soon be friends. . . . Now, my dear, you know that no one can make any change in our love for one another, and it will be something to know that you are no longer alone. And so I send you my best love and wishes, and pray that all will be well.

In May, Jack ended his long association with the Anzacs when they decided to replace all British officers on their staff with Australians. Being an experienced staff officer, he was posted to general headquarters, British Expeditionary Force, as an assistant military secretary. General Birdwood paid tribute to the hard work Jack had put in for the Anzacs by seeing that he was awarded a Distinguished Service Order (DSO). With typical humility, Jack wished that there were a suitable decoration other than the DSO, which he felt properly belonged to the fighting troops. But, in that "age of medal ribbons," as he described it, he would wear it with pride. He got a home leave that summer and saw Goonie and the children in Oxfordshire.

Jennie and Montagu Porch were married at Harrow Road register office on June 1, 1918. Winston, Clemmie, and Goonie were the witnesses. She was sixty-four and he was forty-two, and although he was quite slim, his hair was white and he looked older than his years. He had money and large family estates. This time there would be no dramatic change of name. Jennie would remain Lady Randolph Churchill. Porch had to continue working in Africa, and, because of wartime restrictions, Jennie was refused a passport to join him, not even for a visit. Within three weeks of the marriage, Jennie was as lonely as ever. Porch had bought Jennie the lease on a new and more prestigious house, 8 Westbourne Street, Hyde Park, and she put all her energies into redecorating and furnishing it.

Jean Hamilton recorded in her diary, on June 14, 1918,[12] how Clemmie and Frances, Lady Horner of Mells Manor, had to leave a dinner party at Lord Haldane's[13] house at 11:00 P.M. to work a night shift at the Hackney Canteen. Clemmie was at that time four months pregnant with her fourth child, but she had not allowed the pregnancy to deter her from her duties. There were many worries beginning to accumulate for Clemmie. The Ministry of Defense had decreed that farmland had to be cultivated as part of the war effort, and straitened financial circumstances meant that Winston could not afford to cultivate Lullenden Farm. Also at around that time the cost of the lease on 33 Eccleston Square was being increased, and the Churchills could not afford to renew it. They had been plunged into genteel poverty when Winston lost his job as First Lord of the Admiralty and then his parliamentary pay when he went into the Oxfordshire Hussars as a soldier, and he had borrowed from Ernest Cassel.

At a dinner party at the Hamiltons' London home, 1 Hyde Park Gardens, on June 18, Clemmie unburdened herself to Jean: Lullenden Farm was obviously too isolated a place to give birth. Clemmie told Jean she could not afford the cost of the birthing in a nursing home, which was twenty-five guineas a week. Jean offered her the use of her home. Then, during a discussion about whether the childless Jean should adopt two children she was fostering, the compassionate Clemmie offered to give her unborn child to Jean, or, if Clemmie had twins, she was to have one of them.[14] It was, however, a momentary crisis, and when the child, a little girl, Marigold, was born, kindly Aunt Cornelia, Lady Wimborne loaned the Churchills her house for Clemmie's confinement. Mary, the Lady Soames, Clemmie's youngest daughter, told the authors in an interview that all her life her mother worried about money, which would explain her state of anxiety.[15] Winston, who knew nothing of the conversations between Clemmie and Jean, had earlier borrowed money in an attempt to see both families through the war, and their financial circumstances were still rather difficult due to the huge outlay on Lullenden Farm.

AFTER FOUR YEARS of war, events began rapidly to move in favor of the Western Allies. In June 1918, Jack found himself working for his old chief, General Birdwood, on the staff of Fifth Army. His letters home describe the victories, along with news of the interior collapse of the German army. He also thanked Jennie for her kind offer to pay Johnny's school fees—though one of her checks had bounced.

Then, on November 11, 1918, the German plenipotentiaries signed an armistice that brought the fighting to an end.

Nineteen

POSTWAR BRITAIN

1919–1929

A British general election was held in 1918, resulting in a continuation of the coalition government, led by Liberal prime minister David Lloyd George. Winston Churchill retained his parliamentary seat of Dundee in Scotland. In November 1922, Lloyd George resigned, forcing another general election, which the Conservatives won, and the new prime minister was Andrew Bonar Law. Winston lost his parliamentary seat and went out of government. That December, the Irish would be granted an Irish Free State. There was a brief and unsuccessful first Labour government in 1924, led by James Ramsay MacDonald. Another general election that October was won by the Conservatives, with Stanley Baldwin as prime minister, and Winston won the Conservative seat of Epping in Essex. In 1928, female enfranchisement was extended to women twenty-one years and older.

An armistice treaty between the Allies, including the United Kingdom, France, and the United States, and Germany was signed on November 11, 1918, in a railway carriage in Compiègne Forest in France. The principal signatories were Marshal Ferdinand Foch, the Allied commander in chief, and Matthias Erzberger, Germany's representative.

A British general election was held in December 1918. Women over the age of thirty were eligible to vote. Clemmie, Goonie, and more recently Jennie had supported women's enfranchisement and were able to vote for the first time.[1] The election resulted in a continuation of the coalition government of Conservatives and Liberals, with David Lloyd George as Liberal prime minister. In Ireland, a majority political party, Sinn Féin, had replaced the Irish Parliamentary Party of Lord Randolph's day. They had won 73 of the 105 Irish seats.

The end of hostilities in the Great War did not mean that everything immediately returned to normal. An armistice was not peace, and theoretically, the war could recommence at any time. Jack was busy on the staff of the Fifth Army for many more months, at first keeping the army in the field and, later, supervising the demobilization of the citizen soldiers as they were finally allowed home to civilian life. He wrote to Jennie on March 6, 1919:

> I have been hoping to receive orders to come home. My job has practically finished and although I have been fairly busy up to about a week ago—I have now very little to do and am very anxious to get away. . . . I am wanted in the City, where things are beginning to look better. I think Goonie has taken on Bedford Square for 6 months—and we will live there until the autumn—but it is going to be a great struggle.
>
> I hope to see you next week & to return for good. Yrs Jacky[2]

It seems that, on one of his final leaves home, Jack had made useful connections in the City that would guarantee him a job. The house at 41 Cromwell Road was still out on a long lease to raise much-needed funds. Until the lease ran out, Jack and Goonie and family were to live at 44 Bedford Square, London, loaned them by Lady Ottoline Morrell, a society hostess.[3] She then rather ruthlessly put them out as she needed the house, and they had to find another temporary abode in Ebury Street. Jack returned home in March, and later in 1919, he and Goonie and the children finally settled back into their own home.

In May, Jennie moved into her new home 8 Westbourne Street, after making a good sale of Brook Street. Montagu Porch, having left the colonial service for a time, was finally able to join her, and she was very happy living with a man who clearly adored her.

IN THE GENERAL ELECTION of December 14, 1918, Winston won his seat of Dundee in Scotland. Despite the Tory majority in the coalition government, it was fortunate that Winston's friend, David Lloyd George, who remained prime minister, bestrode the world stage as one of the victors of the most terrible war in Britain's history. Despite the cabinet being dominated by Conservatives, the prime minister was sufficiently in command of his government in January 1919 to confidently offer Winston either his old job at the Admiralty or the important role of secretary of state for war, with the added responsibility of the Air Ministry. Winston accepted the double ministries. The dominant Irish party, Sinn Féin, under the leadership of Arthur Griffith, had won 73 of the 105 parliamentary seats in Ireland, and was demanding an independent state rather than just Home Rule.

Winston and Clemmie, with their children Diana, Randolph, and Sarah and their new baby Marigold, were back in their country home at Lullenden, and also had a rented house in London. The ever-sensible Clementine advised Winston to drop the Air Ministry and concentrate on one thing at a time. But he was too keen on all things related to air power to consider her request, having taken flying lessons before the war. On July 18, Winston was piloting a plane over Croydon airfield when it crashed spectacularly. Though badly shaken, he still delivered a speech at a dinner that night. Winston, it seemed, was indestructible.

Winston did not help his reputation greatly by the violence of his reaction to the Bolshevik Revolution, which had taken place in Russia in 1917. With a war-weary nation looking forward to enjoying peace, he kept large numbers of British troops in north and south Russia to fight to maintain an anti-Bolshevik coalition but to no avail. He said that Bolshevism must be "strangled in its cradle." He was instrumental in having arms sent to the Poles when they invaded the Ukraine.[4] This belligerence soured his relations with Lloyd George and encouraged sections of British society to see him as a warmonger.

For the Churchills there was also the government's pressing requirement to cultivate lands for agricultural use due to the chronic shortage of food, vegetables, and fruit in the aftermath of the war. Winston could not afford to buy the machinery or to pay the wages of a farm manager and laborers to work on the land at Lullenden Farm, and in April 1919 he sold it to their friends, General Sir Ian and Jean, Lady Hamilton. There would be other rented houses before they were able to settle into a real family home.

WHEN JACK RETURNED home from the war later that year, he was without a job but followed up his earlier contact. He had been very kind to one of the Rothschilds whom he knew when they were schoolboys together at Harrow School, and this was remembered. Leo de Rothschild was putting money into the stock brokerage firm Vickers da Costa and asked for Jack to be a party to the negotiations. Some time around late 1919, he secured a partnership with the firm as a stockbroker.[5]

From November 1918, Jennie had been busily having her new house done up to the highest standard from the proceeds of the previous house sale. Lady Sarah Wilson, Jennie's sister-in-law, gave a victory ball at her home in London in January 1919. Jennie and Alice Keppel and all the best of society attended, and there were fifty Rolls-Royces parked in the street.[6] A life of luxury for the aristocracy was returning. For Jennie and Monty, as she called Porch, as the year progressed, there were new and exciting people for them to meet at the parties — Stravinsky, Picasso, Ravel, Proust, James Joyce. Jennie, effervescent as ever, particularly enjoyed entertaining younger people. In September, she agreed to act as cohostess at a party in a large country house, Chateau de Villegenis, south of Paris.

Clemmie had not much time for her mother-in-law and her gallivanting about, spending money, and, as she thought, making rather a fool of herself remarrying at her age a man twenty years younger.[7] Jean Hamilton wrote in her diary:

> Clemmie, when she [Jennie] 'phones to them to come and dine with her, just casually says "Oh, it's too far, we won't go, we must not begin this kind of thing." They now live at Westminster . . . but they have two motors and it can't take more than ten minutes.[8]

That December, Jennie and Porch also went again on holiday to Ireland to Leonie and Jack Leslie at Castle Leslie, set in a peaceful and idyllic setting, with thousands of acres of land and woods and seven lakes.[9] Leonie's husband had finally succeeded his father as 2nd Baronet, and Leonie was, from 1916, Lady Leslie.

The seclusion of the remote Leslie home and its incumbents was a world apart from the real situation in Ireland. A very different set of circumstances prevailed there after the victory of the Allies in France. Unlike London, there was no euphoria or celebrations in the streets. In 1916, there had been the Easter Rising, and riots and battles were frequently fought in the streets between the people and the police. In March 1920, 9,500 hurriedly trained ex-soldiers were sent from the United Kingdom to support the police. Dressed in khaki army uniforms, they were nicknamed the Black and Tans. Winston was, from 1918, moving steadily to the right in his politics. He approved the creation of this auxiliary police force. In an increasingly ugly guerrilla war for Irish independence, these men committed some notorious atrocities by way of retaliation for Irish attacks on British establish-ments. They attacked the ordinary population as well as the rioters and became a hated force.

Winston was now engaged in negotiations to grant Home Rule to Ireland with a parliament in Dublin and one in Belfast in the north, but the Unionists there were not keen on the idea. When the Home Rule Act was passed on December 23, 1920, to which Winston was a signatory, it was already out of touch with the demands of both the dominant political party, Sinn Féin, and the opposing Unionists, the latter residing mainly in the province of Ulster in the north.[10] Sinn Féin wanted an inde-pendent Irish Free State, and the Unionists wanted Ireland to remain British, though they would eventually agree to the partition of Ireland.

As secretary of state for the colonies (February 13, 1921–October 19, 1922) Win-ston was involved in the lengthy negotiations with the Irish leaders on the treaty to establish an Irish Free State. Clemmie was most eager for a solution in Ireland, and wrote to Winston in February, urging him to participate in bringing about a just set-tlement. She asked him to put himself in the place of the Irish leaders in order that he might understand that they would not be "cowed by severity and uncertainty."[11] Win-ston was a signatory to the Anglo-Irish Treaty, establishing the Irish Free State, which came into being on December 6, 1922. Twenty-six counties in the south of Ireland be-longed to the new state, with a parliament in Dublin, while six in the north remained in a separate British state called Northern Ireland, in the United Kingdom, with a parliament at the Stormont building in Belfast.

AT 41 CROMWELL ROAD, family life was returning to normal for Jack and Goonie, following a five-year separation during the war. Clemmie now had three girls, and Goonie longed for a girl. In June 1920, she got her dearest wish; a daughter was born, christened Anne Clarissa Nicolette (she was always known as Clarissa). Goonie would lavish a great deal of love on this precious child, her last.

Johnny, aged eleven, had artistic tendencies, and Peregrine, nine, was already showing an interest in engineering. Both boys followed in the footsteps of their fa-ther and uncle and built up a huge collection of toy soldiers, with a fine transport section. Their model electric railway covered the entire ground floor of their home, and they collected model ships. Their mechanical model of the Battle of Jutland, the largest naval battle of the war between the British and the Germans, May 31–June 1, 1916, in the North Sea near Denmark, was so accurate that it impressed two of the British admirals who had participated, David Beatty and Roger Keyes, when they were invited to see it. It would later be taken to Chartwell to show Uncle Winston, who at the request of Arthur Balfour had written a report of the battle. (In May 1915, Balfour had succeeded Winston as First Lord of the Admiralty.)[12]

1921 WAS OTHERWISE to be a terrible year for the Churchills. Clemmie's younger brother, William (Bill), who had given her away on her wedding day, had been in command of HMS *Thorn,* a torpedo destroyer ship, during the war. He now lived in Paris and had become a heavy drinker and a debt-laden gambler. In February, Winston, who was extremely fond of him, had tried to straighten him out, encouraging him to give up gambling and to pay off his debts. Bill had apparently done so and had given Winston his solemn promise that he would not gamble at cards again.[13] Winston and Clemmie had then left at the end of February on a long trip to Cairo, as Winston was to attend a Middle Eastern Conference to settle affairs in that part of the world. In Jerusalem, Winston reasserted the British government's policy of allowing a Jewish National Homeland of Palestine.[14] The Churchills had only just returned home, when a few days later, suddenly and without warning, on April 14, Bill shot himself dead in his Paris hotel room. For Winston, as a cabinet minister, it was a shocking revelation in the press. Winston was filled with grief and remorse, lest the promise he extracted from Bill had tipped him over the edge to suicide.

At the end of May, Jennie went to one of the marvelous house parties at Mells Manor, Somerset, the home of the Horner family. Frances, Lady Horner and her family were great friends of the Churchills. Jennie, having recently been to Italy on holiday, was wearing new Italian shoes, and normally a maid would scour the soles to make the new leather less slippery. It seems this was not done, and Jennie took a very nasty fall downstairs and broke her ankle. A local doctor set it, and she was taken back to London by ambulance.

Jennie's leg turned black, and Winston, upon seeing it, brought in a surgeon for advice. Jean Hamilton was to go to the theatre with Jennie and arrived at her house on the afternoon of June 10. Leonie was there, looking after Jennie, and told Jean at the door about Jennie's accident and that gangrene had set in, and they thought her foot was to be amputated. Jennie was taken by ambulance to the hospital that day, where her leg was amputated. She had been very brave, telling the surgeon to "be sure and cut high enough." After the operation, Jennie seemed out of danger and was cheerful. Then she suffered a sudden hemorrhage on the morning of June 29. By coincidence, Bourke Cockran and his third wife were visiting London, and Bourke drove Leonie Leslie across London to Jennie's bedside. When they arrived, she was still breathing, but she never regained consciousness. She died later that day, aged sixty-seven. On a hot July day her coffin was transported to Oxford by train, accompanied by her family. Jennie was laid to rest in the cemetery at St. Martin's Church, Bladon, beside Randolph. All their lives, Winston and Jack had adored their mother. They lined her grave with white roses and lilac orchids, which were her favorite flowers.[15]

Afterwards, Jack looked after poor Montagu Porch, who, having returned to work in Nigeria, rushed back, arriving too late to attend his wife's funeral.[16] He declined to inherit any of Jennie's property, and it was Jack who was left to sort out her estate. She left debts of approximately £70,000/$336,000, mostly owed to Rothschild's Bank.[17] Immediately after her death, her creditors were demanding large sums, and Jack had to pay the most persistent of them out of his own pocket to keep the bailiffs at bay until an auction of her property could take place to raise funds. Winston and Jack retained items only of sentimental value, which included some of her jewelry and furniture and a fine library. Settling her financial affairs was no easy matter. It would be 1927 before Jack was able to complete this task.[18]

While Winston was busy with the affairs of the Colonial Office, Clemmie had searched out a new London home for them, 2 Sussex Square, and they moved in that August.

That August, Goonie rented for their holidays Menabilly, a house in Cornwall, which was leased by the Horners but is more famous as the home of the novelist Daphne du Maurier.[19] They spent an idyllic summer there by the sea, visiting many friends, including Clemmie and the Horners. Jack could only get down for three weeks as he was sorting out his mother's estate, but everyone said how much better he looked when he left than he did when he arrived. Clemmie wrote to Winston from Menabilly, asking him to look after Jack. It seems that, with all the servants from 41 Cromwell Road gone to Cornwall with Goonie and the family, Jack was being cared for by one housekeeper, a policeman's wife, "who nourishes him exclusively on salted haddock."[20]

Clemmie remarked to Winston how much she would like a country home, if only to be able to see more of the "Jagoons," the delightful collective noun the Churchills gave to the family of Jack and Goonie. This would spark the search that ended with the finding of Chartwell.

In early August, there had been more sorrow for Winston. Thomas Walden, Lord Randolph's old and faithful valet, died. Walden had accompanied Lord Randolph on the world tour in 1894. At his death in 1895, Walden had become Winston's servant, accompanying him to all his wars and taking care of him. But the hardest blow of all was about to strike.

Marigold, aged two years and nine months, their adored "Duckadilly," died unexpectedly, on August 23. She had previously had coughs and colds, but it was not known that she was very ill until it was too late. She died of septicemia, while Clemmie sat by her bedside singing her favorite nursery song to her.[21] Winston and Clemmie were utterly devastated by their loss, and were plunged into deepest mourning for a beloved child. Winston took his other children to see the grave. A story is told today by the guides at Kensal Green Cemetery, in London, where Marigold is buried, that the wartime prime minister would arrive in an official limousine and stop and get out and sit on a bench there for a time, meditating in silence.[22]

MUCH JOY WAS restored in September 1922 with the birth to Clemmie and Winston of their daughter Mary, today the Lady Soames and the Churchills' only surviving child.

Things may have been looking up for them, for Winston bought for £5,000/$24,000 a fine country house in Kent, Chartwell, set in lovely grounds but needing a good deal of work done before it was truly habitable for a family. Winston's great-grandson, Randolph Churchill, recently told the authors that he had discovered that General Sir Ian Hamilton (who was a lifelong friend of Winston's) had the shooting rights of the Chartwell estate from the previous owners prior to Winston's time there. Randolph thinks the likelihood is that it was Hamilton who told Winston when the place came up for sale.[23]

That October, Winston suffered from appendicitis and was hospitalized and had to undergo an operation, which took him out of political life at a crucial moment.

At loggerheads with his Conservative partners, David Lloyd George resigned as prime minister in October 1922, forcing a general election, which was held on November 15. The Liberal Party was split between those who followed Lloyd George and those who followed Herbert Asquith, the previous Liberal prime minister.

Clemmie set off to Dundee to Winston's constituency to campaign for her husband. Taking baby Mary with her, she arrived on November 5. Clemmie addressed six public meetings, making speeches on her husband's behalf. Winston wasn't able to visit Dundee until November 11, just four days before polling. He had bombarded the electorate with letters and manifestos, but again erred on the side of extremism. He attacked the Labour Party candidate, the irreproachable E. D. Morel, trying to paint him as a bloodthirsty communist. Despite Clemmie's best efforts, it all backfired terribly. Winston was thrashed into fourth place. On his forty-eighth birthday, he was out of office and out of Parliament altogether. The Conservatives won the election,[24] with Canadian-born Andrew Bonar Law becoming prime minister.[25] They had no place in their ranks for Winston, who they still viewed as a turncoat.

Winston and Clemmie went on a long winter holiday in the south of France. He tried to put a brave face on things, but the "black dog" of depression sat heavily upon him.[26] He found solace in his painting and began to sketch out plans for his monumental history of the period 1914–1919, _The World Crisis._

Having lost his Dundee seat, Winston had time on his hands and was working on _The World Crisis,_ between the years 1923 and 1931. As each volume was published, the Churchills' finances steadily improved. This encyclopedic work on the origins, conduct, and aftermath of the Great War was an opportunity for Winston to explain many of his decisions and to vindicate his stand on such major issues as Gallipoli and the Dardanelles campaign. The work is criticized as being very partial in its presentation of the history of the war, insofar as Winston could portray the decisions he made in the best possible light. Even the friendly reviews in the press found it "remarkably egotistical";[27] Arthur Balfour described it as "Autobiography, disguised as a history of the universe."[28] But the books had been supported in the writing by, and drew praise from, naval authorities and all those who opposed the attritional fighting on the Western Front. What we can add to the story, from papers that have come to us from Peregrine, is that, once again, Jack Churchill assisted with the preparation of the book, for which he would get no acknowledgment whatsoever. He read accounts and biographies, especially of the Gallipoli campaign, which he then summarized and sent to Winston, to guide him in his writing.

Over the years the political landscape had been slowly changing with the rise of a labor movement of trades unionists, who were demanding policies to improve the lives of working-class men. James Ramsay MacDonald had been involved in British politics as a socialist in the working-men's Labour Movement for a number of years.[29] He joined the newly formed Labour Party in 1906. In that year, in the general election held between January 12 and February 8, he was elected to Parliament for the first time as member for Leicester (along with twenty-eight other Labour Party members). In 1911, MacDonald, having formerly been chairman of the Labour Party, became its leader. Following the decline of the Liberal Party, the Labour Party had been slowly growing in strength. In 1922, MacDonald was again leader, and the Labour Party was now the main opposition party to the Conservative government of Stanley Baldwin.

In November 1923, MacDonald was invited to form a minority Labour government, and it took office in January 1924.[30] This was anathema to Winston. He, like many others, feared the very worst, as the rise of the working classes was somewhat associated with the Russian Revolution. It turned out to be a very timid and short-lived Labour administration. Being still out of Parliament, at the earliest opportunity, February 1924, Winston fought a by-election for the constituency of Westminster. There was the curious stance of Winston being backed by most of the national leadership of the Conservative Party though reviled and rejected by the local party because of the number of years he had been a Liberal. He stood as an independent Constitutionalist candidate, promoting himself as an anti-Socialist, even though there was an official Conservative candidate also standing in the election. He ran a fine campaign, helped by the young Brendan Bracken, a businessman who was also eager to get elected to Parliament.[31] Winston missed victory by only 43 votes. The Conservatives won, and Winston had helped beat the Labour candidate, Fenner Brockway, into fourth place. His path back into the Conservative fold was now wide open.

MEANWHILE, FAMILY MATTERS at home required attention. The Churchill children were growing up, and needed to be educated. Jack sent both his sons, Johnny and Peregrine, to Harrow Public School, while Winston chose Eton Public School for Randolph. Both Johnny and Peregrine were good at athletics, especially acrobatics and diving. Less is said of their academic record. Jack, whose own handwriting was described by one of his masters at school as "educated and scholastic looking,"[32] did criticize Johnny's letters for the poor writing. Jack gave both his sons lots of practical advice, like getting to know the Custodians well. These men, a sort of school police, could help a scholar out of a jam if they liked him. Johnny's artistic temperament developed, and, in 1925, aged fourteen, he sold his first work, a poster for the Great Western Railway. He painted the ceiling of his uncle Winston's summer-house, the Marlborough Pavillion, in the grounds at Chartwell in 1934, and again in 1949. The scenes celebrate the success of John Churchill, the 1st Duke of Marlborough, at the Battle of Blenheim, Bavaria, fought on August 13, 1704. Jack treated his sons with care and consideration. He introduced them in their midteens to the pleasure of good wine, especially port. Jack and his friend from Harrow school days, Lionel de Rothschild, were in the habit of pooling their resources to buy really fine wine and shared the cellar.

Johnny, in his autobiography *Crowded Canvas*, provides a portrait of domestic probity at 41 Cromwell Road.[33] Johnny thought his parents got on very well but spoke very little. After dinner they might play a little mah-jongg; more often Jack retired to his study to read the newspapers or books by one of their many author friends. Goonie held court every morning—elevenses with digestive biscuits and port, and a constant stream of writers and artists calling to see her. Jack would go round the house closing shutters; Goonie would follow and open them! Goonie's great foible was the poking of fires, often poking them to death. The British aristocracy had large houses with high ceilings and ill-fitting windows, which were drafty, and it was the job of a maid to keep an eye to poking the fire to let the heat out. Goonie's friends took to hiding the pokers when she came to call upon them, lest she leave them with desolate hearths.

The social graces were imparted by Jack, with lots of practical advice. He insisted that the boys always present themselves "clean, shaved, and powdered," for the ladies at close quarters notice every detail. Goonie advised them to pause before entering a gathering and run a wet finger over their eyebrows and eyelashes. It made one look fresh and alert. When they returned from a social event, Goonie would sit up late into the night discussing with Johnny all the finer points of the evening's proceedings.[34]

IN SEPTEMBER 1924 Winston was adopted as the Conservative candidate for Epping in Essex, and he was duly elected on October 30 with a majority of nearly 10,000 votes over his Liberal opponents. His critics suggest that, once again, he had managed to change parties just as his new friends swept to victory. What is truly astonishing is that the Conservative prime minister, Stanley Baldwin,[35] to the amazement of large sections of his party, promptly handed Winston one of the great offices of state, making him a cabinet minister as Chancellor of the Exchequer (November 6, 1924–June 4, 1929), meaning he would oversee and decide the amount of money each government department would spend, on the armed forces, on welfare benefits, and so on. After all those years in storage, Winston could finally wear his father's robes. Winston seized the offer as if he had never been away from government and, with his usual burst of energy, began imposing new limits on all government departments.

Winston and Clemmie were able to sell 2 Sussex Square, and move into the house at 11 Downing Street that went with his job. At the first budget he presented in 1925, Winston benefited greatly from the caution of the previous Labour chancellor, Philip Snowden, from whom he inherited a surplus of some £37 million/$177.6 million. He was very severe on the armed services, cutting naval estimates and eschewing any continental alliance with France.

The Churchills' country home, Chartwell House, required a great deal of repair and refurbishment, as well as the program of bold and imaginative alterations to the grounds instituted by Winston. A mortgage had to be raised on the property to finance all of this. Once again, Jack came to the fore in the family's monetary affairs. In April 1926 the solicitors were writing to him as a trustee to see if he was happy for a loan of £10,000/$48,000 to be raised on a property valued at £18,000/$86,400. "As this is a family transaction, the question of a forced sale is hardly likely to arise . . . but, of course, this does not affect your responsibility as a Trustee to see that a proper security is obtained."[36]

Trouble in Britain's coalfields arose in 1926. With their export markets destroyed by the strong pound and the cheap German coal being dumped around Europe to pay off war reparations, the mine owners simply cut the pay of their workers. Not unreasonably, the miners withdrew their labor, and a bitter eighteen-month dispute set in. In May 1926, the Trades Union Congress (TUC) tried to force a decision by calling a general strike in support of the miners' claim. Winston saw this as a call to arms. Paternal reforms for the workers was one thing; seeing the organized working class making demands of the government was quite another. This was the socialist menace he had feared and campaigned against since 1917, writ large. With the Fleet Street newspapers shut down by sympathy strikes, Winston got approval for the creation of a semiofficial newspaper, the *British Gazette,* to keep the public informed about the course of the strike and what the government was doing to combat it. Run by volunteers, with paper commandeered from Fleet Street, and with editorials thundering forth in typical Winston style, the circulation peaked at two million copies a day.

There was no revolutionary intent in the TUC, and the strike was called off after just nine days. It is entirely in character that Winston then became one of the chief contributors to an effort to find a peaceful settlement between the doughty miners and their equally stubborn employers. "Beer and sandwiches," a British working-class expression meaning for both sides to sit down together and talk rather than going on strike, were employed long before the Wilson governments of the 1960s and '70s earned a reputation for using such diplomacy.[37] The mine owners were recalcitrant, and the miners were literally starved into submission.

Winston produced useful budgets each year, something he never seemed to manage for his own household, and he found plenty of time for long holidays.

The general election of 1929 put the Tories out of office and gave Ramsay Mac-Donald's Labour Party its first real chance to govern. It was the Labour Party's misfortune to be in office when the great recession hit the world's economies. Winston held his seat but returned to the backbenches, for far longer than he imagined.

Twenty

FROM THE POLITICAL WILDERNESS TO DOWNING STREET

1929–1940

In May 1929, the Conservatives in Britain lost power to the Labour Party, still led by James Ramsay MacDonald. Soon afterward, the Wall Street stock market crash of 1929 led to a world economic recession. In 1931, MacDonald formed a National Government. The majority of members were Conservatives; they gradually assumed the reins of power though he remained as prime minister. In 1935, MacDonald retired due to ill health, and the Conservative leader Stanley Baldwin took over until 1937. That year, Arthur Neville Chamberlain became Conservative prime minister. On September 3, 1939, Chamberlain declared on the radio that Great Britain was at war with Germany. When he resigned, in May 1940, Winston Churchill became prime minister and minister for defense until 1945.

A general election was called in May 1929, and the Labour Party won 289 seats, the Conservatives 260, and the Liberals 58. James Ramsay MacDonald was still leader of the Labour Party, having moved his parliamentary seat from Wales to Seaham Harbour in County Durham, England. MacDonald again formed a minority government, the Liberals holding the balance of power in the House of Commons.

Winston retained his seat at Epping but, having no ministerial responsibilities, decided to go on a lecture tour. Jack had never taken more than three weeks holiday at a time in his life, so in the summer of 1929, he expressed a new sense of solid well-being by accompanying Winston on a three-month trip to North America. Randolph and Johnny, both down from university for the summer, would accompany their respective fathers for part of the holiday. Goonie expressed no desire to be so long away from England, and, to everyone's regret, Clemmie was not well enough for the journey. They sailed on August 3 on the *Empress of Australia* and traveled in great comfort. Winston found time to write two major essays for publication and began an intensive course of reading in preparation for his proposed study of John Churchill, the 1st Duke of Marlborough.

Once in Canada, the Canadian Pacific Railway Company provided them with excellent accommodation for their tour across from Quebec to Vancouver. The trip paid for itself with a series of lectures made along the way. After twenty-six days in Canada, they spent twenty days in California. They were often the guests of very wealthy Americans, and took great delight in visiting the locations and stars of the film industry in and around Los Angeles.

During their absence, Clemmie was recovering from minor operations and illnesses. She was sustained at home by her loving daughters, Diana, Sarah, and Mary, and by Goonie, who, with "Pebin" (Peregrine) and Clarissa, was a frequent visitor to Chartwell. She wrote on September 30 to Winston that the sixteen-year-old Peregrine and the (nearly) fifteen-year-old Sarah "seem more wrapped up in each other than ever."[1] In another curious reprise of family history, Johnny, who had grown up a bit of a handful, was always in scrapes with the equally rambunctious Randolph, and now rebelled against sobriety in favor of bohemianism, while Peregrine had grown into a serious, quiet young man, always with his nose in a book if he wasn't pondering some problem of practical engineering.

In mid-August Charles M. Schwab, the head of Bethlehem Steel Company, provided the train that took the touring party back to the East Coast of America. From there Randolph and Johnny, due back at university in September, were sent home. Winston and Jack extended their holiday with a visit to the battleground at Gettysburg and other Civil War sites. By the end of October the great Wall Street Crash had devastated the American economy and sent shock waves around the world. Winston estimated that his investments shrank by £10,000 ($16,384) in the twinkling of an eye, and, no doubt remembering his own upbringing, he felt a great anguish about his family's finances and prospects. In a throwaway remark in his memoirs, Johnny would say, "Certainly our families avoided the tragedy which overwhelmed so many others."[2] It was a blessing at this time to have a well-established stockbroker like Jack in the family.

The crash brought retrenchment in the extensive work planned to take place at Chartwell in the months ahead. Only the study was kept in use, and the family repaired to a cottage that had been intended for a butler. Winston embarked on such a sustained program of writing for money that they kept their heads well above water, and could even take out long leases on quite comfortable London homes. The year 1930 saw the publication of the very successful *My Early Life*. This humorous, charming, and engaging memoir has influenced most subsequent books about Winston. It was followed in 1931 by *The Eastern Front* (a supplementary volume to *The World Crisis*, after criticism that he had badly neglected that aspect of the war); an abridged edition of *The World Crisis*; a collection of essays, *Thoughts and Adventures*; and then the four-volume *Marlborough* (between 1933 and 1938).

Jack was back in his office at Vickers da Costa in November, wrestling with the turbulent stock markets in the wake of the financial disaster in New York. He could do little to recover their position in America, where things were bad and getting worse. But Vickers da Costa was paying close attention to world market trends, and Jack was able to make short-term purchases and quick sales to keep a small flow of profits coming back to the family. He managed the family's affairs, ordering their debts into a sequence for payment (putting everything off for as long as possible), setting losses made on the Chartwell farm against tax liabilities, and steering their investments along safer lines, toward basic commodities that would always be in demand and companies with a brighter future: copper in Rhodesia, oil in Alberta, and into Marks and Spencer, Gaumont British Films, and Sherwood Starr Gold Mining.

WHILE THE NEW Labour government was beset by worldwide recession, the Conservative opposition shadow cabinet ministers met only infrequently. This suited Winston, who was hard at work with his writing. But he soon found himself once again at odds with the party leadership. Stanley Baldwin, still leader of the Conservative Party, was steering the party toward some partial recognition of India's demand for self-government. In another extreme stance, Winston was utterly opposed to this. He spoke of the benign Mohandas Gandhi as if he were the devil incarnate. He was egged on by Tory press barons, hostile to any weakening of the Empire, and found himself entrenched in a very right-wing segment of the Conservative Party. In February 1931, Winston formally resigned from the shadow cabinet in protest, and when Baldwin entered into a National Government with Ramsay MacDonald in 1931, he was not offered any ministerial position by the dominant Conservative Party. He was well and truly in the wilderness politically, and without allies.

At the end of 1931, with Clemmie now recovered, they were able to travel together to America, where Winston embarked on what was expected to be a successful lecture tour, scheduled to bring in some £10,000/$48,000. But, soon after the first talk, while attempting to find a private address in New York to which he had been invited, he was knocked down by a car on Fifth Avenue. It was a nasty accident. He spent eight days in the hospital and all of Christmas and the New Year confined to bed at the Waldorf-Astoria Hotel. Three weeks of convalescence in the West Indies helped a lot, but he was depressed at this turn in his fortunes. He was very sad at what he considered three great blows in the last two years — the loss of money in the crash, the loss of office in the Conservative Party, and now the road accident — and he wondered if he would ever recover completely from this trio of woes. He gamely tried to complete the lecture tour, but was able to manage only about half of it.

Winston was writing on an industrial scale by now and began negotiations with the publishers Cassel for the major work that would become his epic *History of the English-Speaking Peoples*. An advance of £20,000/$96,000 was most acceptable, especially for a work not due to be delivered until the latter half of the decade.[3] Although Winston dictated his words to efficient secretaries, he always employed first-rate researchers, usually rising stars in the world of history,[4] to assemble the raw material on which he worked.

In May 1932, Winston's son, Randolph, left Oxford University before his finals to take up a career in journalism. Thanks to his father he secured a job on Lord Rothermere's *Sunday Graphic* and was soon reporting on the elections in Germany. Winston had very high hopes for Randolph. Having determined that his own parents were too distant, Winston had vowed to be a good father to his own children. He lavished care and attention upon his children, but they may have found that "living under the shadow of a great oak tree the small sapling does not perhaps receive enough sunshine,"[5] and being Winston's child was more of a strain than anyone realized at the time. Diana would endure two broken marriages. Randolph is variously described as "thorny, patrician, overbearing, comprehensively disliked," and even "a fascist beast." He, too, had two unhappy marriages, and is remembered as a heavy drinker, gambler, and womanizer. Sarah, full of charm and vitality, was won over by the amateur dramatics engaged in at Chartwell and Blenheim to a life on the stage and in films. Of her three marriages, the first ended in divorce, and the second in separation and the suicide of her ex-husband. After the terrible loss of Marigold in infancy, what a blessing the lovely and balanced Mary would prove to be.[6]

With Johnny embarked on an artistic career, Jack and Goonie were glad to see Peregrine safely into Cambridge University to study engineering, for which he had always displayed a natural affinity. Goonie had so longed for a daughter that she lavished an ocean of love and affection on Clarissa. This was so pronounced that it drew comment from others, including cousins and their nannies, who felt it to be almost unhealthy.[7]

Winston's continued extremist stand on Indian freedom alienated him from many Conservatives who might otherwise have shared many of his ideals, like Anthony Eden,[8] Harold Macmillan,[9] and Alfred Duff Cooper,[10] all of whom were experienced MPs. It has been observed that, had Winston passed away at some time before 1939, he would have been remembered as a rather fine writer and journalist, a good and improving painter, and a failure as a politician, in the sense that he might have achieved so much more had he been less of a maverick.

In August 1932, Winston traveled extensively in Germany, a country he admired, visiting the battlefields of the 1st Duke of Marlborough. In Munich, he saw at close quarters the burgeoning influence of the Nazi Party on the brink of assuming complete control of the nation-state. While he, in common with most people at the time, did not outwardly disapprove of the new regime in Germany, he does seem to have instinctively grasped the danger it would pose for Europe. He witnessed Germany's rearmament, in blatant disregard of the terms of the Treaty of Versailles that ended the First World War. On his return to England he wrote articles for the *Daily Mail* in October and November, highlighting the dangers of aerial bombardment by the rapidly expanding German air force, advising a corresponding growth of the Royal Air Force, and generally warning of the danger posed by a well-meaning pacifism in the face of Germany's aggressive intent.

WINSTON'S EXPERIENCE in Germany made him fiercely opposed to fascism and reaffirmed his belief that a strong army and navy were required in the United Kingdom, lest it should come under attack. January 1933 saw Hitler appointed chancellor of Germany. The Nazis moved quickly to seize the apparatus of the state, making their removal impossible. In February the Oxford University Union debating society passed the motion "That this House refuses in any circumstances to fight for King and Country." A week later, addressing the Anti-Socialist and Anti-Communist Union, Winston denounced this "abject, squalid, shameless avowal" and warned of the "splendid clear-eyed youth" of Germany demanding the rearmament of their country. His powerful talents as writer and speaker swung into action as a warning to

Britain and Europe of the danger they faced. It did not help Winston that people reminded him of his stance, before and after the Great War, against military spending and of the cuts he had made in defense budgets at every opportunity. But he had seen, with a clarity denied to others, the logical outcome of the Nazi accession to power, and he would not desist. There were great moves afoot in Europe to negotiate further general disarmament as a guarantee of peace, and France was put under great pressure to set an example and reduce its powerful armed forces. When Winston suggested that these measures made war more likely, he was shouted down in the House of Commons. His old reputation as a war lover, however unjustified, was at odds with the mood of the country.

ON MAY 13, 1934, Johnny had married the beautiful Angela Culme Seymour. Their marriage failed, and when Angela left him, he was left with a child, Cornelia (called Sally), to care for. Some months later, when he returned to London expecting his parents to assume the care of little Sally, he was in for a shock. Jack and Goonie did not wear their religious beliefs lightly. Jack and Angela had both declared themselves to be atheists, and his parents had disapproved of the irreligious marriage they had gone through. It had been conducted by the *podesta,* or mayor, at Portofino Town Hall (a small Italian fishing village in the province of Genoa on the Italian Riviera), and they had refused to take the oath on the Bible required for a Christian marriage. Now Jack and Goonie refused to take the child into their household on a permanent basis. They did look after the innocent child until Johnny could get set up in London and arrange for Sally to be taken into the Marchioness of Tweeddale's residential crèche. Johnny was not told at the time that both his mother and his father were quite ill. Jack was looking after Goonie, a heavy smoker, already in the early stages of lung cancer, while he had been told by his own doctors that an aneurysm in his chest might give him only two years to live.

In Parliament and the press Winston continued to warn of the danger of disarming in the face of German rearmament. He realized that he was having little impact on majority opinion in the country. While he maintained that his writing, and his idyllic life at Chartwell, sustained him, there were many "black dog" moments and a noted increase in the enormous pleasure he took in alcoholic beverages.

The region to the west of the Rhine had been demilitarized as part of the Versailles Peace Treaty at the end of World War I. On March 7, 1936, German troops reoccupied the Rhineland without any protest from the Western powers. The obsession with maintaining peace at any cost saw the West turn a blind eye to aggressions by militarist Japan in Manchuria, by fascist Italy in Abyssinia, and now by Nazi Germany in Europe—the policy that would later be denounced as "appeasement." By now the pretense of a unified National Government in the House of Commons was over. The Conservatives had assumed the reins of office from June 1935, with Stanley Baldwin again as prime minister. If Winston had hoped for a moment that he might be invited back into government, he was soon disappointed, for he was not offered a cabinet post.

Winston predicted that 1937 would be a "mournful year." His anticommunism, deep-seated since the Russian Revolution of 1917, colored his attitude to the Spanish Civil War. He was content to see General Franco's rebellion against an elected left-wing government succeed, despite the active support given to it by Germany and Italy. He received a constant stream of letters in his parliamentary mailbag, and reports and visits from his supporters who viewed the increasing military might of Germany with alarm. It is clear that brave individuals in the armed services and the Civil Service risked their careers by passing on classified information to Winston, spelling out the dangerous shift in the balance of military forces, especially in the air, in favor of Germany and against the Western Allies, as Germany massively rearmed in flagrant violation of the Treaty of Versailles. The British Establishment continued to feel that Winston was endangering the international situation by his public stance on these issues.

In May 1937 Stanley Baldwin retired, and Neville Chamberlain, Conservative Chancellor of the Exchequer since 1931, became prime minister. If his accession saw the first steps toward an increase in military readiness on the part of Britain, it also coincided with a more determined effort to engage with Hitler and secure peace by international treaty, which was anathema to Winston. In October, Chamberlain, on receipt of yet another published volume of essays, expressed his ardent admiration for Winston's writing, but there was to be no place for him in government in these dangerous times. But official permission was finally given to several senior officers to correspond with Winston in answering his questions on defense issues. He had gradually drawn closer to Conservative members like Anthony Eden and Alfred Duff Cooper, and a growing band of parliamentarians who were alarmed by the international situation. Eden, who had been appointed foreign secretary by Baldwin in 1935, disagreed with Chamberlain over the policy of appeasement, and resigned office in February 1938. Duff Cooper had been promoted to First Lord of the Admiralty in 1937, and resigned in 1938 over the Munich Agreement that Chamberlain had concluded with Hitler. When Eden resigned, Winston spoke vehemently in his defense. He declared in the House of Commons that it had been "a good week for Dictators," but the band of seers around him remained a tiny minority as the nation prayed earnestly for peace.

BOTH MARY, the Lady Soames, and Clarissa, Countess of Avon, the wife of Sir Anthony Eden, recalled from their girlhoods that, for many years, the whole talk at Chartwell was of the threat of war. Winston and Clemmie took great comfort from their family gatherings. The Jagoons were frequent and popular visitors. Mary described her Uncle Jack as "a peaceful addition to any party." By the late 1930s, Jack was much concerned with Goonie's health, and stoically bore his own problems in that regard without any fuss. Johnny was quite a successful artist now, with regular commissions for mural decoration. With Sally's upkeep, and a studio-cum-shop in London to maintain, he was usually cash-strapped. Jack did make him several substantial gifts of money, and Winston, when he heard of his difficulties, wrote him a generous check. Peregrine was gainfully employed on major engineering projects. Clarissa, in an effort to escape the cloying love of her mother, and displaying great academic ability, went off to the Sorbonne in Paris to study.

It was not long before their Uncle Winston advised both Johnny and Peregrine to get themselves into the army. Johnny at first applied to the Royal Engineers and Signals Board, hoping to use his artistic talent to specialize in camouflage work. There was no vacancy at that time, so the brothers both joined the family regiment, the Queen's Own Oxfordshire Hussars, now a Territorial Army antitank artillery unit.

IN 1938, HITLER threw caution to the wind and absorbed the whole of Austria into Greater Germany, before making territorial demands upon Czechoslovakia for the return of the mainly German Sudetenland to its mother country. It was a sign of the true feelings of Britain at large that Chamberlain could fly to Munich, make shameful concessions to Nazi aggression, and return to a hero's welcome, waving his promise of "peace in our time." If German ambitions could be diverted to Eastern Europe, what need had Britain and France to concern themselves? Winston's group of patriots was roundly denounced as troublemakers, and the machinery of the Conservative Party was deployed to make their political lives difficult. It can have come as little comfort to watch as Hitler promptly invaded and occupied the whole of Czechoslovakia in March 1939, then turned his attention to Danzig. Belatedly, Britain and France began military preparations to face the crisis; despite its lack of geographic contiguity they somewhat bizarrely issued a guarantee—that they would find impossible to deliver—to Poland that its territorial integrity would be protected against German aggression.

Thus it came to pass that, when Germany attacked Poland on September 1, 1939, Britain issued an ultimatum demanding German withdrawal. That ultimatum was ignored, and Britain declared war on Germany on September 3. Chamberlain had to create a war cabinet, and immediately that day Winston was appointed to it as First Lord of the Admiralty. He was at his desk that very evening, and a blizzard of letters to him followed, thanking God that he had kept such a true course for the best part of a decade, and was back in office where his undoubted talents were so badly needed.

After the rapid defeat of Poland, the whole of Europe went into a quiet phase known as the Phoney War. The British Expeditionary Force (BEF) established itself in northern France; Johnny served with them as a staff captain at 1st Corps headquarters, specializing in camouflage work. Peregrine was employed at the Air Ministry as a civilian expert on similar work. Winston saw the Royal Navy win a great success by forcing the pocket battleship *Graf Spee* to scuttle itself after being trapped in Montevideo harbor following the Battle of the River Plate. Once again the frustration of inactivity saw Winston firing off new schemes for action, including some very dangerous ideas about sending the fleet into the Baltic. He was initially interested in the plan to send British and French troops to assist the Finns in their separate war with the Soviet Union, but later argued that it would not impact at all on Germany's war effort. These discussions did draw Allied attention toward Scandinavia and the vital iron ore in Sweden that found its outlet through Norwegian ports like Narvik. Winston became a major advocate of preemptive action in Norway to seize these assets for the Allies and deny them to Germany. Preparations were well under way for an intervention in Norway when the news came that Germans were massing in their northern ports with a similar plan in mind.

Both sides set out on April 7, 1940; the Germans, having a much shorter journey, arrived first and in strength. Denmark was overrun, Norway invaded. The Royal Navy had some remarkable successes against the German fleet, but Allied land forces were contained and driven back by the German army and Luftwaffe. Before April was out, the Allies were planning for the very difficult evacuation of their beleaguered troops from Norway. A mounting tide of criticism of the whole handling of the campaign inevitably made Winston something of a target. How extraordinary that, in the ensuing parliamentary debate, he should emerge the victor.

Twenty-One

THEIR FINEST HOUR

1940–1945

After the surrender of France in June 1940, Britain stood alone against Nazi Germany, sustained by the "bulldog spirit" of Prime Minister Winston Churchill. Hitler's attack on Russia in June 1941, and Japan's attack on the United States in December 1941, created the great Allied coalition that would eventually grind down the enemy after much difficult fighting. Germany was forced to surrender in May 1945, and Japan in August 1945. By then the Western Allies were already at odds with the Soviet Union, and the foundation for the cold war was laid.

The British attempt to forestall the German invasion of Norway saw an unprepared expeditionary force overwhelmed by the ruthlessly efficient enemy they met in the snowy fjords and mountains. Though he was as culpable as anyone for the fiasco in Norway, Winston emerged strongly from the debate in the House of Commons on May 7 and 8, 1940. On May 9, Neville Chamberlain tried to cobble together a new coalition government, but the Labour Party refused to serve under him. There was such a tide of opinion running against him that a vote of censure reduced the government majority from 213 to 81. Chamberlain left the chamber on May 10 to cries of "Go! Go! Go!" That day the Germans launched a huge offensive against Holland, Belgium, and France. Chamberlain tendered his resignation to the King and, when asked to nominate a successor, advised that Winston Churchill be called upon. Winston's reputation, established as an experienced wartime minister between 1914 and 1918, and later built over several years as the siren voice warning about Nazi aggression, now made him the natural choice for wartime leader, and on May 10 Winston became prime minister immediately.

This was the moment Winston was born for. The stubborn streak in his character; his love of British history and institutions; his certainty in the correctness of his own opinion—all this came together at the hour of his country's greatest need. His unflinching leadership over the next couple of years is why he was, is now, and always will be regarded with the greatest admiration by freedom-loving people in Britain and throughout the world. His utter refusal to contemplate a negotiated peace with the most evil regime in history was what carried an ill-prepared and battered nation through many trials until more powerful allies stepped up to take the strain of the war.

He would face many more humiliating military defeats, and the pressure of responsibility would see many more "black dogs" of depression gnawing at him. Throughout his travails a close and loving family would sustain him. They made a vital contribution to Britain's success in war in this, their own way.

As WINSTON EMBARKED on his career as prime minister, Jack, himself having been diagnosed with an aneurysm at his heart, and devoting all his spare time to nursing Goonie, gamely went out every day to work in his office in the City.

In 1939, Randolph had married the beautiful Pamela Digby,[1] an English socialite, and the daughter of Edward, 11th Baron Digby, of historic Minterne Magna House, Dorset. In 1940, Randolph was returned unopposed as the Conservative member of

Parliament for Preston, Lancashire. In January 1941 he went out to the Middle East with No. 8 Commando, and was frustrated to be kept in Cairo, doing various liaison jobs, by commanders too afraid of his father to put him in harm's way. Diana served in the Women's Royal Naval Service but had to leave in February 1941 to look after her two small children and her husband, Duncan Sandys, who had been seriously injured in a car accident. Sarah continued her acting career until she parted from her husband, Vic Oliver, in 1941. She then joined the Women's Auxiliary Air Force and worked on photographic interpretation. By September, when Mary joined the Auxiliary Territorial Service and immediately applied for active service with a mixed antiaircraft battery, the whole family was in uniform.

The matriarch, Clementine, was the guiding genius of the family. She was as perceptive as ever, realizing that a well-meant attempt to get Johnny's daughter Sally evacuated to America as part of a general government scheme to evacuate children from the London bombings would look like the Churchills were abandoning the country. She moved swiftly to get the passage canceled and the child relocated elsewhere in England. She frankly warned Winston in June 1940 that his "sarcastic and over-bearing manner" was alienating the friends he must work with.[2] She was sure this was just the strain of his work, but the value of such timely advice was beyond calculation. Clemmie embarked on a punishing schedule of work and visits in her own right to investigate the condition of air raid shelters in London and make many practical suggestions for their improvement.

It was not long before the home of Jack and Goonie, 42 Chester Terrace, Regent's Park, received bomb damage in 1940. Goonie moved to live in the country, and Jack moved into 10 Downing Street. He spent a good deal of time in the extensive bombproof shelters belowground, "in quarters resembling third-class accommodation on a Channel steamer," according to "Jock" Colville, Winston's wartime assistant private secretary.

Between working in the City, where he said things were rather flat, and traveling down to see Goonie every weekend, Jack helped Winston by using his organizational and financial skills to set up and run a canteen for Winston's immediate staff at the Downing Street–Foreign Office complex. Their productivity in the service of this most demanding of masters was enhanced by being able to have their meals at any time at their place of work. Lord Moran, Winston's doctor, remembered Jack dining with the secretaries every night, always "the life of the party." Moran knew that Jack was seriously ill and marveled that "he went on his way as if he had no care in the world."[3] Jack's office skills, shorthand, typing, and administration, were called upon for some of Winston's most private correspondence.[4]

Winston's great energetic attitude to work saw him constantly moving about the country, visiting installations, inspecting units, and meeting officials. Jack was an inseparable companion for much of the time. He was always there when asked, but would make himself scarce when secret matters were discussed. The presence of his brother helped Winston through some difficult times, and when the chance to relax at Chequers, the prime minister's official country home, came, he needed as many of his family and friends about him as could be arranged. Winston refreshed himself for the fight in this setting and with these people.

The British and French armies were defeated in France by June 1940, and had to be evacuated across the beaches at Dunkirk. A desperately weak Britain stood in imminent danger of invasion. It was at this time that Winston made some of the greatest speeches of his career, inspiring the nation to stand firm in its resistance to the seemingly invincible enemy and the ensuing bombing campaign we know as the Blitz. The defiance in Winston's great speeches was as powerful a weapon as the scarce resources available to Britain's armed forces. The sustained bombing of British cities that autumn was stoically borne, while the might of the Royal Navy and the extraordinary dedication of the Royal Air Force and antiaircraft services during the Battle of Britain kept Britain's shores inviolate.

Not content with resisting the fascist enemy, Winston declared that he sought nothing less than complete victory and the extirpation of the enemy creed from the world. All the while he devoted himself to drawing that great arsenal of democracy, the United States of America, into the war on Britain's side. Though many leading Americans recognized the threat posed by a victorious Nazi Germany, there were as many and more who agreed with the majority of the American people that this was a European civil war, best avoided by the United States.

Winston must have hoped that his half-American heritage would appeal to the decision makers in America. His direct appeals to President Franklin D. Roosevelt, by cable and personal meetings, drew much sympathy but no commitment to enter the war. America, to the great benefit of its depressed economy, sold arms and equipment to Britain until the entire gold reserves of the country had found their way to Fort Knox, and then Roosevelt sent Harry Hopkins over with the offer of lend-lease, a sort of deferred payment scheme that suggested Britain was only borrowing the sinews of war to keep its armed forces in the fight.

All this was a prelude to the first of the two great acts that would ultimately lead to Germany's downfall. On June 22, 1941, Germany and its allies attacked the Soviet Union, unleashing the greatest and most violent campaign in military history. Winston, the inveterate enemy of Soviet communism, began immediately to offer assistance to his new ally, Joseph Stalin. In justifying his calls to assist the Soviet communist leader, he quipped that if the Germans invaded Hell, he could be relied upon to make at least a favorable reference to the Devil in the House of Commons! The Soviets suffered such a string of massive defeats in 1941 and 1942 that many doubted that they could last much longer, but they fought the Germans to a standstill at the very gates of Moscow and then secretly brought in troops from Siberia to launch a powerful counterattack that showed the world that the Germans could be defeated in the field.

ON THE EXTENDED Churchill family, so completely taken up with the war, a great sadness now descended. Goonie, who had continued to be a heavy smoker, had bravely fought lung cancer for some three years with Jack by her side. She knew she was getting weaker, and she raged against her fate. She resented the idea of dying at the age of only fifty-six. Early in July 1941, a severe chill developed into pneumonia, and she died on July 7. The letters and tributes to her were, quite simply, astonishing. A tidal wave of love and affection, private and public, was released, to the great comfort of her family.

One poignant little card from her mother, who survived her by a year, read, "Now comes peace, my darling." Lord David Cecil,[5] a younger son of Lord Salisbury, the former prime minister, wrote the lyrical obituary that appeared in *The Times:*

> Lady Gwendeline Churchill's extraordinary charm was implicit in her appearance, her subtle twilight beauty, the fastidious grace of her dress. But it disclosed its power, fully, only in intimate conversation. . . . She was like the single flower of a high civilization, bred through generations to bloom once only for the wonder and delight of mankind.[6]

It was the kind Katharine Asquith, widowed daughter-in-law of Herbert Asquith, a former prime minister, who, when Goonie died, directly addressed the role Jack had played during the long illness: "I know the terrible strain you have been under for three years—and how you dreaded the pain and suffering for her—and how wonderfully you took it. Your love must have been a great protection for her."

The devout Roman Catholic Lady Gwendeline Spencer Churchill was buried on July 10, 1941, at Begbrook Convent, some three miles from Blenheim Palace.

ON DECEMBER 7 the Imperial Japanese Navy, without a declaration of war, attacked the U.S. naval base at Pearl Harbor in the Hawaiian Islands. Astonishingly, in the second great act of folly referred to, either in a fit of Hitlerian madness or a bowing to inevitability, Germany at once declared war on the United States of America. Winston could hardly contain his glee. He felt that the war had been won from that moment forward. There would be much hard fighting for more than three years, but in slightly more than one year the battles of Midway in the Pacific, El Alamein in North Africa, and Stalingrad on the Eastern Front decisively wrested the initiative away from the Axis powers.

It would be some while before the full might of the United States, industrial and military, could be fully mobilized. For most of 1942, the Allies endured further reverses that seemed all the more bitter after the jubilation released by America's entrance into the war. A Russian offensive failed, and its armies were driven back to the Volga and the Caucasus Mountains. The Japanese burst out over Southeast Asia and the Pacific. The surrender of Singapore to the Japanese was arguably the worst disaster in British military history. An experimental amphibious raid on Dieppe in France was bloodily defeated. The Royal and merchant navies suffered grievous losses in the Pacific and Atlantic Oceans and the Mediterranean Sea. With his deep knowledge and understanding of military history, Winston saw these setbacks as the episodes they were. In July 1942, he faced down a vote of no confidence, which had been tabled in the House of Commons in June. Success for the British against the Germans and the Italians in North Africa, soon followed by the Soviet counterattack at Stalingrad that surrounded the German Sixth Army, was seen as a sign that the fortunes of war were turning in the Allies' favor. Success secured Winston's position as Britain's war leader against any further critics at home.

Once again, as had been the case in the First World War in relation to France, Britain was a junior partner in a great war coalition, and, while the Soviets were actively fighting the vast majority of the German armed forces, the Americans were pouring troops and equipment into Britain, anxious to open a second front in France at the earliest opportunity. Winston had a larger strategic vision that he found increasingly difficult to sell to the Americans. As the Soviets gradually assumed the initiative on the Eastern Front, he determined to develop an Allied offensive in the Mediterranean that would bring British and American troops into Central and Eastern Europe long before any invasion of France could be mounted from the west. It was to forestall the Soviets in the long term that Winston inveigled the Americans into joining attacks on Sicily and then Italy. The German defense of Italy neutralized that strategy, and the Americans were able to impose their will and press ahead with plans for the cross-channel invasion.

From November 1943, when Roosevelt and Stalin worked together at the Teheran Conference to insist on a second front opening in France the following summer, Winston finally lost control of the overall strategy of the war. The conference also guaranteed that the Soviets would be in Central Europe in force before the Western Allies and laid the foundations for the cold war that ensued. Perhaps Winston was right to try to forestall the Soviets in Central Europe, but with Soviet allies dying in such numbers in such savage fighting, it was impossible to spell out his visionary understanding at that time.

Winston, approaching his seventieth birthday, kept up a punishing schedule of work. He spent a lot of time overseas, at summit meetings or with his service chiefs.

Jack was always there to greet him on his return, often escorting Clemmie. Mary recalls that Clemmie drew strength and comfort from the constant and calming presence of Jack through these difficult years. The strain ultimately began to tell on Winston, and his health began to suffer. Clemmie, too, was ordered by her doctors to convalesce by the sea in April 1943. Ten days' rest at Weymouth, with the amiable Jack for a companion, saw her return to the fray in the best of spirits.

Clemmie did important war work as president of the YWCA's Wartime Appeal. She did not enjoy public speaking, but her delivery improved as she took her duties seriously and spoke up with spirit, appealing for money to help women war workers and service women adjust to the demands of war. She was a diplomatic host to the energetic and outspoken Eleanor Roosevelt during her three-week visit to the United Kingdom. But her most triumphant work was as head of the Red Cross Aid to Russia campaign. This nonpolitical appeal to send medical aid to embattled Russia was an ideal way for all political classes to express their support for a real fighting ally. The Russians were demanding recipients; polite pleasantries did not figure in their vocabulary. But Clemmie drove the appeal along forcefully, raising £2.25 million by December 1942. She deliberately let the fund get overdrawn as it shipped aid off as fast as it could be collected. A fine New Year's appeal saw the overdraft cleared in a trice, and the fund boomed along—over £4 million raised by October 1943, and £6 million by December 1944. It actually ran on until June 1947, by which time over £7.5 million had been raised. The Soviet authorities were moved to honor her on behalf of all the volunteer workers associated with the Red Cross.

The Royal Family did not sit idly by either. In 1944, Princess Elizabeth (later Queen Elizabeth II), who was the elder daughter of King George VI and Queen Elizabeth, joined the Auxiliary Territorial Service (ATS) and trained as a motor mechanic. Elizabeth could change the wheel of a car as well as any man. As wartime prime minister, Winston was a great favorite of the Royal Family. The King and Queen went out on walks about London, viewing the bombed areas and meeting the working-class people whose homes had been destroyed. They were photographed visiting people in the East End. The Royal Family refused to move out of Buckingham Palace in the center of London to a safe location. When the palace was struck by a German bomb, the Queen most famously said, "I'm glad we've been bombed. It makes me feel I can look the East End in the face."[7]

AFTER THE ALLIED breakout from the Normandy bridgehead in August 1944, the German armies were chased back to the frontiers of the Fatherland. Their success against the airborne landings at Arnhem in September, and the last desperate counterattack in the Ardennes in December, could not prevent their ultimate defeat. In particular, they could not prevent the armed forces of the Soviet Union pouring across the 1941 frontiers and driving into Romania, Bulgaria, Hungary, Czechoslovakia, Austria, Poland, and Germany itself.

Late in January 1945, Winston flew out to Yalta, on the Black Sea, for an important conference with Stalin and Roosevelt. Churchill was acutely aware that, with Soviet armies storming into Eastern and Central Europe, and those armies responsible for killing four out of every five of all the German soldiers killed throughout the entire war, he would be facing a triumphalist Marshal Stalin intent on securing the borders of the Soviet Union as far to the west as he could manage. President Roosevelt was already a dying man, and the Western leaders were not able to put up as firm a front as would be needed to restrain Soviet ambitions.

In March 1945, as Winston watched the British assault across the Lower Rhine between Wesel and Düsseldorf, Clemmie flew out, via Cairo, to begin a seven-week tour of the Soviet Union as the honored guest of the Red Cross. She and her companions, Grace Hamblin, Winston's secretary who worked at Chartwell, and Miss Mabel Johnson (secretary to the Aid to Russia Fund), were lodged in the State Guest House. A full program of visits to hospitals, children's homes, factories, and the ballet, and of official lunches and dinners, and one interview with Joseph Stalin himself, was laid on. The Soviet Red Cross awarded Clemmie the Distinguished Red Cross Service Badge amid stormy applause. They had traveled to Odessa, via the Crimea, for May Day, and returned to Moscow on May 5. She was there when the news of Germany's surrender finally came through. The next day, Clemmie broadcast over Moscow Radio a message from her husband looking forward to friendship and understanding between the British and Russian peoples. Clemmie was home by May 12. Winston, unable to break the habits of a lifetime, was late in arriving to meet her.

Jack's illness, despite his courageous attitude to it, was gradually wearing him down. In the last week of April he suffered a heart attack while staying at the Royal Dorset Yacht Club, Weymouth. After a week he was judged fit to be moved to London. Winston was in daily touch with the doctors for the fullest details of Jack's condition, and he visited him in the hospital several times. Jack spent time recuperating at Chequers, although that facility was soon to be removed from the family.

BY 1945, THERE had been no general election in Britain for ten years. With victory in war guaranteed, the political parties began to turn their attention to the demands of peace after such a protracted and expensive struggle. Partisan attitudes began to replace coalition cooperation. Winston greatly offended the organized working class, as represented by the Trades Union Congress, by refusing to consider an amendment to the Trades Disputes Act of 1927, still resented as an act of vengeance after the general strike. The Labour Party became more assertive, and the party conference at Blackpool in May declared that it was not prepared to wait for victory over Japan before insisting on an election. The coalition ended on May 23, and Winston technically headed a caretaker Conservative government until the election.

Winston worked on his electioneering speeches over the first weekend in June at Chequers. In his public addresses his old Labour colleagues immediately became Socialists, abhorrent to a free Parliament. Despite the predictably sensible advice of his wife, who warned him not to antagonize the electoral supporters of his wartime colleagues, Winston inserted into a political speech on the radio the idea that such a party could only govern with some sort of Gestapo to nip free opinion in the bud. The broadcast unleashed a storm of protest and did irreparable harm to the Conservative campaign. He may have realized, too late, that he had blundered, but he still campaigned as vigorously as one would have expected.

The election was held on July 5, but the result would not be declared for three weeks, to allow all the service votes to come in from around the world. On July 15, Winston flew out to the Potsdam Conference, outside Berlin, where the Allied powers were to discuss the continuation of the war against Japan and the many intractable issues about the settlement of postwar Europe. He returned to London on July 25 for the declaration of the results. He expected a victory; the Labour leader, Clement Attlee, himself expected to lose by a narrow margin. Winston was returned unopposed in his constituency of Woodford (formerly Epping), but the Conservative Party crashed to one of its greatest ever defeats. The British might have loved "Winny" and admired his defiant stand at the moment of the nation's greatest peril, but they could not forgive his party for the hardship of the thirties and the drift to war that had blighted so many lives. They did not trust the Conservatives with their future and turned in decisive numbers to the program of social reform heralded by the Labour Party.

Twenty-Two

THE END OF IT ALL

1945–1965

The Labour Party won the July 1945 general election, and their leader, Clement At-
tlee, became prime minister until 1951. The United Nations was set up to prevent
war in the future. Winston Churchill would eventually be returned as prime minis-
ter. Despite his advancing years, he became a world leader of some stature, both by
standing up to the Soviet Union and by seeking diplomatic understanding with them.
Ill health forced him to quit politics at a time when he was becoming idolized as the
greatest British statesman of all time.

W hen the results of the first postwar British general election were declared on July 26, it was a landslide majority of 145 seats for a Labour government, led by Winston's former deputy, Clement Attlee. Clemmie, concerned at the enormous strain the war years had put on his constitution, remarked to Winston on the night the results were declared that electoral defeat might well be a blessing in disguise.[1] He replied that it seemed quite effectively disguised! Admitting to himself that the size of the Labour majority made him feel slightly ashamed, it was not immediately obvious to Winston that not having to cope with the enormous problems of demobilization and reconstruction in a long-drawn-out age of austerity would actually work entirely to the advantage of the Conservative Party and its embattled leader. As his daughter Mary wrote: "Nothing and nobody could really soften the bitterness and humiliation of the blow."[2]

The Churchills had to leave 10 Downing Street, and a new house had to be found in London. A new role for Winston as leader of the opposition was embarked upon, and a well-earned holiday was arranged. Villas in the possession of two wartime colleagues, Field Marshal Harold Alexander, a British military commander who had served with distinction in the war,[3] and General Dwight D. Eisenhower,[4] who was supreme commander of the Allied forces in Europe, were made available in Italy and the south of France. Eisenhower was not staying at his villa at Cap d'Antibes but, having met up with Winston in Monte Carlo, pressed him to go and stay there. Winston did so, and completed some fine paintings, which must have helped to calm his frayed nerves. He submitted two paintings anonymously to the Royal Academy in 1947. Both were accepted for the summer exhibition.

A priority for the victorious nations was to create institutions by which war could be prevented in the future. The term "United Nations" was first used by Winston Churchill and Franklin D. Roosevelt in the 1942 Declaration, which united the Allied countries of World War II under the Atlantic Charter. The United Nations, as an international organization, was founded on October 24, 1945, to replace the League of Nations, which had clearly failed to prevent war. The chief aim of the UN was to provide a platform for dialogue as an alternative to war. There were five permanent members of the Security Council: France, the Republic of China, the Soviet Union, the United Kingdom, and the United States. The first meetings of the General Assembly, with fifty-one nations represented, took place in Westminster Central Hall, London, in January 1946. The hope of building a new world order around the UN met with disappointment as the former Allies in the fight against Germany and

Japan now engaged in a new cold war for world supremacy based on their respective ideologies.

Jack Churchill's health, meanwhile, continued to deteriorate and the aneurysm had caused a swelling in his chest. Following the heart attack he suffered in 1945, he had moved in with his son Johnny and his second wife, Mary (Cookson), at their home at Camden Hill, London. He was in such pain a lot of the time that Mary had to inject him with morphine at regular intervals. When he improved in health, he insisted on returning to his office in the City, traveling each day by subway train. Later that year, Johnny and Mary found him a nice apartment of his own at Bayswater, London, where he could have all his personal books and possessions around him. It was next door to an old friend, Katherine (Katie) Crichton, wife of the Honorable Arthur Crichton, and daughter of Colonel Walter Trefusis. Jack took great pride in being finally (after previous failures) elected to the exclusive Turf Club, Piccadilly, and he took pleasure in entertaining his family there. Peregrine, who was as yet unmarried, spent much time with his father in his last years. It was during these years that Jack imparted much of the family history to his younger son.

IN OCTOBER 1945, when Winston was awarded an honorary degree from Westminster College in Fulton, Missouri, he received an invitation to give their next annual lecture. He was encouraged to accept by a promise from President Harry S. Truman to introduce him to the audience, as Missouri was his home state. On March 5, 1946, in this small Midwestern college, Winston delivered one of the great speeches of his life. The speech was the product of his deep understanding of history and his worries about the effect on Europe of a resurgent Soviet Union. It was made famous by the dramatic description of Europe divided by "an iron curtain," though he had used the phrase many times before and it was not original to him. But it was thanks to this speech that the term made newspaper headlines.

In Fulton, Winston warned against a new appeasement and stated that the Soviets understood strength and despised weakness. He recognized that the Soviets had legitimate state interests, but warned that they could only be contained by a united English-speaking world, which shared a special relationship. It was a warning to the West not to drop its guard in the face of new perils. Condemned by some as the first shot fired in the cold war, and fiercely denounced by Stalin as a call to war, the speech gradually assumed a mantle of wisdom as the way to avoid future conflict, from a position of strength, rather than to drift into catastrophe through weakness and irresolution.

The defeated premier returned home from his American vacation as a world statesman reborn. He launched immediately into the preparation of his war memoirs, presented as a magisterial general history of the war (a planned five volumes would

eventually become six). Winston had always said that personal reputation was vin-
dicated by history[5] and that he would make certain that he was the historian. He negotiated a remarkable series of contracts with British and American publishers,
guaranteeing the most enormous income. He then set about recruiting a powerful
team of researchers and writers, including the up-and-coming historian William
Deakin, a war veteran and Winston's literary assistant, who had been a brilliant Oxford graduate, and the consummate staff officer, General Sir Henry Pownall, who
had been chief of staff of the British Expeditionary Force in France and Belgium.
Winston wrestled with the Whitehall Civil Service bureaucrats to be allowed un-
precedented access to all the state papers relating to the war. Many of his wartime
colleagues had been refused permission to quote from state papers in their personal
memoirs, but Winston, as the prime minister who had led his country to victory, was
granted privileged access.

It was a remarkable achievement for a septuagenarian, absorbing the work of
several assistants, editing their texts, and dictating his own linking narrative. The
succeeding volumes were always published first in the United States, the most lu-
crative market, and then in Britain. The first volume, *The Gathering Storm,* came out
in 1948; *Their Finest Hour* in 1949; *The Grand Alliance* in 1950; *The Hinge of Fate*
in 1950–51; *Closing the Ring* in 1951–52; *Triumph and Tragedy* in 1953–54. In all, 1.6
million words of text and nearly three hundred thousand words of appendices were
produced. He earned easily ten times what he was ever paid as prime minister. Indeed, all his books took on a new lease on life, and booming sales made him, really
for the first time, a wealthy man.

Like Winston's *The World Crisis* and its treatment of the First World War, this
project was not an entirely objective study of history; rather it was based on the careful selection of primary documents that show Winston's decision-making process in
the best possible light. It also repeated the fault of the earlier work through a complete lack of balance concerning the colossal and decisive fighting between the Germans and the Russians on the Eastern Front.[6]

IN THE MIDST of this tremendously strenuous work, in the hard winter of 1946–47,
Jack's health collapsed for the last time. Sir Charles Wilson (later Lord Moran), Winston's personal physician, recorded in his diary how Jack's illness had developed into
an aneurysm, which "throbbed under his breastbone like a great engine," threatening to burst and kill him at any moment.[7] In late February 1947, Jack's personal doctor, Lord Horder, told the family that the end was near. Winston received telephone
updates almost hourly. He gave a stream of advice to the nurses in attendance, encouraging Jack to fight to the finish.

On February 22, Winston was at Jack's bedside with Johnny, waiting for the end.
Lord Moran remembered Winston telephoning him with news of the illness. "Win-

ston was sad about Jack. He has a tender heart."[8] Johnny left the two brothers together for the final moments. With much shedding of tears, Winston sat with Jack as he slipped away on February 23, aged sixty-seven.

Winston had always loved Jack and felt his loss keenly. He busied himself greatly with the funeral arrangements, revealing a prodigious knowledge of suitable prayers, hymns, psalms, and incidental music. He discussed with Johnny the order of service and then, in a curiously Winstonian moment, pulled out a copy of his early book on the Sudan campaign, *The River War,* and read from it for some thirty minutes, seemingly to console them both at such an emotional time.[9]

In a final sadness, Winston was not able to see Jack buried. In the bad weather of that terrible winter, Winston's doctors would not allow him to attend the funeral at St. Martin's Church, Bladon, which was several hours' drive from London. Since 1945, Winston had a hernia and was wearing a truss, awaiting an operation to take place in June.[10] Jack was laid to rest beside his father and mother. Winston was able to attend the memorial service held later in London.

Of Jack's children, only Clarissa is alive at the time of this writing. Johnny continued his career as an artist, specializing in murals, and married twice more. He died in 1992, leaving only Sally (Sarah Cornelia, Lady Ashburton), who survives and is married with a family, to continue Jack's line. Peregrine became a successful civil engineer, developing a line of prefabricated housing of enormous benefit to the third world. He was keen to write about his father's role in the family, but he died unexpectedly, without issue, in 2002. His widow, Yvonne, survives him. Clarissa (Countess of Avon) married Sir Anthony Eden in 1952 as his second wife, and there were no children of that marriage.

DESPITE A MINOR stroke in 1949, Winston was back on form and able to lead his party into a general election the following year that almost wiped out the huge Labour majority of 1945. By October 1951, he had returned as the duly elected prime minister of a Conservative government. (In May 1940 he had become prime minister by acclamation of the House of Commons without a general election.) It was his sixteenth general election, and he was feeling all of his seventy-seven years.

There would be a last flourish of that great heart. In 1953, Anthony Eden,[11] the foreign secretary, had to take a long leave from the Commons because of ill health. Winston took over the duties of foreign secretary, and the extra work seemed to rejuvenate him. Thus it was that he was in post when Joseph Stalin died in March. Winston took the opportunity to issue a warm, friendly invitation to the new Soviet leadership to a summit conference, and even referred to the possibility of a pan-European security system that would, presumably, replace the power blocs of the cold war. The speech seems to have been instinctive: It came as a shock to his own party and to the Americans. The Korean War had reached a stalemate, and an uneasy armistice there was pending; the race for the hydrogen bomb was in full spate.

The world was not ready for such bold initiatives as Winston had proposed. A few weeks later another stroke forced him to take a month's leave, and he rested at Chartwell. He did not abandon his hopes for a reduction in tensions between the Soviet Union and the West, but circumstances were not conducive to success. War in Indochina and icy meetings between American and Soviet leaders militated against his idea that peaceful relations could be restored among the great powers.

In the postwar years of the late 1940s and 1950s, a great cult of admiration developed around Winston, with a constant stream of adulatory books about his life and times leaving the printing presses. In the United States, Dwight D. Eisenhower encouraged the cult by the several forewords he provided to biographies of the great man. In the 1950s, Winston was rapidly assuming the status of the greatest living Englishman, and one of the greatest figures in British (and world) history. The British government, at the behest of the new young Queen Elizabeth II, had already awarded him a state funeral by 1953. The planning began based on the last great civilian state funeral, that of William Gladstone.[12]

Winston was offered a peerage in 1955 with the highest category of Duke; Duke of London was a suggested title. He refused, perhaps because it would have interfered with his son Randolph's parliamentary aspirations. But in 1953 he was installed as a Knight of the Garter, and later that year he personally assisted in making the coronation of Elizabeth II a great morale booster for the British people, who were only just recovering from wartime and postwar austerity. In this triumphant year also, Winston was awarded the Nobel Prize in Literature. There is a faint, and commendable, suggestion that he would have preferred to win the Peace Prize.[13] A signal honor was paid to Clemmie when she was asked to accept the Nobel Prize in Literature on Winston's behalf (normally, if a recipient is unwell, his or her country's ambassador to Sweden accepts the prize).

For a man up in years, 1953 was strenuous, with the Garter investiture and the coronation. At a large Downing Street dinner on June 23, Winston had a serious stroke, and his condition, kept secret, deteriorated over the next few days. He was taken to Chartwell to rest, and the prognosis was not good. By the time speculation about his condition reached the British press via news stories from America, Winston appeared to have made a remarkable recovery.[14] Clemmie was anxious that he should retire from office sooner rather than later. But he battled on, first to wait until the "Party leader in waiting," Anthony Eden, recovered from a series of operations, and then to hold the position while the Queen and Prince Philip went on their long Commonwealth tour. He tired easily, and could get depressed, but still he managed to attend cabinet meetings and the party conference in October.

The Churchill family had its tribulations in those years. Diana suffered a nervous breakdown that made relations with her mother more than usually fraught.

Randolph, a successful journalist, seemed intent on offending as many people as was humanly possible, and Clarissa broke with him completely over a spiteful attack he made on her husband, Anthony Eden, in his book *The Rise and Fall of Anthony Eden*,[15] in which he spoke of "Eden's ill-planned, ill-timed and abortive invasion" of the Suez Canal in 1956. Sarah had separated from her second husband. Clemmie suffered acutely from neuritis, which gave great pain to her right arm and shoulder.

Winston's eightieth birthday, in 1954, was a national event of the highest importance—30,000 cards (one simply addressed to "The Greatest Man Alive, London") and 900 presents were delivered. A collection by 30,000 subscribers raised £259,000 for a Churchill Trust that would go toward the creation of Churchill College, Cambridge (in 1958).

As part of the birthday celebrations Clement Attlee presented an illuminated address from both Houses of Parliament to him, together with a specially commissioned portrait by Graham Sutherland. This uncompromising picture of an elderly gentleman, which Winston famously described as a remarkable example of modern art, was not at all how he wished to be remembered, and Clemmie was perfectly happy to throw it on the fire. Civic freedoms, prizes, and awards poured in. The celebrations were a tremendous, rejuvenating boost to Winston, though Mary Soames recorded in her diary that her mother collapsed with fatigue.

Senior members of the Conservative Party were now openly asking Winston to set a date for handing the premiership over to Anthony Eden. Winston would have liked to see another summit meeting to discuss the implications of the advent of the hydrogen bomb, but the Russians could not be brought to the negotiating table. Finally, the date for retirement was set for April 5, 1955. Anthony Eden took over as prime minister. Queen Elizabeth was present at a celebratory dinner at 10 Downing Street on April 4. Her presence was a sign of the enormous respect and personal regard the Queen felt toward her prime minister, since the time as a young princess when she had personally served in Britain's armed forces during the Second World War. A party for all the staff at Downing Street was held the next day. Chartwell and life as a private citizen beckoned. At last he could get on and finish his latest book, *The History of the English-Speaking Peoples*, which he had contracted to write nearly twenty years before.

THE LONG AND gradual decline of Winston's life set in from 1958 when a bout of pneumonia left him much weakened. A fall in 1960 led to the breaking of a small bone in the neck, but a worse tumble in 1962, while staying at the Hotel de Paris, saw the breaking of a hip bone. That had longer-term consequences. His London home, 28 Hyde Park Gate, was fitted with lifts to enable him to get about, but he was not able to travel down to his beloved Chartwell for a year. Deafness, for which he resolutely refused to wear a hearing aid, and increasing bouts of lethargy led to long periods of brooding silence.

As always, family life brought both joy and tragedy. Great comfort was taken from visits by his grandchildren (two Churchills, three Sandyses, and five Soameses) and the first great-grandchild (to Diana's daughter Edwina). The Soames family (who lived at Chartwell Farm) were a constant source of pleasure. Sarah's third marriage, to Henry Tuchet-Jesson, 23rd Baron Audley, on April 26, 1962, promised much happiness but was tragically ended after just fifteen months as Henry succumbed to a massive heart attack. The heaviest blow of all was the death of Diana, in October 1963, by an overdose of sleeping tablets.[16]

Winston remained the Conservative member of Parliament for Woodford through the general elections of 1955 and 1959, with substantial, if slightly declining, majorities. His last attendance at the House of Commons was in January 1961. The question of how long he could remain a member was being increasingly discussed, not least by Clemmie, who thought it really was time he stood back from public life. As a general election approached in 1964, Winston took the decision not to seek reelection.

The Conservative government of Sir Alec Douglas-Home, who in 1960 had been foreign secretary, planned, on Winston's retirement, to put before the House of Commons a vote of thanks for Winston's long and distinguished services to Parliament, which would then be conveyed to him at his London home. When Clemmie saw the utterly banal appreciation offered, she was deeply displeased. She carried out some research and looked up the stirring address made by the Speaker of the House when the Duke of Wellington left Parliament and compared it to the "mangy address" to her husband. Winston made a final visit to the House on July 28, and the next day a much more fitting tribute was passed, paying proper respect to his wartime leadership, remembering "above all, his inspiration of the British people when they stood alone, and his leadership until victory was won."[17]

Winston had been made an honorary citizen of the United States of America in the spring of 1963; his ninetieth birthday, in November 1964, saw more national celebrations. But another stroke on January 11, 1965, left him semiconscious. A priest was called to pray over the unconscious Winston, but he clung to life. On January 22, Winston was gravely ill, and Clemmie was keeping a close watch over him. Some cheerful news arrived that their grandson Winston's wife, Minnie, had given birth to a baby son; they named him Randolph. He endured until early on January 24, 1965, when, with two or three long sighs, he died at his London home, 28 Hyde Park Gate, exactly seventy years to the day, and almost to the hour after his father, Lord Randolph.

From January 26 to 30, Winston's body lay in state at Westminster Hall. The funeral coffin was borne to and from the gun carriage by men of the Grenadier Guards;

the carriage was towed in procession by naval ratings. After the service at St. Paul's Cathedral, attended by some three thousand people, the coffin was carried by motor launch from Tower Pier to the Festival Pier at Waterloo. It was then that the dockside cranes along the river were dipped in silent salute by their operators. Winston was laid to rest at Bladon Church in the bosom of his family. His place in history was secured forever.

WINSTON CHURCHILL's grave is visited by many thousands of tourists each year. It lies close to that of his father, marked, appropriately, with a Celtic cross as a symbol of the Ireland he loved, and of his mother. We are frequently asked where Jack is buried. His grave is beside his father and mother, in the row immediately in front of Winston and Clemmie.[18] Clemmie died on December 12, 1977, and was laid to rest with her husband. Winston and Clemmie are survived by their youngest daughter, Mary, the Lady Soames.

By his iron will, the product of his family history and character, Winston became his country's savior and, by extension, an important element in the fight against one of the greatest threats to freedom in the history of the world. His reputation as one of the great statesmen of the Western democracies is strong and well earned.

Authors' Note

U ntil now, Lord Randolph Churchill has been viewed by historians and biographers primarily through the eyes of his elder son and some of his in-laws. This has led to statements relegating him to being "a busy father who did not like children and who treated him [Winston] with calculated coldness."[1] Until we discovered the truth about Lord Randolph's will, it was believed that at his death he had left Jennie virtually penniless with two sons to provide for. Winston's cousin, Sir Shane Leslie, 3rd Baronet, would write the damning assertion: "Few fathers have done less for their sons."[2] Jack is not mentioned or considered in these assessments of Randolph's life.

A closer reading of the family's letters about and between all four members has painted a very different picture of the Churchills. Lord Randolph was certainly a busy man, often leading the fight for, and—because of the high moral positions he struck—just as often against, his own political party. He attracted a great deal of opprobrium from the Tory-dominated press. Through all this he suffered from very poor health, often exhausting himself and requiring frequent rest cures. But it is no longer possible to say that he ignored and neglected his son Winston. His letters to and about Winston and Jack display great affection, but also an increasing exasperation with the intractability of Winston to apply himself to his studies at any school he attended.

This annoyance, which could be impassioned, can only be understood if compared to the model behavior of young Jack, who applied himself diligently at all the schools he attended, and won the affection of as many teachers as Winston managed to antagonize. Through all this Lord Randolph was trying to secure the future of both his boys, and he went to a good deal of trouble on their behalf, for which he previously received no consideration whatsoever. For this reason our book has spent a good deal of time explaining the life and times of both parents, in order to provide a better understanding of their relationship with, and the development of, their two sons.

In 1930, Winston published a highly entertaining account of his upbringing, *My Early Life*.[3] It is witty and compelling, and the stories and basic assumptions in it are repeated in numerous subsequent accounts of his life. However, this memoir needs to be read with a critical eye. It too easily creates an image of parents who took little interest in him as a child. This, together with a highly colored account of his schooling, is probably meant to leave the reader with the impression that Winston achieved so many great things entirely by his own efforts and against a tide of circumstances impeding his general progress.

Winston and Jack were the sons of a Victorian aristocrat and his wife. Notions of child rearing in nineteenth-century England were very different from today, though children could still be spoiled by doting parents and nannies. It was entirely the norm at the time for children to be handed over to nurses and governesses and to be sent away to boarding school. By the standards of the day this was as much to develop their character as for their education. The surviving letters of both Winston and Jack are a cacophony of requests for more letters, more visits, more parcels, and, above all else, more money. Taken alone, this correspondence could be seen as "evidence" of neglect. We have come across many instances where such letters are quoted only partially to reinforce this general impression, in accordance with the story according to Winston, but which is not borne out by the writings of young Jack.

The fact is, the correspondence is anything but complete. It needs to be read carefully and analytically. Then patterns begin to emerge. Letters are often acknowledging the receipt of other letters, gifts, or visits, for which no other record exists. The letters between both parents and their two sons were often read out aloud at home and shared between all parties. Thus, cross-referencing between letters gives a much fuller picture of a close and loving family. It is worth remembering that when Lord Randolph or Jennie talk of sending the boys postal orders or cash of one or two pounds sterling, the equivalent of four or six dollars, we should multiply the value by anything between fifty and seventy times to get an idea of its worth in today's terms. When Lord Randolph shared his racing winnings with his boys, sending them three or five pounds, he was making a gift equivalent in value to over three hundred dollars today.

It is also true that Jennie's own account of her life in *Reminiscences,* published in 1907–08, and written at a time when she was desperately short of money, exaggerated many aspects of her early social life to appeal to the buying public, especially in her native America. This added to an image of her as a feckless mother, constantly enjoying herself, which reinforced Winston's descriptions of her being worshipped from afar by a lonely little boy. Throughout her life, Jennie did everything she could to promote Winston from his school days and through his army and political career.

OVER A HUNDRED years have gone by since the marriage in Victorian times of Lord Randolph Spencer Churchill and Miss Jennie Jerome. Gradually, over the years, due to Winston's elevated status as a world leader during and after the Second World War, the Churchill family has been a constant focus of interest for historians, biographers, the press, and television. Speculation about certain circumstances of their lives has given rise to stories of a damaging nature that have grown up around them. Thanks to our special relationship with the Churchill family, we are able to provide explanations of how some of these stories came about and have produced evidence to show that they are untrue.

The first story, a scandal about Lord Randolph, was written by a journalist, Frank Harris, in his own biography, *My Life and Loves,* in 1922,[4] alleging that Randolph died of syphilis, with which he had been afflicted since he was a student at Oxford University. The book was banned in the United Kingdom, United States, and other countries around the world for its sexual explicitness. Harris published it himself in France in 1922. Peregrine Churchill described the situation that prevailed in relation to Winston's political career in the 1920s:

> Winston was out of favor with both the Liberals and the Conservatives and . . . out of Parliament for two years. The party propaganda machines wanted to keep him out and the Frank Harris story, among others, was pertinent. . . . When Winston re-entered Parliament it was as an "Independent Constitutionalist." A pirated copy [of Harris's book], however, found its way to the Conservative Central office and was used as propaganda depicting Winston as infected [with syphilis] through a degenerate father and a drunkard in order to keep him out of the Conservative Party. A member of the Cabinet Office told me that in 1940 they did not believe Winston would last more than a few months because of his instability. Such is the power of propaganda![5]

Another origin for the rumor that Lord Randolph had syphilis is to be found in the writings of Leonie Leslie's granddaughter, Anita Leslie, who wrote a biography of Jennie.[6] Leslie alleged that he caught syphilis from a maid at Blenheim Palace during the time Jennie was pregnant with Winston. It has therefore been assumed by several writers that Jennie was sexually estranged from Randolph from that time because of the risk of infection. This led to obvious implications for Jack Churchill's paternity, which will be discussed later. As we have shown through the letters between Jennie and Randolph, particularly up to 1882, some of which were written from hotels when the couple were apart, it was quite obvious that normal sexual relations were continuing between husband and wife. If Randolph had syphilis, he would have infected Jennie, his unborn child Winston, and later Jack.[7]

Lord Randolph died on January 24, 1895, and his death certificate says he died of pneumonia. Pages were dedicated to him in the *Illustrated London News* on February 2, 1895. On page 3, it is stated that "ill-health, nervous prostration, and finally paralysis, had done their work."[8] If the Churchills had any idea at that time that Lord Randolph had died of syphilis, they would never have given these details to the press. His "paralysis" was clearly not seen as being associated with syphilis in the brain. Syphilis in Victorian times was a feared and dreaded disease, much as AIDS is today. To imply in the press that it afflicted Lord Randolph would have been detrimental to the family. When Winston entered politics, the scandal would have threatened to destroy his career.

In 1995, Peregrine S. Churchill asked Dr. John H. Mather, M.D., to investigate the issues relating to Lord Randolph's health from a medical perspective. Dr. Mather obtained Lord Randolph's medical reports from a relative of Dr. Thomas Buzzard, the main Victorian specialist in neurological diseases who attended Lord Randolph in the last months of his illness before he left with Jennie on the world tour in June 1894, and after his return in December 1895. The file also contained some reports by Dr. Robson Roose, the Churchills' family doctor. The authors also perused copies of these reports in Peregrine's papers.

Dr. Mather made a two-year study of Lord Randolph's reports and also considered the allegation by Frank Harris that he may have picked up an infection while at university. Dr. Mather described the genital discomfort described by Harris as not even remotely similar to a primary syphilis chancre and as being that of only mild herpes. Dr. Mather looked at Randolph's symptoms of 1893–94—mood swings, speech problems, dizziness, and palpitations of the heart. Randolph was able to write cogently until his final days, as his August 1894 twelve-page letter discussing the politics of the day, sent from California to Sir Edward Hamilton, private secretary to Gladstone, clearly shows.[9] Dr. Mather also studied his handwriting of the period. He noted: "His script slowly becomes shaky, but never, ever, unintelligible. The thoughts expressed in writing remain rational and cogent."[10] It was not therefore Lord Randolph's mind that was affected by his illness but his ability to express his ideas in words. He made his last speech in the Commons in June 1894, on the subject of Uganda, but his inability to find his words was such that his friends, the MPs Michael Hicks-Beach and Arthur Balfour, had to help him out.[11] When Beach paid him a private visit at home, Randolph told him, "I know what I want to say but damn it I can't say it."[12] Dr. Mather makes the point that this is not a symptom of syphilis affecting the brain, and pointed out that those symptoms are quite different, consisting of "muddled thoughts, memory lapses and profound confusion,"[13] none of which he found present in Randolph's medical reports or in the accounts of him in his last days. Dr. Mather maintains that the "psychic seizures" that Randolph suffered were "strongly suggestive of a variety of epilepsy found in deep parts of the brain, close to the speech area," and says that such symptoms "would be consistent with a developing brain tumor, possibly an aberration of the blood vessels . . . a left side brain tumor, for which no surgery was available."[14]

Such a condition would also have been consistent with the problems Randolph had experienced of the gradual onset of numbness, and bad circulation in his hands and feet, which would have been exacerbated by his chain smoking and would have been "symptomatic of Raynaud's disease."[15] Nicotine clogs the arteries, constricting the blood vessels, and hence the blood circulation around the heart. Dr. Mather wrote: "Spasms in the arteries reduce circulation which causes numbness and pain due to lack of oxygen in the tissues."[16] He then went on to make a quite crucial point, that there was no medical record of Lord Randolph ever having shown signs of any of the *secondary* symptoms of syphilis, "such as a rash over much of the body." Doctors Roose and Buzzard had treated Randolph for "pain" with "laudanum," and for "heart failure" with "belladonna and digitalis." The damage that two such powerful drugs could inflict on Randolph's frail constitution, along with their harmful side effects, is known today, but was not known in Victorian times. Dr. Mather also found that Randolph's doctors had not prescribed treatment for syphilis. He concluded:

> If Dr. Buzzard had been convinced that Lord Randolph Churchill had advanced syphilis, he would have treated him with mercury and with potassium iodide, which he strongly espoused for all neurosyphilitic patients. But Buzzard makes no mention of such treatments in any of his papers during Randolph's illness.[17]

Since no secondary signs of syphilis in the form of a rash had ever been evident in any of Lord Randolph's photographs, some of which were taken in the last year of his life, some authors have suggested that he grew a beard to cover them. He only grew a beard during the time he was living in the bush in South Africa. It was less convenient there to shave every day, and the beard would have protected him from the searing heat of the sun. Peregrine said his grandfather kept the beard after his return because beards had become fashionable, especially as the Prince of Wales had grown one.

Another source of the syphilis smear was Jennie's sister, Leonie Leslie. Jennie was the best looking of the Jerome girls, the first married, and, consequently, the recipient of the most generous settlement by their father. Clara Jerome married next, and by the time Leonie married, there was only a few hundred pounds left for her to inherit. Genteel poverty affected this ultraconservative society snob considerably, and would not have been helped by her being in receipt of hand-me-down clothes from Jennie,[18] and hand-me-down toys for her children.[19] A degree of jealousy hovered beneath the surface. Leonie kept a diary and provided her granddaughter Anita Leslie with stories about the Churchills for her books.

Frank Harris also implied in his biography that Lord Randolph was mad with syphilis; he said that Leonie told him he drew a gun in his cabin on board one of the ships in which they traveled during the world tour and that Jennie wrestled him and took it away from him. Leonie's dislike of Randolph undoubtedly stemmed from the time when, as secretary of state for India, he denied the Duke of Connaught the post of commander in chief of the Bombay District. In 1895, Leonie had started an affair with the Duke of Connaught that lasted for the rest of his life.[20] When Lord Randolph resigned as chancellor and leader of the Commons in 1886, on a matter of principle, she replied to her mischievous friend, Lady Charles Beresford (the Duchess Lily), "Liver or madness? Let us hope the latter, and that he will shut up before he can do further mischief." As to the gun incident, Jennie revealed in *Reminiscences* that around mid-September 1894, when they took a trip on a steamer up the Pearl River while making a flying visit to Canton, because of the Japanese-Chinese war going on at the time, the situation was rather dangerous. Jennie wrote that as they boarded the ship:

> I caught sight of stacks of rifles in the saloon, with printed instructions to the passengers to use them if necessary. This did not make me feel at all safe, these river steamers having been known to be attacked by pirates. At Hong-Kong we were advised not to go to Canton, since, owing to the war and their defeat, the Chinese were in rather a turbulent state.[21]

It is possible therefore that in his fragile state, if Randolph had a gun for his own protection and someone like Jennie came suddenly into his cabin, he might have reached for it.

It was stated in a Channel 4 documentary drama program titled *Lady Randy*[22] that Jennie knew when they left on the world trip that her husband was dying and that she secretly had a lead-lined coffin loaded into the hold of the ship to bring him back in. The witness said: "She doesn't want him to froth and decompose." As has been seen in chapter 10, the coffin was only taken on board the ship at Singapore, and even then at Lord Randolph's bidding, so that, if he died, he could be buried at sea.

It has also been said by several authors that when the party arrived back from their travels on Christmas Eve 1894, Lord Randolph was brought home in a strait-jacket because he was violent. Peregrine told the authors that when his grandfather's arm became numb with his illness and he could not lift it, Dr. Thomas Keith, who had accompanied them on the trip to look after him, put it in a sling to prevent injury. Peregrine said that his grandfather was brought home by ambulance to the Dowager Duchess's house, 50 Grosvenor Square, London. Some press reporters were waiting around in the street and saw him and assumed he had been restrained.[23]

Lord Randolph Churchill, never in the most robust of health, died of a brain tumor in the early hours of the morning of January 25, 1895. How then, and why, has the syphilis smear taken such a hold?

In a most extraordinary request, Dr. Thomas Buzzard was asked by Sir Richard Quain (physician to Queen Victoria), in a letter of December 31, 1894, to supply details of Lord Randolph's illness for perusal by the Prince of Wales. Setting aside this invasion of privacy, Buzzard replied, on January 1, 1895, with his usual description of the illness that he specialized in, general paralysis:

> Dear Sir Richard Quain,
> As you are aware Lord Randolph is affected with "General Paralysis" the early symptoms of which, in the form of tremor of the tongue & slurring articulation of words were evident to me at an interview two years ago. I had not seen him for a long while—a year or two, I think—previously, so that it is impossible to say how long he has been affected with the disease.[24]

It will be noted that there is no specific reference to any sexually transmitted disease. Buzzard, the great expert of neurosyphilis and later stages of the disease, is reckoned to have diagnosed 95 percent of his patients as syphilitic.[25] The period he refers to, when he did not attend Randolph, was from April 1891 until January 1892, when he was fit and well and living in the bush in South Africa searching for gold. The family letters show that the onset of Lord Randolph's final illness began shortly after his return with a numbness in his arm, which with bathing went away. Then gradually his speech problems set in, and he was attended by Buzzard and Roose. While Buzzard would normally have referred to terminal syphilis in the brain as "General Paralysis of the Insane," in his letter to Quain he only referred to Lord Randolph's condition as general paralysis, leaving open the interpretation.

The eminent doctors attending Lord Randolph included, besides Buzzard, the family doctor of a number of years, Dr. Robson Roose, and after his return from the world trip, Sir John Russell Reynold and Dr. Gowers; they were doing their best in an age that knew nothing of definitive blood tests or sophisticated neurological testing, and with no imaging techniques, such as CAT scans and MRIs. The spirochete responsible for causing syphilis was not discovered until 1905.

We have already noted the interest the Prince of Wales took in Lord Randolph's illness. He, of course, was more interested in the availability of Jennie for his pleasure. (We might ask, as an aside, whether he would have been quite so interested if she was the wife of a known syphilitic.) At the time of Lord Randolph's death, the Prince was about to throw over his current mistress of nine years, Frances, Lady Brooke (always known as Daisy), now the Countess of Warwick, wife of the 5th Earl.

Daisy was such a gossip that her nickname was the Babbling Brook. She had squandered her great fortune and was in debt. Being in possession of large numbers of very indiscreet letters the Prince had written her over the years, she was looking to make money. In 1901, the Prince became King Edward VII, and in 1910 he died. In June 1914, Daisy attempted to blackmail the King's son, King George V. She threatened to publish the letters in her memoirs to raise large sums of cash. Rich friends of the King arranged for the letters to be purchased and destroyed. Some of these letters, addressed to "My darling Daisy wife," survived, and were the basis of a book on her life by Theo Lang.[26] The earliest record of Daisy's blackmail attempt is contained in the diaries of Jean, Lady Hamilton, the wife of General Sir Ian Hamilton, on Wednesday, November 4, 1914. Lieutenant Colonel Stephen Hungerford-Pollen, who had been equerry to the Prince of Wales and King Edward VII, and now, in 1914, to his son King George V, told the Hamiltons about it over dinner at their house.[27] Daisy's agent, planning big publishing deals in the United States, was none other than Frank Harris, the very man who spread the rumor of Randolph's syphilis. We can assume that he would have acquired the full news of Lord Randolph's last illness, as communicated in Buzzard's letter, from Daisy Warwick, and couldn't resist working the story into his book in 1922.

By coincidence, Harris was also agent to Winston Churchill when he was writing *The World Crisis* in the 1920s. They had a serious falling out, probably over money,[28] which left Harris an implacable enemy to Winston. The stories he published about Lord Randolph in his biography in 1922 were possibly an act of revenge, and they were seized upon by Winston's enemies in the Conservative Party. Peregrine remembered an incident when he was a boy at Summerfield Preparatory School, in 1924, aged eleven. He was, he said, taunted by the son of an MP, who said, "My Daddy says all you Churchills have revolting diseases, and are quite mad."[29]

Gradually, however, informed opinion is changing about the nature of Lord Randolph's final illness. Robert Rhodes James,[30] Lord Randolph's biographer, wrote that syphilis was now almost the last thing anyone should think he died from. A proper understanding of his generally poor health should end the unpleasant stories that he was not Jack's father, and help us to recognize that he died of an undiagnosed and inoperable brain tumor.

THE SECOND STORY relates to speculation about Winston Churchill's birth. The *Daily Mail* published stories asking whether Winston was illegitimate.[31] The same question was raised in the earlier mentioned Channel 4 documentary. The origins of this allegation stems from speculation about letters written by Lord Randolph. He wrote to Jennie after he had been to Paris during the time of their engagement. Having stayed in the Hôtel du Rue de Rivoli, he wrote, on March 6, 1874: "I like to think of you being in my room. You can't think darling how I long to be back it is after the first day or two that one feels the separation most."[32] This letter has been taken out of context to mean Jennie had been with him in his bedroom and had sex with him before they were married, and that she became pregnant with Winston out of wedlock.

When Lord Randolph stayed in a hotel, he took a suite of rooms, which was customary for the aristocracy and particularly the son of a duke. He had a bedroom for himself, another bedroom next door for Thomas Walden, his lifelong valet, a bathroom, and a sitting room, plus the use of the hotel lounge. When Jennie visited Randolph at his hotel, she was in company with her maid, and the room referred to was obviously the sitting room. An unmarried girl like Jennie, only twenty years old, had to be chaperoned by her maid or another female relative when in company with a man, even if they were engaged. If Jennie had slept with Randolph before they were married, her reputation would have been ruined, and he would have formed the opinion that she had been with other men, and he would not have married a girl who was not a virgin.

It was said by an interviewee on the Channel 4 documentary that there was an "extraordinary letter" at the Churchill Archives in which Lord Randolph had written to Jennie that he liked to think of her in his bedroom, meaning at the hotel. This claim is quite inaccurate. The wording in the letter is as above in the original, and the word "bedroom" does not appear in any of Lord Randolph's or Jennie's letters until after they were married. Randolph had written in a letter to Jennie the previous day, March 5, "I think I had better not kiss you again until we are married," which would rather contradict the notion that any sexual relations had taken place.[33] Lord Randolph and Jennie were married on April 15, 1874, and Winston was born on November 30. The doctor in attendance, Dr. Frederick Taylor, stated that the child was premature but healthy; the Duchess of Marlborough described him as "strong and healthy."

Speculation about Winston's birth has also arisen out of a letter Lord Randolph wrote to Mrs. Jerome, who was still living in Paris and must have been much vexed about missing the arrival of her first grandson. Randolph was a proud and dutiful father and wrote at 12:30 P.M., November 30, 1874, "The boy is wonderfully pretty so everybody says dark eyes and hair and very healthy considering its prematureness."[34] These remarks have prompted some authors to claim that Winston was born with a full head of hair.[35] As a redhead Winston would have been bald at birth, and his father was not to know that all newborn babies have blue eyes, but he probably only caught a glimpse of his infant son in the early hours of the morning in the lamplight, as Winston was born at 1:30 A.M. His father's description of Winston to Mrs. Jerome was clearly slanted to give the impression that Winston was dark and took after Jennie's side of the family. It was an obvious attempt to cheer Mrs. Jerome and to compensate for her having missed the birth of her first grandchild.

Peregrine told the authors that there was a medical problem at the neck of Jennie's womb. It was thought that one of the several falls this fearless young horsewoman suffered had caused a pelvic injury that made it hard for her to carry her babies to full term.[36] From the date of the marriage to the date of Winston's birth was thirty-three weeks. Our medical adviser for this part of the study, the consultant Mr. Rodney Croft, has analyzed the situation thus:

> Pregnancy is 280 days or 40 weeks from the first day of the last menstrual period (LMP). Assuming Jennie had regular periods lasting circa five days and that she would have wished not to have been menstruating at the time of her wedding, it can be postulated that her LMP might well have been the latter end of March and the early part of April. Winston's birth date would therefore normally have been during the first two weeks of January 1875. Based on these calculations the baby was born between four and a half and possibly as much as six weeks premature. The latter figure concurs with the seven months routinely stated in the past.[37]

Peregrine told the authors something that has not been known previously. At birth, Winston's jaw was fractured and required surgery.[38] Peregrine also left a written record in which he said at birth, "Winston suffered a defective jaw which needed surgery."[39] Mr. Croft says:

> This type of injury would have occurred because Winston's jawbone (mandible) was not properly formed and therefore weaker and more prone to injury. His jaw bone was weaker because he was premature.[40]

It has been suggested by some authors that such a healthy baby as Winston could not have been premature. In Victorian times few premature babies of seven months would have survived, but the statistics compiled for infant mortality are misleading. They are taken as a generality and were based on the majority of the babies who were born to impoverished and working-class mothers. There are no separate figures for the survival rates of babies born to the wives of aristocrats or well-to-do mothers who, like Jennie, were healthy and well nourished, and where the feeding and aftercare of the infant was excellent. The Duchess of Marlborough had appointed a wet nurse from Woodstock while Jennie was still in labor, which meant the baby was fed soon after he was born.[41]

THE THIRD STORY follows on from the syphilis theory relating to Lord Randolph's health. It has been assumed by several authors, who have mentioned Jack only in passing, that since his father was suffering from syphilis from early on in the marriage, he must have been fathered by someone else. A number of names have been suggested over the years as potential fathers for Jack. The first was John Strange Jocelyn, the 5th

Earl of Roden,[42] who stood sponsor for Jack at baptism. Peregrine was particularly upset to see Roy Jenkins's successful 2001 biography of Winston, entitled *Churchill*,[43] repeat the slander that Jack had been fathered by Jocelyn. Jenkins wrote: "If the legitimacy of Jack Churchill is challenged, a more likely candidate seems to be the Dublin-based Colonel John Strange Jocelyn."[44]

The story of Jack's birth as related by Peregrine (who obtained it from his father) was that, like Winston, he was a premature baby. Jack was born also at seven or eight months, and Peregrine said he was at birth a "blue baby," and they thought he might die. Mr. Rodney Croft advises that:

> "blue baby" describes a newly born infant who is cyanotic (blue) due to a lack of adequate circulating oxygen. Oxygenated haemoglobin (the blood pigment) is red, hence a pink hue and deoxygenated blood is blue, hence the lay term. It can be caused by traumatic birth (if the umbilical cord is strangulated or premature separation of the placenta before the child is born and can breathe).[45]

John Strange Jocelyn had newly become the 5th Earl of Roden on January 10, and Jack was born in Dublin on February 4, 1880. Jocelyn did not live in Ireland; he lived on his estate in England with his wife and daughter, and was a man of fifty-seven years of age, while Jennie was a young woman of twenty-six. Jocelyn arrived in Ireland in January to take charge of the estate at Tollymore House,[46] Bryansford, outside Newcastle, County Down (today in Northern Ireland), which he had inherited with his new title.[47] Tollymore, set in a forest, is over a hundred kilometers from Dublin. The connection between Jennie and Jocelyn has been made by several authors on the complete misunderstanding that he owned and lived in a neighboring estate in Dublin, and that Jennie went riding with him there and came back pregnant by him. The present Earl of Roden wrote to us confirming that Jocelyn first signed the house book at Tollymore in January 1880. He also sent a photograph of Jocelyn, and Jack looked nothing like him.

Jocelyn was a close friend of the 7th Duke of Marlborough and was a signatory to his will. He had come to visit his friend and was staying in the Viceregal Lodge when Jack was born. Peregrine described to the authors how Jocelyn was roused from his bed in the early hours of the morning to stand sponsor so that baptism could take place immediately in case Jack died before he was christened. Mr. Rodney Croft says:

> The cyanotic condition is also associated with blood disorders and serious congenital heart defects. It was the possibility of the latter which may have prompted the immediate baptism.[48]

Peregrine had a letter published in the *Sunday Telegraph* on April 29, 1990, clarifying the situation regarding his father:

> The Rodens allowed me some years ago, to copy their family records and the facts are as follows: "John Jocelyn . . . lived in England and was there during 1879. He arrived in Dublin after my father's birth."

The second name associated with Jack's paternity was Evelyn Boscawen (later 7th Viscount Falmouth).[49] Boscawen was military secretary to the 7th Duke of Marlborough during the time that he was viceroy of Ireland and the Churchills were living in Dublin. The story that Boscawen was Jack's father was told by Leonie Leslie's two sons, Shane and Seymour Leslie. Shane wrote in a letter to Anita Leslie: "You can calculate when they [Jennie and Boscawen] first met by the time Jack was born."[50] Seymour told her that, when he was a boy, his family lived in a flat across the road from Boscawen's London home.[51] The impression is thereby created that the Leslie brothers observed a relationship between Jennie and Boscawen in Ireland, and later in London.

At the time of Jack Churchill's birth in 1880, Leonie Jerome was unmarried and lived with her mother in Paris. Leonie met John Leslie (later 2nd Baronet) at a banquet in Dublin Castle in 1883, and they were married in New York the following year. Their first child, John (who in adulthood changed his name to the Irish Shane), was born in 1885, followed by Norman in 1886 and Seymour in 1889. It will be recalled that the Churchills returned from Dublin to live in London in April 1880. The Leslie brothers could not therefore have had any knowledge of an affair between Jennie and Boscawen prior to Jack's birth or for a long time afterward, as they were not yet born. The Leslie family lived at Castle Leslie, Glaslough, in County Monaghan (today in the Republic of Ireland). Boscawen, who was nicknamed the "Star" or "Star Man," was a friend, and almost certainly a lover, of Jennie's. But his name only appears for the first time in Jennie's secret diary of 1882, two years after the Churchills return from Dublin to London.[52]

Other names are recorded as being possible fathers to Jack, but as it is unlikely any of them ever set foot in Ireland, it is not worth considering them. The best proof of all of Jack's paternity is that, in his photographs, his elder son, Johnny, was the image of Winston, and his younger son, Peregrine, was the image of his grandfather, the 7th Duke of Marlborough.

THE FOURTH STORY relates to Jennie's mother's ancestry. Some authors have suggested that there was Native American blood in the family. Mrs. Jerome's grandmother, Mrs. Clarissa Hall (née Wilcox), was from Massachusetts, and it has been alleged that she was raped by an Iroquois Indian. This ridiculous story was told in fun by Jennie's sisters, Clara and Leonie.[53] It came about because in her old age her daughters thought their mother looked Indian and the girls laughingly called her Big Chief Sitting Bull.

Apparently, Mrs. Jerome's grandmother and her sisters had jet-black hair and dark eyes, which had given rise to speculation about the rape. The story had become a legend, having been passed down among the generations.[54] Mrs. Elizabeth Churchill Snell,[55] who lives in Canada, investigated the story and found that there were no Iroquois Indians or Indians of any kind living within many miles of Clarissa Wilcox's homes, and there was no likelihood that she would have come into contact with Indians.

THE FIFTH STORY, which appeared in the *Daily Mail* in 2009 and was discussed in the Channel 4 documentary, was that Jennie had two hundred lovers during her lifetime.[56] No source was provided for this allegation. The authors have, however, traced its origin to George Moore,[57] who was an Irish artist, novelist, and journalist.[58] It is unlikely that Moore, who was considered to be something of a disreputable character, ever knew Jennie.

While we accept that Jennie had a few lovers, considering that she married three times, it is unlikely that they numbered more than a half dozen. The names of men appear in her life after the death of Lord Randolph, and before she met George Cornwallis-West. When George left her for the actress Mrs. Patrick Campbell, Jennie wrote an outpouring to George's mother, on August 14, 1910, assuring her that she had been true to George all during their marriage: "I have loved him more than anyone on earth and have *always* been true and loyal."[59]

Given Lord Randolph's difficult and ongoing health problems from 1882, and the fact that Peregrine thought his grandfather was more or less impotent from that time, there are few today who would hold it against Jennie that she took Count Charles Kinsky as her lover of ten years.[60] She was then just twenty-eight years old. It probably helped her to cope with her husband's ill health and the stress of life in a marriage to a rising political star.

It was claimed by an interviewee on the Channel 4 program that Kinsky "was never going to commit to marrying someone like Jennie who was possibly damaged goods." This is untrue. Kinsky would have married Jennie when she became widowed, but his father, Prince Kinsky, forced him to announce his engagement to a young heiress, the Countess Elizabeth Wolff Metternich zur Gracht (Lily), when Jennie was absent on the world trip.

Peregrine Churchill could relate how Kinsky's great friend, George Lambton, said that his father forced him into the marriage under the threat of disinheriting him if he did not, and Kinsky had heavy debts. What Jennie never knew, as it was only revealed in Anita Leslie's biography of Jennie in 1969, was that when Kinsky found out that Lord Randolph was dying, he wanted to break off his engagement to Lily but his father brought such pressure to bear on him that he had to go through with the marriage.[61] Kinsky never got over the loss of Jennie. His young wife was delicate and died of cancer thirteen years into the marriage without producing an heir. On the morning of her marriage to George Cornwallis-West, Jennie received a card edged in black as though it were a bereavement. It was from the Chancellor of the Austro-Hungarian Embassy, St. Petersburg. It contained just third words: "Toujours en deuil" (Always in mourning), signed Charles Kinsky. As Prince Kinsky, Charles came back to Jennie after his wife's death and her divorce from George Cornwallis-West, and he would have married her then. They became friends and he bought her a clock for Christmas, but she would not have him even for the title of Princess. Peregrine said she never forgave him for his betrayal, and she married Montagu Porch instead.

While Jennie was living in wedded bliss with Porch, Prince Charles Andreas Kinsky died, on December 11, 1919. George Lambton wrote, "If ever a man died of a broken heart, Charles Kinsky did."[62] Lambton had been to see Kinsky during the final stages of his illness, and he observed that the only picture in his room was a portrait of Jennie hanging above his bed.[63]

Winston Churchill is mentioned in print and broadcast media on an almost daily basis. He was, undoubtedly, one of the great figures in world history, with his lasting fame ensured by his leadership of the United Kingdom during the Second World War. His skill as a writer and communicator added to his fame. His own account of his life, coming as he did from one of the great political families of Britain, is captivating. However, this greatness did not exist in a vacuum, and his rise to fame cannot be understood without fully understanding the family that produced him. His father was a great politician, a "man of the people," whose health failed before he could achieve the high office he might have expected. His beautiful American mother did everything in her power to advance Winston's career. Finally, by bringing his younger brother Jack back into the family story, we are better able to understand the role of the parents in providing for both their sons. In doing this they gave us a leader in the struggle for human freedom whose fame will live for all time.

Acknowledgments

The authors acknowledge the gracious permission of Her Majesty Queen Elizabeth II for allowing them access to the Royal Archives, Windsor Castle, and for allowing them to publish extracts from Lady Randolph Churchill's letters to HRH the Prince of Wales.

The late Mr. Peregrine Churchill, and Mrs. Churchill: enormous thanks and gratitude are due to the late Peregrine and Mrs. Churchill for their support, and for allowing us unrestricted access to all their private papers, letters, and photographs.

His Grace the 11th Duke of Marlborough: thanks are due to His Grace for allowing photographs to be taken at Blenheim Palace of the Jerome family rocking chair (bequeathed by Peregrine Churchill), and for granting us permission to reproduce photographs.

The Lady Soames, LG, DBE: thanks and gratitude are due to Mary for two lengthy afternoon interviews in 2005, and for much help and guidance with this book.

The Countess of Avon: thanks and gratitude are due to Lady Avon for an interview, and her hours of painstaking work in helping us understand her family history.

Mrs. Minnie Churchill and Mr. Simon Bird: thanks are due to Minnie and Simon for their kindness.

The Honorable Celia Sandys, author of *Churchill Wanted Dead or Alive:* thanks are due to Celia for her kind help at the outset when we were writing this book.

Mr. and Mrs. Randolph and Catherine Churchill: thanks are due for their kindness and hospitality at their home, and for allowing us access to their library and paintings.

Mr. Andrew Lownie, our literary agent: much thanks are due to Andrew for his hard work and excellent choice in placing our book with Palgrave Macmillan.

Sir John Leslie, 4th Baronet, Castle Leslie: thanks are due for granting us an interview and for receiving us with great courtesy and kindness, at Castle Leslie.

The Earl of Roden: we are most grateful to the Earl for supplying us with a photograph of his ancestor the 5th Earl of Roden, John Strange Jocelyn, and supplying helpful information.

Mr. Ian Hamilton: thanks are due to Ian for his kindness in granting permission to use several passages from his Great-Aunt Jean Hamilton's diaries. Thanks are also due to Mr. and Mrs. Hamilton's two sons, Felix and Max.

Mrs. Barbara Kaczmarowska Hamilton (Basia): more thanks than can ever be recorded are due to Basia, who introduced us to Mr. and Mrs. Peregrine Churchill in 2001. Basia has been an enthusiastic supporter throughout the writing of this book.

Dr. John H. Mather, MD, CIP, FACPE, President, UNI-CORN LLC: enormous thanks are due for an interview and for most generously allowing us to quote from his papers, *Lord Randolph Churchill: Maladies et Mort,* and *Sir Winston Churchill: His Hardiness and Resilience.*

Mr. Rodney J. Croft, MA, MChir, FRCS, FACS, Consultant General and Vascular Surgeon: enormous thanks are due for his time and painstaking medical opinion on Winston Churchill's birth.

Mr. Richard M. Langworth, CBE; Editor, The Churchill Center: was a great friend of Peregrine Churchill and fully understands Jack's role in the family.

Mrs. Rita Boswell Gibbs, MA, RMSA, Archivist, Harrow Public School: thanks are due for providing copies of examination results and other help and guidance from the public school where Winston and Jack Churchill were educated.

Miss Pamela Clark, Registrar, The Royal Archives, Windsor Castle: thanks are due for help on several occasions with information of a historical nature.

Mr. John Forster, former Head of Education, Blenheim Palace: thanks are due for his painstaking help on Churchill letters and his knowledge of the family and Blenheim Palace.

Mr. Richard Cragg, photographer, Blenheim Palace: thanks are due for wonderful photographs of the "historic" Jerome family rocking chair, and for providing us with a copy of the wedding portrait of Major John and Lady Gwendeline Churchill.

Mrs. Claire Aston: thanks are due for the story of how Winston Churchill used to stop the official car outside the cemetery and visit the grave of his deceased daughter, Marigold.

Mr. Geoffrey Bailey: much thanks are due for academic and other advice, acquired through his many years of experience in the publishing industry.

Mr. Robin Brodhurst, Head of the History Department, Pangbourne College: for advice on relevant books to read in relation to the politics of Ireland.

Dr. Robin Darwall-Smith, Archivist, Magdalen College, Oxford: thanks are due for painstakingly produced figures of the costs involved for a student taking a degree at Oxford in 1897–98.

Mr. Julian Mitchell: thanks are due to Julian, the co-author of *Jennie: Lady Randolph Churchill — A Portrait with Letters,* published in association with Thames Television's film *Jennie: Lady Randolph Churchill,* for which Julian was the scriptwriter.

Mr. Allen Packwood, Director, Miss Katharine Thomson, Mr. Andrew Riley, and the staff of the Churchill Archives, Churchill College, Cambridge: more thanks are due than can ever be recorded. When we visited the impeccably arranged Churchill Archives, every help was provided to us.

Mr. Andrew Roberts: Andrew is a well-known historian and author, and more thanks than can ever be recorded are due to him for his opinion.

Mrs. Elizabeth Snell: thanks are due for most generously allowing us access to her writings on the ancient Earls of Abingdon, the ancestry of Lady Gwendeline Bertie.

Mr. Paul Strong: thanks are due for putting us in touch with Sir John Leslie, 4th Baronet.

Mr. Hugo Vickers: thanks are due for an interview and for his knowledge of Jack Churchill's employment at Vickers da Costa.

Miss Tatiana Roshupkina: thanks are due for organizing a Churchill family tree and preparing photographs for reproduction.

Mr. Thad Uehling: thanks are due for enhancing photographs for reproduction.

Mr. Gordon Wise and Miss Shaheeda Sabir, Curtis Brown Ltd.: more thanks than can ever be recorded are due for their painstaking help and guidance on copyright matters.

Thanks are due to Alessandra Bastagli, Colleen Lawrie, Erica Warren, and all the staff at Palgrave Macmillan in New York for their care and attention to the publication of our book.

Notes

In 1945, the late Sir Winston Churchill's widow, Clementine, gave her husband's papers dealing with his life after 1945 to Churchill College, University of Cambridge.

Sir Winston's papers for the years before 1945 remained in family ownership, though also housed at Churchill College, Cambridge.

In 1995, the British government bought these papers for the nation.

In 1973, the present-day Archives Centre was built onto Churchill College, University of Cambridge, to house all the papers of Sir Winston Churchill.

The copyright of all the late Sir Winston Churchill's papers is owned by his grandson, also Mr. Winston Churchill, who lives in London. The copyright of all of Sir Winston Churchill's papers is taken care of on Mr. Winston Churchill's behalf by the literary agency Curtis Brown in London. In the following notes the abbreviation CHAR followed by the reference means the papers are at the Churchill Archives, University of Cambridge. Please note that the prefix CHAR originated from the time that the papers were stored at Winston's home Chartwell House.

Mary, the Lady Soames, LG DBE, also donated the papers of her mother, Clementine, Baroness Spencer Churchill, to Churchill College, Cambridge. The copyright of Clementine's letters and papers is owned by Lady Soames, and is also taken care of by Curtis Brown. Mrs. Peregrine Spencer Churchill, widow of Peregrine, and daughter-in-law to Major John Strange Spencer Churchill (brother of the late Sir Winston Churchill), owns privately all of the following papers and letters, which are housed at the Churchill Archives, University of Cambridge:

- The letters and papers, both public and private, belonging to Lord Randolph Spencer Churchill
- The letters and papers, both public and private, belonging to Lady Randolph Spencer Churchill (Jennie)
- The letters and papers, both public and private, belonging to Major John Strange Spencer Churchill (Jack)
- The letters and papers, both public and private, belonging to Lady Gwendeline Spencer Churchill (Jack's wife)
- The letters and papers, both public and private, belonging to Peregrine Spencer Churchill (whose registered names are Henry Winston)
- The letters, etc., belonging to Mrs. Peregrine Spencer Churchill herself

In many instances we have given an endnote where something we have quoted has been published in another format. That is by way of letting the reader know it appeared somewhere else. It does not alter the fact that the original letter or paper is owned by Mrs. Peregrine Spencer Churchill.

It has therefore not been necessary to include endnotes for many of the above letters that we have quoted.

Letters that Jennie wrote to her younger sister, Leonie, Lady Leslie, are with the Leslie papers in the National Library of Ireland in Dublin. The letters Jennie wrote to her elder sister, Mrs. Clara Frewen, are owned privately by Jonathan Frewen. The copyright is owned by Mrs. Peregrine Spencer Churchill. Other Leslie letters and papers are in the possession of Mr. Tarka King, Anita Leslie's son. Winston Churchill's letters to Miss Pamela Plowden, later the Countess of Lytton, form part of the Lytton Papers, which were sold in recent years to a private collector.

INTRODUCTION

1. Michael Ryan, "Who Is Great?" *Parade Magazine,* June 16, 1996.
2. *Finest Hour,* the journal of the Churchill Society.
3. H. Lawrence, Officer in Economic History Services, *Exchange Rate between the United States Dollar and the British Pound 1791–2000,* EH.net (a website maintained by Miami University and Wake Forest University).
4. "Inflation: The Value of the Pound 1750–2001," House of Commons Research Paper 02/44, July 11, 2002.

CHAPTER 1

1. Queen Victoria had several residences. Her main home was Buckingham Palace in London, and she had Sandringham House in Norfolk in the English countryside and Balmoral Castle in Scotland.
2. The color of Jennie's eyes seems to cause a deal of confusion among writers. An unknown artist painted a portrait of Jennie from a sepia photograph of her that he had bought from a professional photographer. It is a stunning portrait, but as the artist had never met Jennie, he did not know the color of her eyes and thought they were amber. He sent the portrait to Jennie, who was delighted with it, and, in view of the pains he had taken with the work, even including a corsage of American orange blossoms on her gown, she did not have the heart to tell him her eyes were a blue gray.
3. Memorandum titled *Early Recollections* written circa 1906 by Jennie, Lady Randolph Churchill, detailing her first meeting and her romance with Lord Randolph Churchill. Copy in Peregrine S. Churchill's papers; quoted in *Jennie—Lady Randolph Churchill,* ed. Peregrine Churchill and Julian Mitchell (William Collins, 1974), pp. 17–42, 269.
4. Ibid.
5. Ibid.
6. CHAR 28/112/8.
7. Conversations with Peregrine S. Churchill, 2001–02.
8. Churchill and Mitchell, pp. 23–25.
9. Conversations with Peregrine Churchill, 2001–02.
10. Ibid., p. 32.
11. Ibid.
12. Ibid., p. 61.
13. Jennie's letters to Randolph frequently discussed politics both in the United Kingdom and in Paris.
14. Ibid.
15. Ibid., p. 35.
16. Conversations with Peregrine S. Churchill, 2001–02.
17. Ibid., undated letters between the duke and Lord Randolph ca. mid-October 1873; it was known in political circles that a general election for Parliament would be called soon.
18. Ibid., cable sent ca. beginning of November 1873.
19. Ibid., Jennie to Lord Randolph, January 1, 1874.
20. Lord Randolph's aunt was taken very seriously ill in Ireland, and he went there instead.
21. Ibid., undated letter sent from the Jockey Club, New York.
22. Anita Leslie, *Jennie: The Mother of Winston Churchill* (George Mann, 1992), p. 35; conversations with Peregrine Churchill, 2001–02, about Jennie's dowry.
23. Ibid., p. 28; also copy in the papers of Peregrine S. Churchill.
24. Lady Camden, formerly Lady Clementina Augusta Spencer Churchill, daughter of the 6th Duke of Marlborough.
25. Conversations with Peregrine Churchill, 2001.
26. Undated letter, circa summer 1875, in the private collection of Peregrine S. Churchill.
27. Undated, circa autumn 1876, CHAR 28/5/6.
28. Ibid. Undated, circa October 1875, in the private papers of Peregrine S. Churchill.
29. Churchill and Mitchell, chap. 4, pp. 87–104.

CHAPTER 2

1. Many Anglo-Irish aristocrats and gentry already owned a substantial home or country estate in England, visiting Ireland for the hunting, shooting, and fishing seasons only.
2. Mrs. George Cornwallis-West, *The Reminiscences of Lady Randolph Churchill* (Century Co., 1908), p. 103.
3. Viscount Edgar Vincent D'Abernon, *Portraits and Appreciations* (Hodden and Stughton, 1931).
4. Winston S. Churchill, *Lord Randolph Churchill,* vol. 1 (Macmillan, 1906), p. 66.
5. Ibid., p. 82.
6. Address to the House of Commons at the end of 1877, ibid., pp. 82–83.
7. Conversations between the authors and Peregrine S. Churchill, 2001–02.
8. Christine Kinealy, *This Great Calamity: The Irish Famine, 1845–52* (Roberts Rinehart, 1995). Between 1845 and 1852, the Great Famine years, one million people died of starvation in Ireland, and one million emigrated, mainly to America.
9. Winston S. Churchill, op. cit., pp. 110–11. The Duchess of Marlborough wrote to *The Times* of London, December 12, 1879, to appeal for funds. Queen Victoria donated £500/$2,750, and the Prince of Wales £250/$1,373.
10. Alan Bott and Irene Clephane, *Our Mothers* (Victor Gollancz, 1932). Victorian workhouses were supported by the ratepayers (taxpayers). Unemployed men and women went to live there when they lost their jobs and their homes. They were given some menial work to do and were provided with one meal a day and a bed for the night, sometimes in a wooden onion box.
11. "Mainland Britain" is a term for the countries of England, Scotland, and Wales, which are joined geographically; Ireland is separated from them by the Irish Sea.
12. Winston S. Churchill, *Lord Randolph Churchill,* vol. 1, pp. 110–11. The Duchess of Marlborough's fund continued after the Churchills left Ireland.
13. Randolph S. Churchill, *Winston S. Churchill,* vol. 1, *Youth* (Heinemann, 1966), pp. 36–37.
14. Peregrine Churchill told the authors that his grandparents were horrified when they saw the poverty and squalor in which the Irish people were living.
15. In the sixteenth and seventeenth centuries, most of the land in Ireland was confiscated by the British government from Irish Catholic landowners during the Plantations of Ireland and granted to British settlers who were members of the established churches (the Church of England and the Church of Ireland).
16. Quoted in Winston S. Churchill, op. cit., p. 90. Lord Randolph spoke at the Agricultural and Horticultural Show, Woodstock.
17. Ibid., pp. 90–91.
18. Charles Stewart Parnell was a rich Protestant Anglo-Irish landowner, educated at Magdalene College, Cambridge, and was first elected to the British Parliament as a Home Rule League member of Parliament on April 21, 1875. He was the son of John Henry Parnell and his American wife, Delia Tudor Stewart, of Bordentown, New Jersey, daughter of the American naval hero, Admiral Charles Steward, the stepson of one of George Washington's bodyguards.
19. Quoted in Winston S. Churchill, op. cit., p. 104, in a letter to Sir Charles Dilke, undated but the last week of February 1878, as Randolph says he will be in London on February 26.
20. Ibid., undated letters, p. 37.
21. Ibid.
22. Lord Randolph to Jennie, Dec. 23, 1877, CHAR 28/5/117–18.
23. Winston S. Churchill, *My Early Life* (Butterworth, 1930), pp. 16–17.
24. Ibid. The Fenians, that is, the Fenian Brotherhood and the Irish Republican Brotherhood, were organizations in the nineteenth and twentieth centuries dedicated to establishing a Republic of Ireland, independent of the rest of the United Kingdom. The movement had been founded in America in 1858 by John O'Mahony.
25. Ibid., p. 16. Winston wrote that this happened because they thought they saw a "long dark procession of Fenians approaching," and the pony was startled and started "kicking." It may have been "the Rifle Brigade out for a route march."
26. Winston S. Churchill, *Lord Randolph Churchill,* vol. 1, pp. 109–10.
27. Winston S. Churchill *My Early Life,* pp. 17–19.
28. Ibid.

29. Ibid.

30. Ibid., pp. 16–17.

31. Ibid., pp. 18–19.

32. Peregrine S. Churchill manuscript, April 2000, p. 5, owned privately by his wife.

33. This Jerome family heirloom had gone first with them to Paris. Jennie brought it to London for Winston and then took it to Dublin. Jack and Lady Gwendeline (Goonie) S. Churchill used it to rock their three children. It was inherited by Peregrine, who remained childless; he bequeathed it to Blenheim Palace, where it is now on public display in the room where Winston was born.

34. Churchill, *My Early Life*, p. 19.

35. The exact date they moved into their new home is not known, but a letter from Jennie to Leonie on headed notepaper bearing that address was dated May 30, 1880.

36. Winston S. Churchill, *Lord Randolph Churchill*, vol. 1, p. 118. The Conservatives went from 351 seats to 237, the Liberals from 250 to 353 (an absolute majority), and Parnell's Irish Home Rule Party (renamed, in 1882, the Irish Parliamentary Party) from 51 to 62. William Gladstone became prime minister.

37. Ibid., p. 118.

CHAPTER 3

1. Charles Bradlaugh was forced into the position that he had to resign and fight his seat in his constituency on four consecutive occasions. Each time he won, which explains why an alternative wording was agreed upon for his swearing into Parliament.

2. Robert Rhodes James, *The British Revolution—British Politics, 1880–1939* (Methuen, 1976). W. H. Smith was a cabinet minister (1885–86), leader of the House of Commons (1887–91), and head of the chain of W. H. Smith Newsagents.

3. Alfred Henry Ruegg, *A Treatise Upon the Employers' Liability Act, 1880* (Butterworth, London, 1901), chap. 2. The Employers' Liability Bill had been under debate in the Commons from 1877, and had been withdrawn in July 1879. The government brought the bill back to the Commons in 1880, and it went into force in January 1881, when it became an act.

4. Winston S. Churchill, *Lord Randolph Churchill*, vol. 1 (Macmillan, 1906), pp. 135–44.

5. Benjamin Disraeli (1804–1881) was twice prime minister; in his second term (1874–80) he was raised to the peerage as 1st Earl of Beaconsfield in 1876. The Primrose League was named after his favorite flower.

6. Winston S. Churchill, op. cit., p. 55.

7. The aristocracy was able to buy boxes at theatres. The box was in the gallery and was closed in at the back and sides, separating its occupants from the rest of the audience, and was entered by a door at the back. Jennie meant that a rich friend had invited her to use his/her box free of charge.

8. Anita Leslie, *Jennie: The Mother of Winston Churchill* (George Mann, 1992), p. 70.

9. Winston S. Churchill, op. cit., pp. 189–90.

10. R. Barry O'Brien, *The Life of Charles Stewart Parnell, 1846–91* (Thomas Nelson & Son, 1900).

11. Anita Leslie, op. cit., pp. 77–78.

12. Henry Drummond Wolff, *Rambling Recollections* (Macmillan, 1908).

13. Jennie's handwritten diary for 1882 is owned privately by Mrs. Peregrine S. Churchill.

14. Mrs. E. M. Ward, *Reminiscences*, ed. Elliott O'Donnell (Pitman, 1911).

15. We have not been able to trace any of Jennie's paintings. There is a fine portrait of Randolph, on public display in Winston's studio at Chartwell House, Westerham, Kent, now owned by the National Trust. Peregrine told us he believed it was painted by Jennie. She sold several paintings in Ireland, and we think some may survive there and in the United States. There is no record of her painting portraits of either of her sons. There is a painting somewhere in the United States, as a photograph of it has survived. It is titled "Oil by Jenny [sic] Jerome mother of Winston Churchill—Pompey New York 1863"—which presumably means it is a copy of another painting of that time. There are two small houses or huts perched on a green grassy bank above a river in which there is a small boat.

16. Sir Oscar Clayton (1816–1892); educated University College and Middlesex Hospital; extra surgeon-in-ordinary to the Prince of Wales (later King Edward VII) and his wife, Princess Alexandra, and their children; specialist in typhoid fever; knighted, 1882. Source: *British Medical Journal*, January 30, 1892.

17. Jennie's 1882 diary, owned privately by Mrs. Peregrine S. Churchill.

18. Celia Sandys, *From Winston With Love and Kisses* (Sinclair-Stevenson, 1994), p. 39.

19. Winston S. Churchill, *Lord Randolph Churchill,* pp. 225–27.

20. Ibid., pp. 314–16.

CHAPTER 4

1. Robert Arthur Talbot Gascoyne-Cecil, 3rd Marquess of Salisbury (known as Lord Salisbury) (1830–1903); prime minister, 1885–Feb. 1886; 1886–Aug. 1892; 1895–July 1902.

2. Randolph S. Churchill, *Winston S. Churchill,* vol. 1 (Heinemann, 1966), pp. 48–49.

3. Sir Francis Laking (1847–1914); Surgeon Apothecary in Ordinary to Queen Victoria; Physician in Ordinary to the Prince of Wales.

4. Sir William Withey Gull, 1st Baronet (1816–1890); attended the Prince of Wales during his attack of typhoid fever in 1871.

5. Lord Randolph S. Churchill's letters and copyright are owned privately by Mrs. Peregrine S. Churchill.

6. Ibid.

7. Lady Randolph S. Churchill's letters and copyright are owned privately by Mrs. Peregrine S. Churchill.

8. Randolph S. Churchill, op. cit., pp. 53–55.

9. Virginia Woolf, *Roger Fry* (Random House, 1940).

10. Winston S. Churchill, *My Early Life* (Butterworth, 1930), pp. 25–26; in Winston Churchill's autobiography he disguised the name of the school as St. James's.

11. Lord Randolph possessed what is today called photographic memory.

12. Conversations with Peregrine S. Churchill, 2001–02.

13. Ibid.

14. In the region of two hundred notes and letters from the Prince of Wales to Jennie are preserved in the Churchill Archives, University of Cambridge.

15. Anita Leslie admitted that she could not say for certain if sexual relations took place between Jennie and the Prince of Wales. The affair (detailed later in chapter 9) took place in London, and as Jennie's sister Leonie, who was Anita's grandmother, lived in Ireland she may not have known about it. Anita admitted that in this respect she had not probed deep enough into her great-aunt Jennie's life. Anita Leslie, *The Marlborough House Set* (Doubleday, 1973), chap. 16, "Jennie and the Prince," p. 159.

16. Peregrine S. Churchill told the authors that Jennie started her serious affair with Count Kinsky when he won the Grand National in 1883.

17. Peregrine S. Churchill.

18. Anita Leslie, *Edwardians in Love* (Arrow Books, 1974), pp. 13, 14.

19. Conversations with Peregrine S. Churchill, 2001–02.

20. Peregrine S. Churchill.

21. Mrs. George Cornwallis-West, *The Reminiscences of Lady Randolph Churchill* (Century Co., 1908), p. 149.

22. Ibid.

23. Randolph S. Churchill, op. cit., pp. 50–51.

24. Winston S. Churchill, *Lord Randolph Churchill,* vol. 1, pp. 245–50, 273.

25. It has been customary to have a statue made of British prime ministers, each of which is placed in the central hall of the Palace of Westminster.

26. Ibid., pp. 256–61. Membership peaked at over 1.7 million in 1906.

27. Winston's School Report from St. George's School; the Churchill Archives, University of Cambridge.

28. Randolph S. Churchill, op. cit., pp. 48–50.

29. Winston S. Churchill's letters are housed at the Churchill Archives. Many of his childhood letters have been printed in Celia Sandys's book *From Winston With Love and Kisses* (Sinclair-Stevenson, 1994).

30. Celia Sandys, op. cit., p. 49.

31. Winston's Report from St. George's School; Churchill Archives, University of Cambridge.

32. Ibid.

33. Maurice Baring, *The Puppet Show of Memory* (Heinemann, 1922).

34. Dr. Robson Roose to Lord Randolph Churchill, Mar. 15, 1886; copy in Peregrine S. Churchill's private papers; also Peregrine S. Churchill's manuscript, owned privately by his widow.

35. It was most unusual for a boys' preparatory school to be owned and run by women. The vast majority were run by men with all male masters.

36. Randolph S. Churchill, op. cit., p. 62.

37. Copy letter in the private papers of Peregrine S. Churchill.

38. Winston S. Churchill, *Lord Randolph Churchill*, p. 130.

39. There are several spellings for King Theebaw's name; we have used the spelling of the Victorian period.

40. Copy in the private papers of Peregrine S. Churchill.

41. Sadly it was later stolen in a burglary. She had a miniature made of it, which passed down through Jack and Peregrine.

42. Winston to Jennie, n.d. [Summer 1885], CHAR.

43. Winston to Jennie, Sept. 2, 1885, CHAR.

44. Letters written by Lord Randolph to Winston and Jack have survived with the signature cut out.

45. Members of the hierarchy of the Catholic Church were all educated in English public schools and were Conservative and loyal to the British government.

46. Winston S. Churchill, *Lord Randolph Churchill*, vol. 2, p. 64.

47. The exact date is not known, and the school's records have not survived.

48. Randolph S. Churchill, *Winston S. Churchill*, vol. 1, p. 73.

49. Winston S. Churchill, *Randolph S. Churchill*, vol. 2, p. 79.

50. Copy in the private papers of Peregrine S. Churchill.

51. Churchill Archives, University of Cambridge.

52. Lord Hartington (later the Duke of Devonshire) and Joseph Chamberlain of the Liberal-Unionist Party formed a political alliance with the Conservatives in opposition to the Irish Home Rule Bill.

53. Peregrine Churchill and Julian Mitchell, *Jennie* (William Collins, 1974), pp. 142–43.

54. Letter of October 1886 from Frances, the Duchess of Marlborough, to Lady Randolph S. Churchill. The Duchess of Marlborough's letters are housed in the Churchill Archives, University of Cambridge.

55. Undated letter from Leonie Leslie to her sister Clara Frewen, autumn 1886, quoted in Anita Leslie, *Edwardians in Love*, p. 198.

56. Conversations with Peregrine S. Churchill. One of his other "lovers" was the mistress to the Prince of Wales, Frances, Countess of Warwick (Daisy).

57. Dr. John H. Mather, "Lord Randolph Churchill: Maladies et Morte," in *Finest Hour* 93, Winter 1996/97, pp. 23–28; copy on the Churchill Archives website, University of Cambridge, CHAR.

58. Churchill and Mitchell, op. cit., pp. 147–48.

59. Churchill and Mitchell, op. cit., p. 149.

60. Winston S. Churchill, *Lord Randolph Churchill*, vol. 2, pp. 182–85.

61. Celia Sandys, op. cit., p. 185.

62. Winston S. Churchill, op. cit., pp. 171–72.

63. Ibid., pp. 238–40.

64. Anita Leslie, *Jennie: The Mother of Winston Churchill* (George Mann, 1992), pp. 174–75; Dowager Duchess of Marlborough to Lord Salisbury, Jan. 26, 1895, in the Marlborough letters, CHAR.

CHAPTER 5

1. Robert Arthur Talbot Gascoyne-Cecil, 3rd Marquess of Salisbury (known as Lord Salisbury) (1830–1903); prime minister, 1885–Feb. 1886; 1886–Aug. 1892; 1895–July 1902.

2. Peregrine Churchill and Julian Mitchell, *Jennie: Lady Randolph Churchill* (William Collins, 1974), pp. 156–57.

3. Anita Leslie, *Jennie: The Mother of Winston Churchill* (George Mann, 1992), pp. 116–17.

4. Jennie to Randolph, Feb. 15, 1887; copy in the private papers of Peregrine S. Churchill.

5. Leslie, op. cit., pp. 121–22; Jennie to her sister Leonie (Sniffy), n.d., but as she speaks of arrangements for March 3, it must have been written around the end of February 1887.

6. Churchill and Mitchell, op. cit., p. 162.

7. Lord Randolph to the Dowager Duchess, Aug. 12, 1887; copy in the private papers of Peregrine S. Churchill. Mrs. Peregrine Churchill donated Jack's tiepin, together with other valuable items of his, to the National Army Museum, London.

8. Copy in the private papers of Peregrine S. Churchill.

9. Mrs. George Cornwallis-West, *The Reminiscences of Lady Randolph Churchill* (Macmillan, 1908), chap. 10, pp. 223–25.

10. Ibid., pp. 229–30.

11. Letter from the Dowager Duchess of Marlborough, Dec. 27, 1887; Winston to his mother, Dec. 26 and 30, 1887. Sir Henry Rider Haggard, KBE (1856–1925), was a prolific writer of adventure novels set predominantly in South Africa.

12. Leslie, op. cit., pp. 128–30.

13. Ibid., pp. 130–31.

14. Ralph G. Martin, *Lady Randolph Churchill,* vol. 1 (Sphere Books, 1974), p. 226.

15. Winston to his father, Mar. 6, 1888: "I will take your advice about doing the most paying questions first and then the rest."

16. Winston S. Churchill, *My Early Life* (Butterworth, 1930), pp. 29–31.

17. During Winston's time at Harrow there were many different teaching buildings. Boys were taught in buildings with names like Old Schools, Classics Department, Art School, Music School, and Vaughan Library. Information from Mrs. Rita Boswell Gibbs, Archivist, Harrow Public School, August 2009.

18. The Abbesse won the Portland Plate (£775); in November 1889, she won the Oaks at Epsom (£2,600), and in 1890, the Manchester Cup (£2,200) and the Hardwick Stakes. The total prize money amounted to $26,760.

19. At Harrow the schoolboys were assigned to houses, each with seventy to ninety students, and progressed from one house to another. Within the house there were several classes.

20. Today known as the Royal Military Academy Sandhurst, Camberley, Surrey.

21. Winston S. Churchill, *Lord Randolph Churchill,* vol. 2, pp. 396–97.

22. Conversations with Peregrine S. Churchill, 2001–02; exact date of incident not recalled.

23. Anita Leslie, *Edwardians in Love* (Arrow Books, 1974), chap. 6, pp. 65–66, 285.

CHAPTER 6

1. The term "remove" is used at English public schools for "promote" to a higher form. It can be used in another sense to mean brief holidays.

2. The Churchill Archives, University of Cambridge.

3. Unfortunately, only two of Mrs. Everest's letters to Winston have survived.

4. Jack Churchill inherited his father's racing trophies; he made a gift of the Manchester Cup to the Royal Dorset Yacht Club, and other of the trophies to the Victoria and Albert Museum, London.

5. No papers have survived at Harrow School, giving the system of marking used by each master for classwork. What has survived is the Trial Broadsheet they used, which gives the number of boys in a class and shows a boy's place in his class according to his marks, but it does not give the maximum possible score for each subject or all of the subjects. (Source: Mrs. Rita Boswell Gibbs, Archivist, Harrow Public School, August 2009.) In the examinations, however, the maximum possible scores were given for each subject. Winston's exam paper for June 1892 showed the maximum possible scores as: Latin 2,000 marks, Mathematics 2,500 marks, Essay 500 marks, and so on. (Source: Randolph S. Churchill *Winston S. Churchill,* vol. 1, Companion, part 1, p. 270. Jack's exam papers would have been scored in the same way.

6. This is a reference to an accident that Jack had suffered at the home of the Duchess Lily, The Deepdene, Dorking, when a visiting friend fired some sort of missile that injured his eye. Jack had to wear glasses for a while afterward, but it never interfered with his military service in later life.

7. Astor's home, Cliveden House at Taplow, Buckinghamshire, a huge mansion, exists to this day and is open to the public.

8. CHAR 28/10/20.

9. When Charles Stewart Parnell in 1882 took over the leadership of the Home Rule Party from the moderate Isaac Butt, a Dublin barrister, he renamed it the Irish Parliamentary Party. It has also been referred to by some historians as the Irish Home Rule League.

10. Parnell, who was a single man, owned a country estate, Avondale at Rathdrum, County Wicklow, Ireland, today open to the public. Parnell had been carrying on an affair with Mrs. O'Shea from

1880, and she was separated from her husband. Kitty was the daughter of Sir John Page Wood, 2nd Baronet. Her brother was Field Marshal Sir Evelyn Wood. Kitty was a Liberal and acted as liaison between Parnell and Gladstone during negotiations relating to the First Home Rule Bill in April 1886. That summer, Parnell moved into Kitty's home in Eltham, South East London. They had three children, and got married after her divorce in 1891. Parnell's health collapsed and he died less than four months later, in October, age forty-five.

11. Mrs. Elizabeth Everest to Lady Randolph Churchill, signed "Your Ladyship's Obedient Servant." owned privately by Mrs. Peregrine S. Churchill.

12. Lord Randolph S. Churchill, MP, *Men, Mines, and Animals in South Africa* (Sampson Low, Marston & Co., 1895).

13. G. R. Searle, *A New Oxford History of England: A New England Peace and War 1886–1918* (Oxford University Press, 1999), pp. 155–56.

14. Ibid.

15. CHAR, MARB 1/15. Randolph Churchill to the Dowager Duchess of Marlborough, Jan. 14, 1892. Churchill College, Cambridge.

16. Winston to his mother Jennie, Mar. 16, 1892; copy in the private papers of Peregrine S. Churchill.

17. R. F. Foster, *Lord Randolph Churchill* (Clarendon Press, Oxford, 1981), p. 350.

18. Lord Randolph's old school friend, Lord Rosebery, Liberal MP, later Liberal prime minister (1894), at the request of the Dowager Duchess of Marlborough wrote Lord Randolph's biography, *Lord Randolph Churchill* (Harper & Brothers, 1906).

19. Winston S. Churchill, *My Early Life* (Butterworth, 1930), p. 45.

20. Ibid.

21. Louis Moriarty to Winston S. Churchill, quoted in Randolph S. Churchill, *Winston S. Churchill 1874–1900*, vol. 1, *Youth*, Companion (Heinemann, 1967), pp. 336–37.

22. From a manuscript by Peregrine S. Churchill, owned privately by Mrs. Peregrine S. Churchill.

23. Many of the photographs used today in books and press articles about the Churchills were taken by Jack Churchill. For posterity he would photograph, in particular, his wife, Lady Gwendeline (Goonie), and their children, John George, Peregrine, and Clarissa, and Winston and his family. He also made home movies of their holidays and trips abroad.

24. Roose to Lord Randolph Churchill, Oct. 22, 1892, quoting the diagnosis of Dr. Thomas Keith, in Randolph S. Churchill, op. cit., p. 343.

25. Ibid., p. 350; also report from *The Times*, Jan. 11, 1893.

26. "Winston Churchill: His Hardiness and Resilience," John H. Mather, MD, Research Associate, Institute of Medicine, Johns Hopkins University, School of Medicine; paper presented October 18, 1997, at 14th Annual International Churchill Society Conference, Toronto, Canada.

27. Rev. F. C. Searle to Winston S. Churchill, Mar. 3, 1893, in Randolph S. Churchill, op. cit., p. 370.

28. Capt. Walter Henry James to Lord Randolph, ibid., p. 371.

29. Frances, Countess of Warwick, *Afterthoughts, Etc.* (Cassell, 1931).

30. See Bishop of St. Asaph, *A Handbook on Welsh Church Defence, April 1894.* (The Church of England bishops were opposed to the bill.) See also Hansard, Feb. 23, 1893, vol. 9, CC204–87, for the parliamentary debate (on the Internet).

31. Winston S. Churchill, *Lord Randolph Churchill*, vol. 2, pp. 466–67.

32. Randolph S. Churchill, op. cit., pp. 380–81.

33. Ibid., pp. 388 and 396, letters between Mr. J. Little and Lord Randolph Churchill, Aug. 7 and Aug. 19, 1893.

34. Mr. J. Little to Lord Randolph, Aug. 7, 1893, ibid., p. 388, from the Hotel Sweitzerhof, Lucerne, saying Winston and Jack went boating on the lake the previous Friday.

35. Winston S. Churchill, *My Early Life*, pp. 50–52.

36. Randolph S. Churchill, *Winston S. Churchill*, vol. 1, *Youth*, p. 195.

37. Lord Randolph Churchill to Frances, Duchess of Marlborough, September 3, 1893, quoted in ibid., p. 205, sent from Gastein.

CHAPTER 7

1. Field Marshall Frederick Sleigh Roberts (1832–1914), 1st Earl of Kandahar, one of the most successful army commanders of the Victorian era, was known affectionately as "Bobs."

2. Archibald Philip Primrose, 5th Earl of Rosebery (1847–1951), was a British Liberal statesman, also known as Lord Dalmeny (1851–1868); he was prime minister, March 5, 1894–June 22, 1895.
3. John, Viscount Morley, *Recollections* (Macmillan, 1917).
4. See Author's Note.
5. Winston S. Churchill, *My Early Life* (Butterworth, 1930), pp. 62–63.

CHAPTER 8

1. Dr. Thomas Keith, a specialist in tumors, had attended Jennie in October 1892 when she suffered a swelling behind the uterus.
2. An undated cutting from the *New York Times* in Peregrine S. Churchill's papers; a letter from Jack Churchill to his mother, July 17, 1894, saying Winston had told him their mother was drinking many American drinks. There has been speculation on Internet websites and in articles in journals about whether Jennie invented a Manhattan cocktail, but the date has been wrongly given as 1874, instead of 1894, which has caused confusion; she was not in the United States in 1874, the year of her marriage to Lord Randolph.
3. Conversations with Peregrine S. Churchill, 2001–02.
4. Medical record by Dr. Thomas Keith, copy in the papers of Peregrine S. Churchill. Also, Dr. John H. Mather, "Lord Randolph Churchill: Maladies et Mort," in *Finest Hour* 93, Winter 1996/97, pp. 23–28; copy on the Churchill Archives website, University of Cambridge. Dr. Mather has deduced that this is symptomatic of Raynaud's disease, a serious malady affecting heavy smokers.
5. Conversations with Peregrine S. Churchill, 2001–02.
6. Copy in the private papers of Peregrine S. Churchill; also original in the National Library of Ireland in Dublin.
7. It is unclear who originally contacted Jennie with the news that Kinsky was engaged, but correspondence suggests she knew around August 1894. It is possible therefore that she read it in *The Times*.
8. Copy of letter from Dr. Thomas Keith to Cornelia, Lady Wimborne, in the papers of Peregrine S. Churchill.
9. Quoted in Churchill and Mitchell, *Jennie, Lady Randolph Churchill*, pp. 168–69.
10. Winston S. Churchill, *Lord Randolph Churchill*, vol. 2 (Macmillan, 1906), p. 484.
11. Anita Leslie, *Jennie: The Mother of Winston Churchill* (George Mann, 1992).
12. Winston S. Churchill, *My Early Life* (Butterworth, 1930), p. 76.
13. Winston S. Churchill, *Lord Randolph Churchill*, vol. 2, pp. 464–65.
14. Lord Rosebery, *Lord Randolph Churchill* (Arthur L. Humphreys, 1906).

CHAPTER 9

1. 8th Duke of Devonshire.
2. Of the three trustees, one had died already. Lord Curzon of Kedlestone, a friend of the Churchills and former viceroy of India, was the only remaining trustee. He did not interfere in the family's affairs. Jennie was left in charge.
3. The property in New York, left to Jennie by her father, was the original Jerome mansion on Madison Square. It was rented as a club.
4. Conversations with Peregrine S. Churchill. He looked after his own family's financial affairs and was the executor of his father's will and therefore had access to Lord Randolph's investments and trust fund.
5. The Prince would have been referring to the day Lord Randolph ordered him out of his house on discovering him alone there with Jennie.
6. Anita Leslie, *Jennie: The Mother of Winston Churchill* (George Mann, 1992), pp. 184–85.
7. Ibid.
8. The Churchill Archives, Cambridge. The Prince of Wales hardly ever dated a letter to Jennie, but she kept all the envelopes, which were date stamped.
9. Conversations with Peregrine S. Churchill, 2001–02.
10. Two hundred of the Prince's letters and notes to Jennie are housed in the Churchill Archives, Churchill College, Cambridge.
11. Anita Leslie, op. cit.; the Leslie letters and papers are located in the Leslie Papers in the National Library of Ireland.

12. Cliveden House would become infamous as the place where the notorious, high-class prostitute Christine Keeler in July 1961 seduced John Profumo, the Conservative British secretary of state for war. Keeler was at the same time sleeping with Yevgeny Ivanov, a naval attaché at the Soviet embassy.

13. Quoted in Ralph G. Martin, *Jennie: The Life of Lady Randolph Churchill*, vol. 2, *The Dramatic Years, 1895–1921* (Sphere Books, 1974), pp. 84–85.

14. Ibid.

15. Ibid.

16. The Duchess Lily, widow of the 8th Duke of Marlborough (Blandford), married for a third time, to Lord William de la Poer Beresford (1847–1900), and they lived at The Deepdene, Dorking.

17. Winston S. Churchill, *My Early Life* (Butterworth, 1930).

18. Jennie had brought back rolls of material she bought in Japan during the world trip with Randolph in 1894.

19. Jennie is probably the only one of the Prince's mistresses to be photographed by the press beside him in public. Although Alice Keppel later accompanied him to France and Germany, she walked several paces behind him, and the press air-brushed her out of press photographs.

20. Winston S. Churchill, *My Early Life*.

21. Anita Leslie, op. cit., p. 214.

22. Ibid.

23. Sir Philip Magnus, *King Edward VII* (Macmillan, 1964), p. 260; Magnus said the first time Alice Keppel entertained the King to dinner at her home was February 27, 1898.

24. Winston had written a novel, *Savrola*, and had asked Hamilton to carry the manuscript back to England for him, which he duly did and took it to Jennie at her home with a view to her seeing to its publication.

25. Diary entry for Aug. 15, 1915, in which Jean, Lady Hamilton, recalls earlier years. The diaries are privately owned by the general's great-nephew, Mr. Ian Hamilton.

26. George Cornwallis-West gave the impression in his memoirs that he met Jennie at the Duchess of Devonshire's ball in July, but his letters to Jennie date from earlier that year. He may not have wanted it known in society that Jennie had been visiting a place where army officers were billeted. George Cornwallis-West, *Edwardian Hey-Days* (Putnam, 1930), p. 101.

27. Tim Coates, *Patsy: The Story of Mary Cornwallis-West* (Bloomsbury, 2003).

28. George Cornwallis-West, *Edwardian Hey-Days*.

29. George Cornwallis-West's letters to Jennie are housed in the Churchill Archives, Cambridge.

CHAPTER 10

1. Randolph S. Churchill, *Winston S. Churchill*, vol. 1, p. 255.

2. WSC to Jennie, Nov. 10, 1895, ibid.

3. WSC to Jennie, Nov. 15, 1895, ibid.

4. Winston S. Churchill, *My Early Life* (Butterworth, 1930).

5. Randolph S. Churchill, op. cit., pp. 604–24; and Winston S. Churchill, *My Early Life*, p. 88.

6. Randolph S. Churchill, op. cit., pp. 677–78.

7. WSC to Bourke Cockran, Apr. 12, 1896, in ibid., pp. 668–69.

8. Winston S. Churchill, op. cit., pp. 275–76.

9. Conversations with Peregrine S. Churchill, 2001–02.

10. Randolph S. Churchill, *Winston S. Churchill*, vol. 1, *Youth*; WSC to JSC, January 7, 1897, p. 296.

11. Randolph S. Churchill, *Winston S. Churchill*, companion vol. 1, pt. 2, pp. 696–97.

12. Ibid., companion vol. 1, pt. 2, pp. 701–2.

13. Dr. J. E. C. Welldon to Jack Churchill, Jan. 20, 24, 25, 1895; May 29, 1896; Feb. 2, 9, 19, 1897; owned privately by Mrs. Peregrine S. Churchill.

14. John Colville (Jock), *Winston Churchill and His Inner Circle* (Wyndham Books, 1981), chap. 11, "The Family."

15. Quoted in Randolph S. Churchill, op. cit., p. 288.

16. A medal hunter was a soldier who was interested in obtaining medals for bravery or the like for show or, as is in Winston Churchill's case, to further a political career through press coverage of a heroic nature.

17. Randolph S. Churchill, op. cit., companion vol. 1, pt. 2, pp. 720–21.

18. WSC to Jennie, in ibid., pp. 726–38.
19. Cecil Rhodes, an English-born businessman, was an ardent believer in colonialism and imperialism. He was the eponymous founder of the state of Rhodesia, which, after it gained independence, was renamed Zimbabwe.
20. Conversations with Peregrine S. Churchill. See also Randolph S. Churchill, op. cit., pp. 306–7.
21. Conversations with Peregrine S. Churchill, 2001.

CHAPTER 11

1. David D'Lugio and Ronald Rogowski, "The British Parallel: The Conservatives Near-Defeat," in *The Domestic Basis of Grand Strategy,* ed. Richard Rosecrance and Arthur A. Stein (Cornell University Press, 1993), p. 84.
2. Ibid., p. 84.
3. The letters from Dr. J. E. C. Welldon quoted in this book are owned privately by Mrs. Peregrine S. Churchill.
4. Jennie to WSC, Mar. 5, 1897. In it she said, "800 a year goes to you 2 boys." Winston's allowance from Jennie was £500/$2,400 a year; owned privately by Mrs. Peregrine S. Churchill.
5. Conversations with Peregrine S. Churchill, 2001–02.
6. Randolph S. Churchill, *Winston S. Churchill,* companion vol. 1, p. 866. Jennie to WSC, Jan. 13, 1898, explaining these arrangements, pp. 866–67.
7. Sir Philip Magnus, *King Edward VII* (Macmillan, 1964).
8. Randolph S. Churchill, op. cit., p. 859.
9. Jennie to WSC, Jan. 23, 1898.
10. Conversations with Peregrine S. Churchill, 2001–02.
11. Ibid.
12. Ralph G. Martin, *Lady Randolph Churchill* (Sphere Books, 1974), p. 174; see also headline in *New York Times,* Aug. 4, 1899.
13. Ralph G. Martin, op. cit., p. 176; for Winston Churchill's retraction, *New York Times,* Aug. 5, 1899.
14. Randolph S. Churchill, *Winston S. Churchill,* companion vol. 1, pt. 2, pp. 988–89.
15. Randolph S. Churchill, *Winston S. Churchill 1874–1900,* vol. 1, *Youth,* pp. 424–25.
16. The diaries of Jean, Lady Hamilton, Apr. 15, 1902, recalling an earlier time.
17. Randolph S. Churchill *Winston S. Churchill,* companion vol. 1, pt. 2 (1896–1900), pp. 1022–23.

CHAPTER 12

1. Mary was the daughter of Levi Zeigler, a Chicago millionaire and co-founder of the department store Field & Leiter, now Marshall Field.
2. The first part of the story is from Mrs. George Cornwallis-West, *The Reminiscences of Lady Randolph Churchill* (Century, 1908), chaps. 15 and 16, pp. 361–62.
3. Much of the story of Lady Randolph Churchill's work on the *Anglo-Saxon Review* has been written from the private papers of her grandson, the late Peregrine S. Churchill, which are owned privately by his widow.
4. Mildred Davis Harding, *Air-Bird in the Water: The Life and Works of Pearl Craigie (John Oliver Hobbes)* (Fairleigh Dickinson University Press, 1996).
5. Mrs. George Cornwallis-West, op. cit., p. 367.
6. Ibid., pp. 372–73.
7. Ibid., p. 367.
8. Kings: Charles I, Charles II, Henry VIII, etc.
9. Mrs. George Cornwallis-West, op. cit., p. 362.
10. Part of a copy of Jennie's letter to Bourke Cockran in the papers of Peregrine S. Churchill.
11. Mrs. George Cornwallis-West, op. cit., p. 363.
12. Randolph S. Churchill, *Winston S. Churchill,* companion vol. 1, pp. 997–98.
13. Randolph S. Churchill, op. cit., p. 1018.
14. Jennie to her son Jack Churchill, first week in February 1899.
15. Randolph S. Churchill, op. cit., pp. 442–43.
16. Ibid., chap. 15, "England 1899."
17. Mrs. George Cornwallis-West, op. cit., p. 363.

18. Notes in the papers of Peregrine S. Churchill.
19. Georgiana, Duchess of Devonshire (1757–1806), was even then a historic figure. Born Georgiana Spencer, she was an ancestor of the late Diana, Princess of Wales. The recent film *The Duchess*, starring Keira Knightley, is about this Georgiana.
20. Angela V. John, *Elizabeth Robins: Staging a Life, 1862–1952* (Routledge, 1995).
21. Peregrine Churchill and Julian Mitchell, *Jennie: Lady Randolph Churchill* (Collins, 1974), p. 185.
22. Undated press cutting in the papers of Peregrine S. Churchill.
23. Mrs. George Cornwallis-West, op. cit., pp. 380–81.
24. Access to a copy of the *Anglo-Saxon Review* by kind permission of Randolph Churchill.
25. Churchill and Mitchell, op. cit., pp. 223–24.
26. Mrs. George Cornwallis-West, op. cit., p. 366.
27. Quoted in Ralph G. Martin, *Lady Randolph Churchill*, vol. 2 (Sphere Books, 1974), p. 393.
28. Much of the story of Lady Randolph Churchill's work on board the *Maine* has been written from the papers of her grandson, the late Peregrine S. Churchill, which are owned privately by his widow.
29. The members of the executive committee were Jennie, Chairman; Mrs. Adair, Vice-Chairman; Mrs. Blow, Hon. Sec.; Mrs. Fanny Ronalds, Treasurer; Adele, Lady Essex; Mr. Griffiths, Mrs. Van Duzer, Mrs. Leonie Leslie, Mrs. Arthur Paget, Mrs. Clara Frewen, Mrs. Haldeman, and Mrs. Field. Mrs. George Cornwallis-West, op. cit., p. 400.
30. Ibid., p. 396.
31. Ibid., p. 402.
32. Ibid., pp. 399–460.
33. Ibid., p. 400.
34. Press clipping in the private papers of Peregrine S. Churchill.
35. Anita Leslie, *Jennie: The Life of Lady Randolph Churchill* (Hutchinson, 1969).
36. Randolph S. Churchill, op. cit., pp. 1142–43.
37. Lady Randolph Churchill to HRH the Prince of Wales, Jan. 19, 1900. The Royal Archives, Windsor Castle, Berkshire by permission of Her Majesty Queen Elizabeth II.
38. Mrs. George Cornwallis-West, op. cit., pp. 423–37.
39. Quoted in Ralph G. Martin, *Lady Randolph Churchill*.
40. Quoted in Celia Sandys, *Churchill, Wanted Dead or Alive* (Harper Collins, 1999).
41. Winston S. Churchill, *My Early Life* (Butterworth, 1930).
42. Lady Randolph Churchill to HRH the Prince of Wales, Mar. 3, 1900, The Royal Archives, Windsor Castle, Berkshire by permission of Her Majesty Queen Elizabeth II.
43. Letter from Jack Churchill to his aunt Clara Frewen, Mar. 27, 1900.
44. Report in the *Daily Mail*, Apr. 24, 1900; clipping in the papers of Peregrine S. Churchill.
45. Conversations with Peregrine S. Churchill, 2001–02.
46. *Anglo-Saxon Review*, Dec. 1900, issue 8, pp. 237–38, Impressions and Opinions.

CHAPTER 13

1. Winston S. Churchill, *The River War* (Longmans Green, 1899).
2. Randolph S. Churchill *Winston S. Churchill*, vol. 1, *Youth*, p. 444.
3. Randolph S. Churchill *Winston S. Churchill 1874–1900*, companion vol. 1, pt. 2, pp. 1032–33.
4. Ibid., p. 1033.
5. Ibid., pp. 1035–36.
6. Randolph S. Churchill, *Winston S. Churchill 1874–1900*, vol. 1, *Youth*, pp. 447–48.
7. Randolph S. Churchill, *Winston S. Churchill*, companion vol. 1, *Youth*, p. 1035.
8. Ibid., vol. 1, *Youth*, p. 455.
9. Ibid., p. 448.
10. Randolph S. Churchill, *Winston S. Churchill 1874–1900*, companion vol. 1, pt. 2, pp. 1040–41.
11. Randolph S. Churchill, *Winston S. Churchill 1874–1900*, vol. 1, *Youth*, p. 477.
12. Ibid., p. 476.
13. Telegram of December 22, 1899, from Pamela Plowden to Lady Randolph Churchill, sent from Reigate; Randolph S. Churchill, *Winston S. Churchill 1874–1900*, companion vol. 1, pt. 2, p. 1093.
14. See Winston S. Churchill, *From London to Ladysmith* and *My Early Life*, and Celia Sandys, *Churchill, Wanted Dead or Alive* (HarperCollins, 1999).

15. Conversations with Peregrine S. Churchill, 2001–02. No letters to the effect have survived.
16. Buller to Lady Londonderry, a relative of the Dowager Duchess of Marlborough who was the daughter of Lord Londonderry, quoted in Randolph S. Churchill, op. cit., p. 506.
17. Randolph S. Churchill, op. cit., p. 507. Winston wrote to his mother confirming his appointment, January 6, 1900.
18. Ibid., p. 508.
19. Randolph S. Churchill, *Winston S. Churchill 1874–1900*, companion vol. 1, pt. 2, pp. 1143–44.
20. Winston to Pamela from Government House, Natal, Randolph S. Churchill, *Winston S. Churchill 1874–1900*, companion vol. 1, pt. 2, pp. 1146–47; also Randolph S. Churchill, *Winston S. Churchill 1874–1900*, vol. 1, *Youth*, pp. 509, 510–11.
21. The bullet that shot Jack was mounted on a small chain and kept as a souvenir. It has been donated to the National Army Museum, London, by Mrs. Peregrine S. Churchill, Jack's daughter-in-law. It has recently been on display at the Cabinet War Rooms.
22. Kenneth Griffith, *Thank God We Kept the Flag Flying* (Hutchinson, 1974), p. 344.
23. Anita Leslie, *Jennie* (George Mann, 1992).
24. Randolph S. Churchill, *Winston S. Churchill 1874–1900*, vol. 1, *Youth*, p. 514.
25. Winston to Pamela from Near Colenso, Randolph S. Churchill, *Winston S. Churchill 1874–1900*, companion vol. 1, pt. 2, pp. 1151–52.
26. Randolph S. Churchill, op. cit., p. 524.
27. Winston S. Churchill, *Ian Hamilton's March* (Longmans Green, 1900).
28. Jack Churchill to Lady Randolph, Apr. 3, 1900, CHAR 28/32/1, Churchill College, Cambridge.
29. Jennie, sent from 35A Great Cumberland Place, London, to Winston; copy in the private papers of Mrs. Peregrine S. Churchill.
30. Jack Churchill to Lady Randolph, June 2, 1900, CHAR 28/32/3, Churchill College, Cambridge.
31. Ibid.
32. This child, a girl, Sonia, later Mrs. Roland Cubitt, wrote a book under her maiden name, Sonia Keppel, *Edwardian Daughter* (New York: British Book Centre, 1958).
33. Jack Churchill to Lady Randolph, July 2, 1900, CHAR 28/32/6.
34. Cutting from the *New York Times*, July 29, 1900, in the papers of Peregrine S. Churchill.
35. Jack Churchill to WSC, Sept. 12, 1900, CHAR 28/32/10–13.
36. Jack Churchill to WSC, Oct. 3, 1900, CHAR 28/32/14–15.
37. Bloemfontein fell in March, and Pretoria in June 1900.
38. Original letter in the private papers of Mrs. Peregrine S. Churchill.

CHAPTER 14

1. Randolph S. Churchill, *Winston S. Churchill 1874–1900*, vol. 1, *Youth*, p. 530.
2. Jennie to Jack, June 23, 1900; copy in the papers of Mrs. Peregrine S. Churchill.
3. George Cornwallis-West, *Edwardian Hey-Days* (Putnam, 1930).
4. Anita Leslie, *Jennie* (George Mann, 1992).
5. The diaries of Jean, Lady Hamilton, entry dated December 3, 1903; also on Friday, February 7, 1902, she wrote that Colonel Baring (of the family of Barings Bank) had returned from India thinking he was going to marry Pamela. A mutual friend, Constance Wenlock, had to tell him that Pamela was engaged to Victor Lytton.
6. George Cornwallis-West, *Edwardian Hey-Days*, chap. 10, p. 120. As there was no ban on married men in the army, Jennie believed that the Prince of Wales was behind the action to prevent the marriage.
7. Ibid., pp. 121–22.
8. Ibid., p. 122.
9. The exact date that Jennie's change of title became official is not known, but King Edward VII (formerly the Prince of Wales) addressed her in letters of 1902 as Lady Randolph Churchill, and on August 11 of that year was discussing with her how she should be addressed.
10. Winston had kept in touch with Bourke Cockran, having written to him when he was in South Africa, Nov. 30, 1899, quoted in Randolph S. Churchill, *Winston S. Churchill*, vol. 1, *Youth*, companion vol., pp. 1082–83.
11. Randolph S. Churchill, op. cit., p. 544.

12. Jean Hamilton had been invited to Pamela Plowden's wedding but was on holiday in Paris. She wrote in her diary on Saturday, April 15, 1902: "It is very strange these two should marry. His father and her mother loved each other long ago in Simla. I wonder what old Lady Lytton thinks of it, she can hardly like it, but is always so sweetly reasonable. They will have no money at all."

13. Newspaper cutting of the report in the *New York Times*, April 4, 1902, in the papers of Peregrine S. Churchill.

14. This cup is now at the National Army Museum, London, a gift from Mrs. Peregrine S. Churchill.

15. Raymond Lamont Brown, *Edward VII's Last Loves* (Sutton, 2001).

16. Celia Lee, *Jean, Lady Hamilton—A Soldier's Wife* (privately by the author, 2001), diary entry, Sunday, Jan. 3, 1904, Gopsall House, the home of the Earl and Countess of Howe.

17. David Lloyd George had been elected a member of Parliament at age twenty-seven in 1890.

18. To date Winston had published *The Story of the Malakand Field Force* (1898), which was about India; *The River War* (1899), which was about the Sudan conflict; *Savrola* (1900), which was a novel; *London to Ladysmith via Pretoria* (1900); *Ian Hamilton's March* (1900).

19. Randolph S. Churchill, *Winston S. Churchill*, vol. 2, *Young Statesman, 1901–14*, pp. 134–35.

20. When, in the mid-1880s, Lord Randolph Churchill was rising steadily from one cabinet post to another, the cartoonists, most notably the London magazine *Punch*, published a picture of him with the caption "the coming man," meaning he was on his way to becoming a cabinet minister and a leader in politics.

21. The philanderer Colonel Harry Scobell would spend a weekend at Salisbury Hall with Lady Margerie Orr-Ewing, with whom he was having an affair. Scobell was the hypocrite who played a major part in having his brother-in-law, Colonel Charles A'Court (Repington), thrown out of the army for having an affair with Mary, Lady Garstin, the wife of Sir William Garstin. In 1906, Scobell and Lady Margerie were photographed in the garden at Salisbury Hall (she swathed almost head to toe in a fox fur coat), while Jack Churchill showed them his vegetable patch!

22. Conversations with Peregrine S. Churchill, 2001–02.

23. Randolph S. Churchill, *Winston S. Churchill*, companion vol. 2, pt. 1, pp. 572–73.

CHAPTER 15

1. Pronounced "Barty."

2. Tape-recorded interview with Lady Gwendeline's daughter, Clarissa, Countess of Avon, 2003. When Gwendeline was a little girl, her younger brother could not pronounce her name and called her Goonie.

3. Ibid.

4. Ibid.

5. The exact date of the introduction is not known, as no letters survive to that effect, but it was probably in 1906.

6. Letters from Jack to Goonie of that year survive.

7. Recorded interview with Clarissa, Countess of Avon, 2003.

8. Jack to Winston, Randolph S. Churchill, *Winston S. Churchill*, companion vol. 2, pt. 2 (1907–11): Oct. 25, Nov. 14, Nov. 21, Dec. 19, Dec. 27, 1907, pp. 690, 695–97, 704–5, 728–29; 730–31; Jan. 2, Jan. 10, 1908, pp. 736–37, 742.

9. Margaret, Lady Smith, the wife of Sir F. E. Smith, the attorney general, later Lord and Lady Birkenhead, were also guests in the house, along with several others, including Winston's private secretary Edward (Eddy) Marsh, who escaped wearing only his pajamas and clutching Winston's papers.

10. Mary Soames, *Clementine Churchill* (Doubleday, 2002). The facts of the Hozier children's parentage was not known until the modern age.

11. Randolph S. Churchill, *Winston S. Churchill*, vol. 2, *The Young Statesman, 1901–1914*, p. 263.

12. Ibid., companion vol. 2, pt. 2 (1907–11), pp. 783–94.

13. Author's recorded and written interview with Mary, Lady Soames, Oct. 19 and 28, 2005.

14. Soames, op. cit., chap. 3, "To Thine Own Self Be True." Also, author's recorded and written interviews with Lady Soames, Oct. 19 and 28, 2005.

15. Randolph S. Churchill, op. cit., p. 801.

16. Soames, op. cit., p. 49.

17. Ibid.

18. Randolph S. Churchill, op. cit., p. 803.

19. Ibid., p. 274.

20. Lord Hugh Gascoyne-Cecil was the younger son of the former prime minister Lord Salisbury.

21. Richard Davenport-Hines, *Ettie: The Intimate Life and Dauntless Spirit of Lady Desborough* (Weidenfeld & Nicholson, 2008), pp. 162–63, quoting from Lady Desborough's diary.

22. Press clippings in the papers of Peregrine S. Churchill.

23. The organization the Pearly Kings and Queens survives today, and they still wear their shimmering costumes but are no longer costermongers. They devote their time to charity work.

CHAPTER 16

1. Conversations with Peregrine S. Churchill, 2001–02. Also recounted in Anita Leslie, *Jennie: The Mother of Winston Churchill,* pp. 286–87.

2. George Cornwallis-West to Jack Churchill, letter of condolence, July 9, 1941, owned privately by Mrs. Peregrine S. Churchill.

3. Mary Soames, *Clementine Churchill,* pp. 65–66.

4. While Jennie was visiting her mother in Paris in 1876, Winston was left at home in the charge of Mrs. Everest and his father. Lord Randolph had written to Jennie on June 30: "The baby is very flourishing." And again in July (undated): "He [Winston] came in to see me this afternoon and carried off the paper basket in triumph." CHAR 28/5/36, Churchill College, Cambridge.

5. Soames, *Clementine Churchill,* pp. 66–67.

6. Ibid., diary entry, February 21, 1910.

7. Randolph S. Churchill, *Winston S. Churchill,* companion vol. 2, pt. 2 (1907–11) (Heinemann, 1969), pp. 901–2.

8. Soames, op. cit., p. 81.

9. Lord Randolph Churchill's will, dated 1883, copy in the private papers of Peregrine S. Churchill.

10. To the tune of £600/$993 each—a total of £16,800/$27,812 then, or £840,000/$1,390,626 today.

11. CHAR 28/33/5, Churchill College, Cambridge. This vitally important letter has never been quoted before.

12. George's life with Mrs. Patrick Campbell (Stella) was not a happy one, and she denied him a divorce for many years. At the time of Jennie's funeral he wrote to Jack, saying that parting from her was the biggest mistake of his life. In a sad end, on April 1, 1951, aged seventy-six and suffering from Parkinson's disease and depression, George drew his service pistol and blew his brains out.

13. Peregrine Churchill and Julian Mitchell, *Jennie: Lady Randolph Churchill,* p. 248.

CHAPTER 17

1. See Mary Soames, *Clementine Churchill* (Doubleday, 2002), p. 132.

2. Martin Gilbert, *Winston S. Churchill,* companion vol. 3, pt. 1 (1914–16) (Heinemann, 1977), p. 270.

3. CHAR 28/33/15, Nov. 20, 1914, Churchill College, Cambridge.

4. CHAR 28/121/1, Feb. 1, 1915.

5. Major John S. Churchill, *Gallipoli Diary,* Saturday, Apr. 10, 1915, owned privately by Mrs. Peregrine S. Churchill. The *Gallipoli Diary* is a typed manuscript.

6. Later in the campaign, when this narrow landing place was secured, Jack captured its essence in a poem he sent to the news sheet published by Headquarters MEF:

   Y Beach, the Scottish Borderer cried,
   While panting up the steep hillside
   To call this a beach is stiff
   It's nothing but a bloody cliff.
   Why Beach?

7. Major John Churchill, *Gallipoli Diary,* Thursday, Apr. 28, 1915.

8. Winston Churchill, as First Lord of the Admiralty, was the political head of the Royal Navy, representing its interests in the cabinet and the House of Commons but having no executive authority. Admiral Sir John Fisher, as First Sea Lord, was the commander in chief of the Royal Navy.

9. Letters from Jack Churchill to his mother, CHAR 28/121/9 & 11, June 20 and July 29, 1915.

10. Letters from Jack Churchill to his mother, CHAR 28/121/18–19, Oct. 22, 1915.

CHAPTER 18

1. From the private papers of Peregrine S. Churchill.
2. The Cross of Malta medal was presented by the monarch to women for services rendered, for example, in wartime, making them a Lady of Grace of the Order of St. John of Jerusalem, which is today better known as a branch of St. John's Ambulance. For whatever reason, Goonie did not receive it or any official recognition for her nursing work.
3. Quoted in Frederick, Second Earl of Birkenhead, *F. E.: The Life of F. E. Smith, First Earl of Birkenhead* (Eyre and Spottiswoode, 1960).
4. Ploegsteert Wood, in the Ypres Salient, in 1915 became a quieter section where no major action took place. Army units were sent there to recuperate after heavy fighting elsewhere and to retrain in readiness to take part in future operations.
5. From notes and a press cutting in the papers of Peregrine S. Churchill.
6. CHAR 28/121/37, Churchill College, Cambridge.
7. CHAR 28/121/42.
8. CHAR 28/121/53.
9. See Celia Lee, *Jean, Lady Hamilton (1861–1941), a Soldier's Wife* (published privately by the author), chap. 9, "Gallipoli: The Battle That Would Never End," and chap. 10, "The Dardanelles Commission of Inquiry." See also John Lee, *A Soldier's Life: General Sir Ian Hamilton, 1853–1947* (Macmillan, 2000).
10. *Boche* is a French slang word for "rascal" that was first applied to German soldiers during World War I.
11. Anita Leslie, *Jennie: The Mother of Winston Churchill* (George Mann, 1992), p. 334, quoting the Castle Leslie visitor's book. Castle Leslie, Glaslough, County Monaghan, Ireland, became famous when love blossomed there between Paul McCartney of the Beatles and the model and charity worker Heather Mills. It was in the Church of Ireland in the grounds of the castle that they were married on June 11, 2002.
12. Celia Lee, *Jean, Lady Hamilton,* chap. 8, "Gallipoli: The Battle That Would Never End," and chap. 10, "The Dardanelles Commission of Inquiry."
13. Richard, 1st Viscount Haldane of Cloan, Liberal secretary of state for war, Dec. 10, 1905–June 12, 1912. He is not to be confused with Colonel Haldane.
14. Quoted in Celia Lee, *Jean, Lady Hamilton,* chap. 12, "Love, Sex and Children," pp. 198–99.
15. Interviews with Mary, Lady Soames, Oct. 19 and 28, 2005.

CHAPTER 19

1. On March 28, 1917, the House of Commons voted 341 to 62 that women over the age of thirty who were householders, the wives of householders, occupiers of property with an annual rent of £5/$24, or graduates of British universities could vote in a general election. Several of the women involved in the suffrage campaign stood for Parliament in the 1918 general election, but only Constance, Countess Markiewicz, standing for Sinn Féin, was elected, and she refused to take her seat.
2. CHAR 28/121/82, Churchill College, Cambridge.
3. Lady Ottoline Morrell was a friend of Goonie's and a member of the Bloomsbury Group, an English collective of people whose work influenced literature, aesthetics, criticisms, economics, feminism, pacifism, and sexuality. Virginia Woolf, the well-known writer, and the economist John Maynard Keynes were also members. Lady Morrell had a country home, The Manor House, Garsington, Oxford, where she mostly lived during the war, as did many well-to-do people in the United Kingdom. Once the war was over, she wanted to make use of her London residence.
4. Jeffrey Wallin with Juan Williams, *Cover Story: Churchill's Greatness;* website of the Churchill Centre and Museum, Cabinet War Rooms, London, 2001.
5. The authors' tape-recorded interview with Gwendeline's daughter Clarissa, Countess of Avon, 2003.
6. Anita Leslie, *Jennie: The Mother of Winston Churchill* (George Mann, 1992), pp. 334–39.
7. Author interviews with Mary, Lady Soames, Oct. 19 and 28, 2005.
8. Diary of Jean, Lady Hamilton, May 19, 1919, 1 Hyde Park Gardens.
9. Ibid.
10. There are six provinces in Ireland: Ulster (in the north), and Leinster, Munster, and Connaught (in the south).

11. Mary Soames, *Clementine Churchill*, chap. 14, pp. 234–35.

12. Despite Winston's no longer being First Lord of the Admiralty, Balfour, who was foreign secretary in 1916, asked him to write a full report of the Battle of Jutland (May 31–June 1, 1916). Eugene L. Rasor, *Winston S. Churchill, 1874–1965* (Greenwood, 2000).

13. Mary Soames, *Clementine Churchill* (Doubleday, 2000), pp. 226–27.

14. Ibid.

15. Anita Leslie, op. cit., p. 355.

16. The weather was particularly hot that July, and Jennie's body could not be kept until her husband arrived home from Nigeria, as in those days there was no way of preserving it.

17. Conversations with Peregrine S. Churchill, 2001–02.

18. Peregrine told the authors that after his father's (Jack's) death in 1947, there was £80 still outstanding of monies his grandmother had borrowed from Sir Ernest Cassel, and he settled the account via Rothdschilds Bank, Cassel having died in 1922.

19. It was at Menabilly that Daphne du Maurier wrote *Rebecca*.

20. Mary Soames, *Clementine Churchill*.

21. Interviews with Mary, Lady Soames, Oct. 19 and 28, 2005.

22. The story was related to the authors by Claire Aston, formerly a guide of some years at Kensal Green Cemetery in London, where Marigold is buried.

23. It will be recalled that when Winston was experiencing financial hardship he sold their first country home, Lullenden Farm, to General Sir Ian and Jean, Lady Hamilton. It was bought mainly with Jean's money, as she was the daughter of a Scottish millionaire, Sir John Muir of Deanston, Doune, Perthshire.

24. The Liberal Party was beaten into third place behind the Labour Party, led by John Robert Clynes.

25. Andrew Bonar Law (Sept. 16, 1858–Oct. 30, 1923) was born in Rexton, a small village in eastern New Brunswick, Canada.

26. The modern medical term for Winston's "black dogs" of depression is bipolar disorder. See Dr. John H. Mather's paper "Lord Randolph Churchill—Maladies et Mort," online at the Churchill Archives, Churchill College, Cambridge.

27. Sir Martin Gilbert quotes from a review in the first volume in the *New Statesman:* "He has written a book which is remarkably egotistical, but which is honest and which will certainly long survive him." Martin Gilbert, *Winston S. Churchill* (Heinemann, 1976), vol. 5 (1922–39), chap. 1, "Getting Much Better in Myself," p. 7.

28. Quoted in Geoffrey Best, *Churchill: A Study in Greatness* (Hambledon & London, 2001), p. 70.

29. Up until 1910, MacDonald had spelled his name with a lowercase "d," but after that time it was changed to MacDonald with a capital "D."

30. James Ramsay MacDonald (Oct. 12, 1866–Nov. 9, 1937) was Labour prime minister for less than a year in 1924. Labour returned to power in 1929, but was soon overwhelmed by the crisis of the Great Depression, which split the Labour government. In 1931, MacDonald formed a National Government in which a majority of MPs were from the Conservative Party. As a result, he was expelled from the Labour Party as a traitor. He remained prime minister of the National Government until 1935.

31. Bracken, who was from Ireland, was a big admirer of Winston Churchill. When Winston became prime minister in May 1940, Bracken helped him move into 10 Downing Street. Bracken was sworn into the Privy Council in 1940, despite his lack of ministerial experience. He served as minister of information from 1941 to 1945, following a short stint as Churchill's parliamentary private secretary.

32. Conversations with Peregrine S. Churchill, 2001–02.

33. John Spencer Churchill, *Crowded Canvas: The Memoirs of John Spencer Churchill* (Odhams, 1961).

34. Ibid.

35. Stanley Baldwin was prime minister, 1908; chancellor, Oct. 27, 1922–Aug. 27, 1923; and served three terms as prime minister, 1923–24, 1924–29, and 1935–37.

36. Nicholl, Manisty & Co. to Major John S. Spencer-Churchill, Apr. 20, 1926; in the private papers of Mrs. Peregrine S. Churchill.

37. Harold Wilson served as British Labour prime minister, 1964–70 and 1974–76. He and his government tried to impose wage restraints on British workers, and there were numerous major industrial disputes, with the press referring to the late-night negotiations over "beer and sandwiches at Num-

ber 10. Downing Street" that often took place in an endeavor to resolve disputes and pay claims and avert strikes.

CHAPTER 20

1. Mary Soames, *Speaking for Themselves* (Doubleday, 1998), p. 348.
2. John Spencer Churchill, *Crowded Canvas* (Odhams, 1961).
3. Because of the Second World War, Winston's subsequent six-volume history, *The History of the English Speaking People,* would not actually appear until 1957.
4. Maurice Ashley and Keith Feiling, two of the greatest historians ever produced by Britain, worked on *Marlborough.*
5. Quoted in *Time* magazine, "In the Shadow," June 14, 1968, in an obituary of Winston's son, Randolph, who died two weeks earlier, aged only fifty-seven years. Randolph was a journalist, and in a journalistic piece he had written he said: "When you are living under the shadow of a great oak tree the small sapling does not perhaps receive enough sunshine."
6. Mary is today the Lady Soames. Mary has had two honors bestowed on her by Her Majesty the Queen; she is a Lady of the Garter and a Dame of the British Empire.
7. Interviews with Mary, Lady Soames, Oct. 19 and 28, 2005.
8. Sir Anthony Eden, foreign secretary, 1935–55; Conservative prime minister, 1955–57; married Clarissa Spencer-Churchill, daughter of Jack and Goonie, in 1952, in the registry office in London before the world's press and film cameras.
9. Maurice Harold Macmillan, Conservative prime minister, January 1957–October 1963.
10. Financial secretary to the War Office, 1931; financial secretary to the Treasury, 1934; war secretary, 1935.

CHAPTER 21

1. Pamela Digby (Mar. 20, 1920–Feb. 5, 1997) later remarried twice; the third marriage was to William Averell Harriman, a U.S. businessman who held a number of posts in U.S. Democratic administrations; Pamela became a U.S. citizen in 1971 and as Pamela Churchill Harriman became a political activist for the American Democratic Party. President Bill Clinton appointed her U.S. ambassador to France in 1993.
2. Clementine Churchill to Winston, June 27, 1940. See Mary Soames, *Clementine Churchill* (Doubleday, 2002), p. 325.
3. Lord Moran, *Winston Churchill: The Struggle for Survival, 1940–1965* (Heron Books, 1966), p. 318.
4. Among Peregrine's papers were a number of sheets of notepaper inherited from his father simply bearing Winston's signature at the bottom, suggesting that during wartime Jack was authorized to compose and type letters and send them out "signed" by the prime minister.
5. Lord David Cecil, a writer and poet, became a professor of English literature at Oxford University (1948–70).
6. The *Times,* July 11, 1941.
7. Queen Elizabeth, the Queen Consort, known after her husband's death as the Queen Mother; reported in several British newspapers and now legendary in the United Kingdom.

CHAPTER 22

1. Mary Soames, *Clementine Churchill* (Doubleday, 2002), pp. 424–25.
2. Ibid., p. 425.
3. Field Marshal Alexander was governor-general of Canada, 1946–52.
4. Dwight D. Eisenhower (1890–1969), president of the United States, 1953–61; general of the army, served as supreme commander of the Allied forces in Europe during the Second World War.
5. Eugene L. Rasor, *Winston S. Churchill 1874–1965* (Greenwood Press, 2000).
6. A masterly exploration of the whole work is in David Reynolds, *In Command of History: Fighting and Writing the Second World War* (Allen Lane, 2004).
7. Lord Moran, *Winston Churchill: The Struggle for Survival, 1940–1965* (Heron Books, 1966), p. 318.
8. Ibid.
9. John Spencer Churchill, *Crowded Canvas* (Odhams, 1961).
10. Paper by John H. Mather, MD, Research Associate, Institute for the History of Medicine, Johns Hopkins University, School of Medicine, *Sir Winston Churchill: His Hardiness and Resilience,*

presented on Oct. 18, 1997, at the 14th International Churchill Society Conference, Toronto, Canada; published in *The Proceedings of the Churchill Centre, 1996–1997*, pp. 83–97.

11. Sir Anthony Eden was foreign secretary again in 1955 and prime minister, 1955–57. He was severely damaged by his conduct in the Suez Canal crisis in 1956.

12. John Ramsden, *Man of the Century: Winston Churchill and His Legend Since 1945* (Columbia University Press, 2002).

13. Kjell Stromberg, *The 1953 Nobel Prize;* located on the website of the Churchill Centre & Museum, Cabinet War Rooms, London.

14. Winston may not have entirely recovered from another stroke in 1955, according to Dr. John H. Mather, *Sir Winston Churchill: His Hardiness and Resilience.*

15. Randolph S. Churchill, *The Rise and Fall of Anthony Eden* (Macgibbon & Kee, 1959).

16. Mary Soames, *Clementine Churchill*, p. 253.

17. Ibid., p. 529.

18. Peregrine Churchill has joined his father there.

AUTHORS' NOTE

1. Ted Morgan, *Churchill: Young Man in a Hurry, 1874–1915* (Simon & Schuster, 1982).

2. Shane Leslie, *The End of a Chapter* (Pomona Press, 1916), p. 116. He continues: "Few sons have done more for their fathers," referring to Winston's biography of Lord Randolph.

3. Winston Churchill, *My Early Life* (Butterworth, 1930).

4. Frank Harris, *My Life and Loves* (Frank Harris Publishing Co., 1922).

5. Manuscripts written by Peregrine S. Churchill, August and October 1991, owned privately by Mrs. Peregrine S. Churchill.

6. Anita Leslie, *Jennie: The Mother of Winston Churchill* (Hutchinson, 1969; repr. George Mann, 1992). Anita Leslie is the granddaughter of Leonie Leslie.

7. Lady Soames, Winston Churchill's youngest daughter, told the authors in an interview, in October 2005, in relation to the syphilis smear: "We were all robustly healthy."

8. Kindly loaned to the authors by the great-grandson of the late Sir Winston Churchill, Mr. Randolph Churchill, from Jack Churchill's library.

9. See chap. 8.

10. Dr. John H. Mather, "Lord Randolph Churchill: Maladies et Mort," in *Finest Hour* 93, Winter 1996/97, pp. 23–28; copy at the Churchill Archives, Cambridge.

11. R. F. Foster, *Lord Randolph Churchill, a Political Life* (Clarendon Press, 1981).

12. Authors' conversations with Peregrine S. Churchill, 2001–02.

13. Where the authors have referred in chap. 8 to Lord Randolph's memory being affected, it was in terms of his photographic, or line, memory; instead of giving his speeches from memory, he used notes. His memory was not affected as that of someone suffering from dementia would have been; otherwise he would not have been able to write lengthy letters on politics until shortly before his death.

14. Mather, op. cit.

15. Ibid.

16. Ibid.

17. Ibid.

18. Authors' conversations with Peregrine S. Churchill, 2001–02.

19. Letter from Elizabeth Everest, the Churchill nanny, undated, to Jack, telling him she is sending a lot of his and Winston's old toys to Leonie Leslie for her children and some to Clara for her boys; privately owned by Mrs. Peregrine S. Churchill.

20. Anita Leslie, *Edwardians in Love* (Arrow Books, 1974), pp. 200, 203–18.

21. Mrs. George Cornwallis-West, *The Reminiscences of Lady Randolph Churchill* (Century, 1907–08), pp. 345–46.

22. *Lady Randy,* Channel 4 documentary film, broadcast Tuesday, Nov. 11, 2008.

23. Authors' conversations with Peregrine S. Churchill, 2001–02.

24. The private papers of Mrs. Peregrine S. Churchill.

25. Mather, op. cit.

26. Theo Lang, *My Darling Daisy* (Michael Joseph, 1960). Lang tells the story of Daisy's blackmail attempt in some detail.

27. Lieutenant Colonel Stephen Hungerford-Pollen was married to Lady Hamilton's younger sister, Catherine. Lady Hamilton's diaries are owned privately by General Sir Ian Hamilton's nephew, Mr. Ian Hamilton.

28. Interviews with Mary, the Lady Soames, Oct. 19 and 28, 2005.

29. Authors' conversations with Peregrine S. Churchill, 2001–02.

30. Robert Rhodes James, *Lord Randolph Churchill* (Weidenfeld & Nicholson, 1959).

31. *Daily Mail*, Sept. 8, 2007, and June 13, 2009.

32. CHAR 28/4/30–31, Churchill College, Cambridge.

33. Lord Randolph to Jennie, Mar. 5, 1874, CHAR 28/4/27, Churchill College, Cambridge.

34. Lord Randolph to Mrs. Jerome, Nov. 30, 1874, CHAR 28/4/30–31, Churchill College, Cambridge; also quoted in Peregrine S. Churchill and Julian Mitchell, *Jennie: Lady Randolph Churchill* (Collins, 1974), p. 75.

35. Claimed by a participant in the *Lady Randy* documentary.

36. Authors' conversations with Peregrine S. Churchill, 2001–02.

37. Mr. Rodney J. Croft, consultant general and vascular surgeon, Grenada.

38. Authors' conversations with Peregrine S. Churchill, 2001–02.

39. Peregrine S. Churchill's manuscript dated April 2000, p. 5, owned privately by Mrs. Peregrine S. Churchill.

40. Rodney Croft, op. cit.

41. Authors' conversations with Peregrine S. Churchill, 2001–02; letter from Lord Randolph Churchill to Mrs. [Clarissa/Clara] Jerome, Nov. 30, 1874, CHAR 28/4/30–31, Churchill College, Cambridge.

42. John Strange Jocelyn, 5th Earl of Roden (1828–1897).

43. Roy Jenkins, Liberal MP (Baron Jenkins of Hillhead), author of *Churchill* (Macmillan, 2001).

44. Ibid., pp. 7–8.

45. Croft, op. cit.

46. Jocelyn's father had originally owned Tollymore House and estate and had sold it many years earlier, and Jocelyn had not been back there from his boyhood.

47. The 4th Earl of Roden, Robert Jocelyn, who was unmarried, had died unexpectedly at age thirty-three, in Paris, on Jan. 10, 1880. As there was no immediate heir, John Strange Jocelyn, his uncle, inherited the title.

48. Croft, op. cit.

49. Anne Sebba, *Jennie Churchill: Winston's American Mother* (John Murray, 2007), pp. 98–100. Mrs. Sebba quotes from letters to Anita Leslie in the Tara King private collection in Ireland.

50. Ibid.

51. Ibid.

52. Jennie Churchill's handwritten diary for the year 1882, which has been transcribed by the authors, is owned privately by Mrs. Peregrine S. Churchill.

53. Authors' conversations with Peregrine S. Churchill, 2001–02.

54. Ibid.

55. Elizabeth Churchill Snell is author of *The Churchills: Pioneers and Politicians — England, America, Canada* (Westcountry Books, 1994).

56. *Daily Mail*, Saturday, June 13, 2009.

57. Author of *Memories of My Dead Life* (William Heinemann, 1906).

58. George Moore gave the idea that Jennie had two hundred lovers to Lady Cynthia Asquith (the prime minister's daughter), who published it in her memoirs, *The Diaries of Lady Cynthia Asquith, 1915–18* (Century, 1968).

59. This handwritten draft of a letter, the original of which was presumably sent to Mrs. Cornwallis-West (Mary/Patsy), George's mother, at the time of the first breakdown of the marriage, was found by the authors among Peregrine S. Churchill's papers. It is owned privately by Mrs. Peregrine S. Churchill.

60. Prince Karel Andreas Kinsky (1858–1919) was the son of Prince Ferdinand Buonaventura Kinsky (1834–1904) and Marie Princess von und zu Lichtenstein (1835–1905). In England, Kinsky was known as Charles.

61. Anita Leslie, *Jennie: The Mother of Winston Churchill* (George Mann, 1992), pp. 177–78, quoting Charles Kinsky's cousin, Prince Cleary, who wrote out the details for Anita Leslie. Prince Clary got the story from his grandmother, the Countess Sophie Kinsky.

62. George Lambton, *Men and Horses I Have Known* (J. A. Allen, 1963).

63. Authors' conversations with Peregrine S. Churchill, 2001–02.

Index